In the U.S. Interest

A WORLD RESOURCES INSTITUTE BOOK

In the U.S. Interest

Resources, Growth, and Security in the Developing World

EDITED BY

Janet Welsh Brown

Westview Press
BOULDER, SAN FRANCISCO, & LONDON

Published in 1990 in the United States of America by Westview Press, Inc., 5500 Central Avenue, Boulder, Colorado 80301, and in the United Kingdom by Westview Press, Inc., 13 Brunswick Centre, London WC1N 1AF, England

Library of Congress Cataloging-in-Publication Data
In the U.S. interest : resources, growth, and security in the
  developing world / edited by Janet Welsh Brown.
    p. cm.
  ISBN 0-8133-1053-9
  1. United States—Foreign economic relations—Developing
countries—Case studies. 2. Developing countries—Foreign economic
relations—United States—Case studies. 3. United States—Military
relations—Developing countries—Case studies. 4. Developing
countries—Military relations—United States—Case studies.
5. Developing countries—Economic conditions—Case studies.
6. Economic forecasting—Developing countries—Case studies.
I. Brown, Janet Welsh. II. Title: In the United States's interest.
HF1456.5.D44I39 1990
337.730172′4—dc20   89-48380
                                                                         CIP

Printed and bound in the United States of America

The paper used in this publication meets the requirements of the American National
Standard for Permanence of Paper for Printed Library Materials Z39.48-1984.

10   9   8   7   6   5   4

Contents

Illustrations

VI

Foreword

How important are developing countries to broad U.S. interests and how important are resource management and population growth to these nations' economic and political futures?

In the U.S. Interest: Resources, Growth, and Security in the Developing World sets the stage for thoughtful answers to these vital questions. Through case studies of four countries, this book shows how accelerating deterioration of the resource base, combined with rapid growth of populations that depend more directly than most on natural systems, threatens the economic and political stability of countries vital to U.S. interests.

The four countries analyzed here—Mexico, the Philippines, Egypt and Kenya—include the United States' southern neighbor and third most important trading partner, Southeast Asia's most firmly committed democracy, North Africa's most populous and powerful state, and the East African country with perhaps the most promising future. Yet, all four face ominous trends in environmental degradation and in population growth that are undermining long-term development projects.

Can these countries alter those trends if they get the cooperation of the United States and other comfortable societies of the north that also share a global interest in the outcome? The trends are unmistakable, so action need not await further basic research, and many of the technologies and policies needed to reverse them are known. But whether U.S. policymakers will recognize our national interest in international environmental cooperation has yet to be decided.

From 1983 to 1988, the World Resources Institute brought together policymakers in and out of the government, business leaders, researchers, development experts, and representatives from environmental organizations from both the developing countries and the United States to build understanding of the need for north-south cooperation on population, resource, and environmental challenges. This book is the final product of that long and fruitful process, and it is our hope that it will fuel a policy debate leading to an agreement and concrete action involving the United States and the developing countries—agreements that link shared concerns for environmental protection and economic progress.

For supporting the five-year project on U.S. Stake in Global Resource Issues, we are deeply grateful to the Carnegie Corporation, the Educational Foundation of America, the George Gund Foundation, the John D. and Catherine T. MacArthur Foundation, the Pew Charitable Trust, and the Florence and John Schumann Foundation.

James Gustave Speth
President, World Resources Institute

Acknowledgments

As with any collective effort, this book goes to press with the help of many people over many months. My greatest debt, of course, is to the authors of the country case studies that are the core of the book. I thank them sincerely for their scholarship, their good will, and their enduring patience as we worked through numerous versions.

Each of the country case studies benefited also, in both the planning and review stages, from the experience of colleagues. On the Mexico study, we received advice and assistance from Michael D. Barnes, Robin Broad, Jeff Burnam, Guy Erb, James Hester, Delmus James, John Johnson, H. Jeffrey Leonard, Stephen Mumme, Mario Ramos, Peter Smith, Gary L. Springer, Francisco Szekeley, Cathryn Thorup, and Albert Utton. The case study on the Philippines was expertly critiqued at various stages by Robin Broad, Frederick Z. Brown, John Cavanagh, John Maxwell Hamilton, Eric L. Hyman, Richard Kessler, George Krimsky, Antonio Lim, Charles W. Lindsey, Stephen Lintner, Cynthia Mackie, Collin Rees, Celso Roque, Frances Seymour, and Jack Sullivan. The Egypt case study was improved by the comments and review of Roy Atherton, Raymond Baker, Sally Brandel, Bradley Gordon, David A. Hamod, Peter Johnson, Stephen F. Lintner, Clyde R. Mark, Thomas H. Merrick, George D. Moffet, David B. Ottaway, Don Pressley, Delwin A. Roy, and Richard H. Ullman. On the Kenya study, we had the valued assistance of Tom Blinkhorn, Gary Bombardier, Raymond W. Copson, Pamela Cox, John Gaudet, Charles E. Hanrahan, Molly Kux, Princeton Lyman, Clifford May, and J. Kathy Parker.

While preparing the policy recommendations in the final chapter, I had discussions with Patricia Blair, J. Kathy Parker, John W. Sewell, John Maxwell Hamilton, Jack Sullivan, and many colleagues at the U.S. Agency for International Development and the World Bank. I also found useful the insight and experience of participants in two conferences organized by the project on the U.S. Stake in Global Resource Issues. The first was a public forum that bore the title of this book and was held in Washington on June 22–23, 1987. The second, U.S. Policy in the 1990s: International Cooperation for Environmentally Sustainable Development, also took place in Washington on March 7–8, 1988. It was part of a much larger effort organized by Michigan State University colleagues to review policies guiding U.S. international development assistance programs. Participants in both efforts are listed in the Appendix.

As part of WRI's project U.S. Stake in Global Resource Issues this book has benefited from the overall direction of an advisory panel composed of Kenneth J. Arrow, Harrison S. Brown, Douglas M. Costle, Donald F. McHenry, Edward L. Morse, Henry Rowen, Howard D. Samuel, and Richard H. Ullman and chaired by Daniel Yergin.

Special thanks are due Andrew Maguire, my predecessor, who started the U.S. Stake in Global Resource Issues project, and to WRI President Gus Speth, who conceived the idea of the project, to Vice Presidents Jessica T. Mathews and Mohamed El-Ashry, who provided invaluable intellectual guidance, and to the many colleagues who read and critiqued various parts of the manuscript: Robert Blake, Bill Burley, Peter Hazlewood, Nels Johnson, Jim MacKenzie, Irving Mintzer, Bill Nagle, Diana Page, Bob Repetto, Kirk Talbott, Peter Thacher, and Frederik van Bolhuis.

To Kathleen Courrier, Publications Director, I am most grateful for solid advice throughout the process, to Linda Starke for fine editing, to Hyacinth Billings and Laura Lee Dooley for the final production and to Eileen Powell and Frances Meehan for intelligent, caring processing of numerous drafts. For help in locating and checking sources, I am beholden to WRI Librarian Sue Terry and to Kara Page, Robert Kwartin, Norbert Henninger, and Eric Rodenburg.

To all, for their interest and help, we are grateful, but final responsibility for the substance of this volume rests, of course, with the editor and authors.

Janet Welsh Brown

I

Why Should We Care?

Janet Welsh Brown

Americans have concrete economic and security interests at stake in resolving environmental, resource, and population problems in the developing world. United States trade with these countries has rapidly increased: today more than a third of our overseas markets (and all the U.S. jobs dependent on them) are in Latin America, Asia, and Africa. United States firms have investments throughout the developing world. U.S. banks and U.S. taxpayers hold a disproportionately large share of developing world debt. And United States national security depends on the stability, growth, and self-confidence of numerous key nations in Latin America, Asia, and Africa.

The interdependence of nations is the single most spectacular change in world affairs since World War II—though the voting public and United States policymakers have not yet fully understood that. Although the most prestigious U.S. foreign affairs journals[1] and our daily news continue to focus primarily on a handful of world powers—on trade disagreements with Japan, arms negotiations between the United States and the Soviet Union, the relative value of the mark and yen, and economic summits of the Group of Seven—developing countries are becoming increasingly important players in the new interdependence.

Interdependence makes the United States—like all other nations—more fiscally, economically, and militarily vulnerable to developments beyond its borders. Although generalizing about developing countries usually invites misunderstanding, these nations share some ominous trends of interest to the United States, especially the "spending" of their natural resource "capital," which renders sustainable development uncertain and, in the most ravished countries—Haiti, El Salvador, and Ethiopia among them—impossible. Even better-off "middle-income" countries face natural resource degradation and population growth great enough to call into question confidence in continuing economic and political viability. If the United States wants a prosperous and peaceful developing world in which it, too, may continue to prosper, then developing nations' environmental, resource, and population pressures deserve bigger play in Washington.

Washington policymakers—concerned with trade and budget deficits, preoccupied by rapidly unfolding developments in the Soviet Union, hampered in Central America by a legacy of interventionism and fear of communism, and frustrated by the scale and violence of the drug trade—may be missing the buildup of problems that, if neglected in the next two decades, could devastate developing countries and threaten U.S. interests in the twenty-first century. While the Aquino government struggles to answer critics of the left and right, for instance, a rapid erosion of natural resources threatens the Philippines' fundamental ability to provide for the next generation and raises the question of whether the United States can long count on Filipino respect—and Filipino bases. Mexico, our third largest trading partner after Canada and Japan, shares a long and permeable border with the United States. Yet, few North Americans understand how growing pollution and resource degradation limit Mexico's ability to support its population. Stated U.S. policy concerns for Egypt reflect unresolved Middle East conflicts, the Egyptian military's strength, and President Mubarak's willingness to face up to Qaddafi, but looming ahead is a greater problem: limited land and water resources are not being managed in a way that can possibly support 100 million Egyptians 25 years from now. In Central America, U.S. debate over "democracy" and the degree of Cuban and Soviet penetration pulls attention from the worsening condition of these countries' primary resources: land and people.

In the developing world—even in relatively well-off countries—deforestation, desertification, soil loss, destruction and contamination of water supplies, depletion of marine resources, and air pollution are escalating alarmingly. Although population growth has slowed in most countries, rates are still high, and the base is still large in Mexico, the Philippines, Egypt, and Kenya, the countries discussed in this volume. Developing-country leaders are increasingly worried about these trends, as are a rapidly growing number of indigenous grassroots and community organizations. Although other national concerns are often assigned higher priorities, these issues are no longer considered "soft" or fringe.

In 1990, change and opportunity are in the air. The arrival of *glasnost* and the rehabilitation of U.S.-Soviet relations, the near-resolution of some long-standing Asian, African, and Middle Eastern wars, and a new President in the White House offer room to maneuver. In the United States, public concern focuses largely on economic and, so far, domestic issues, but the context of the debate is changing. Hot Washington summers, high ozone levels, and widespread drought in the farm belt have heightened Americans' concern about the shared global atmosphere. Environmentalists have successfully lobbied foreign assistance agencies, the multinational banks, and Congress to examine environmental impacts of their development programs and to plan for sustainable development.

The spreading scourges of drug addiction and AIDS and their connections to developing countries promise a new level of U.S. attention to Africa, Latin America, and Asia. Developing countries, one way or another, will assume much greater importance for U.S. policymakers in the crucial decade ahead.

U.S. Economic Ties to Developing Countries

The economic importance to the United States of this interdependence seems obvious to some American leaders. David Rockefeller, making the case for foreign assistance, spelled it out bluntly in a speech before the American Banking Association in 1984:

> The primary direct benefits to the U.S. of assisting the developing nations are simple ... the developing nations now provide us a larger export market than all the developed nations put together, excluding only Canada ... the developing nations are an important source for us of commodities and raw materials which are vital to our own productive capacity, as well as to our security and quality of life ... many developing nations are our close friends and allies, cooperating with us on security matters and helping to contain Soviet expansionism. Extreme poverty is the breeding ground for excesses of both the far left and the far right. Such excesses can easily in turn stimulate unrest and prove extremely expensive to close neighbors, and even those far away.[2]

Economic interdependence grew out of the extraordinary dislocations wrought by World War II and the rehabilitation that followed, by the new alliances forged during the cold war, and by the appearance and rapid transformation of 100 new nations since 1945. A communications revolution and great strides in modern transportation accelerated the process.

For the United States, a nation that came of age with a huge territory and a seemingly inexhaustible supply of resources, economic interdependence has changed our lives and our future in ways we have not fully absorbed. Our great banks are tied—by millions of daily transactions—with Tokyo and Bonn, and with a host of lesser money centers that operate around the world and around the clock. Millions of Americans' jobs are affected by production and investment decisions made in other countries—some of them quite small and very far away.

Over the last generation, trade has become much more important to the U.S. economy. In 1960, U.S. exports and imports amounted to only 8 percent of gross national product; by 1985, they totalled 20 percent. The number of partners in that trade has also increased. When the General Agreement on Tariffs and Trade (GATT) took effect in 1948, only 22 countries were signatories. With the accession of Mexico in 1986, the total reached 92, and GATT countries now account for four-fifths of world trade. Thirty other countries abide by GATT *de facto*.[3]

Until World War II, nearly all our trading partners were industrialized nations; after the war, developing countries, particularly in Latin America and Asia, accounted for an ever larger share of U.S. trade. For over a decade, a third or more of American exports have gone to developing countries. In 1983, before the world recession was full-blown, 38 percent of our overseas markets were in developing countries and 37 percent of our imports originated there. From 1986 into early 1989, U.S. trade with developing countries, both exports and imports, hovered steadily around a third of total U.S. trade.[4] With economic recovery and modest growth, those figures could well rise to 50 percent early in the new century. Half of our sales abroad, half of our foreign-exchange earnings, half of our balance-of-payments problems (or successes) will ride on markets in Asia, Latin America, and Africa.

An estimated 2.3 million American jobs were dependent on the manufacture of U.S. merchandise exports to developing countries in 1988. Generally, the public debate about protectionism is couched in terms of losing U.S. jobs to competitors in other countries, but actual job loss in recent years has been due to a loss of exports, "*not* to an inordinate surge of imports." Heavy debt in the Third World meant the loss of an additional 1.1 million U.S. jobs because our trade with those countries failed to grow in the 1980s.[5]

State governments across the country, however, recognize the importance of this trade and have established offices to go after it aggressively. At their Miami meeting in 1985, the Southern Governors Association called for improved language training and international studies in the nation's schools, partly to increase U.S. competitiveness abroad. A 1988 survey by the National Association of State Development Agencies reports that every state in the union provides local businesses with seminars and conferences on how to market to foreign countries. Forty-two states maintain permanent offices overseas; large states maintain several. Ohio has an office in Lagos, Nigeria; Oklahoma has one in New Delhi; Oregon reports that 67 companies are doing business in Malaysia and Indonesia. Most state governments also assign staff people to the job of attracting overseas investments as well.[6]

These aggressive state marketers understand world population figures. The big future markets of the United States and other industrialized nations will be in the developing world, *if* such countries can resume reasonable rates of economic growth.

But growth cannot resume until the crushing international debt burden is alleviated. Debt has created extraordinary hardship in some countries. In Mexico, for instance, real wages declined more than 20 percent between 1980 and 1986. In five debt-ridden countries—Brazil, Venezuela, Argentina, Mexico, and the Philippines—interest payments came to $37 billion last year, equalling about half the value of their combined exports.[7] Back in the United States, banks that hold a considerable share of that debt set aside large reserves to protect themselves against possible default.

Less readily apparent is that debt affects not only U.S. banks, but also U.S. workers. According to a recent U.S. International Trade Commission study for the House of Representatives Ways and Means Committee, debt-related austerity in Brazil, Venezuela, Argentina, Mexico, and the Philippines harmed 40 of the 61 nonservice U.S. industries studied. In 1985 alone, austerity measures in developing countries caused a $5-billion reduction in U.S. exports and the loss of the equivalent of 219,800 U.S. jobs in the 61 industries in question.[8]

Any rise in interest rates in the United States means, among other things, an increase in the debt-service costs for debtor countries. For every 1 percent increase in U.S. rates, annual payments on the Latin countries' debts (an estimated $436 billion in 1989, 68.3 percent of which was loaned at variable rates of interest) goes up by approximately $3 billion. For Brazil and Mexico, holding the biggest debts in Latin America, that would translate to an annual increase of more than one billion each, far outstripping what either country receives in official development assistance.

Debt is the most awesome burden for developing countries' economies today. But it is also very much a U.S. problem—one that affects U.S. banks, workers, and taxpayers.

The U.S. Security Stake in the Developing World

American interdependence with the developing world has political as well as economic ramifications. As Gro Harlem Brundtland, now Prime Minister of Norway, predicted when appointed as Chair of the World Commission on Environment and Development in 1983, "The environmental problems of the poor will affect the rich, as well, in a not too distant future, transmitted through political instability and turmoil." U.S. security is not threatened by attack from any of those countries, and the threat is not that we might get drawn into developing countries' military conflicts. The bedrock issue is that, individually and collectively, the political allegiances and security in the developing world shape the U.S. role and U.S. options in global geopolitics. Environmental and resource problems are sometimes the direct cause of conflict within and between nations, but more often the effects are indirect: environmental degradation, population pressure, and resource stress can endanger the long-term viability of states, opening them to turmoil within, and to mischief from without.

Fresh water resources have long been a source of direct conflict among nations. Rights to the Nile's waters, for instance, figure high on Egypt's international agenda, even though U.S. media reports focus almost exclusively on negotiations with Israel and border tensions with Libya. Completion of the Jonglei Canal in southern Sudan could help improve Egyptian-Sudanese relations, though the canal is also one cause of the conflict between north and south in Sudan's bitter civil war.[9]

Another example comes from the Arab-Israeli experience. Most observers remember the start of the 1967 Arab-Israeli War as Egypt's attempt to block access to the Gulf of Aqaba. But a major unnoticed cause was the struggle for the waters of the Jordan River, the Litani, and other tributaries.[10]

Closer to home, by the mid-1980s United States-Mexican relations reached their worst point in 60 years, with debt, trade, immigration, and drug issues the subject of often acrimonious exchanges. Relations between the two nations are further soured by cross-border tension over air pollution from Mexican smelters, water pollution from Tijuana sewage, salinization in Mexico's end of the Colorado River from irrigation upriver in the United States, and the illegal dumping of U.S. toxic wastes trucked from California and New Mexico into northern Mexico.[11]

Such explanations of conflict might be dismissed as the obsession of a few over-zealous environmentalists if these issues were not also on a 1984 Central Intelligence Agency (CIA) list of global flash points affecting vital U.S. interests. Besides tensions over water, CIA analysts in a still-classified study, "Population, Resources and Politics in the Third World," foresee potential conflict because of extreme population pressure, immigration, and resource depletion. Their analysis suggests that turmoil born of these forces will lead to more authoritarian governments in some cases, and to war in others. Clashes over resources are likely, said the CIA, to become more rather than less frequent causes of conflict, especially in the developing world.[12]

The costs of conflict—both human and material—add up quickly. Eleven million people have died in military conflicts involving developing countries since 1960, some in conflicts with industrialized nations, but most in conflict with each other. One hundred and fifty such conflicts have been fought since World War II. The financial cost has also been high. Besides material damage that is not easily estimated, military expenditures take a significant chunk out of most national budgets. Such outlays in the industrialized countries went up 14 percent from 1976 to 1986, compared with a 63-percent rise in the developing world.[13] At the same time, the World Bank reports that spending on social programs has stopped growing in some of those countries and declined in others.

The more numerous resource-related conflicts, particularly those likely to affect U.S. interests, constitute *indirect* influences. Into this category falls environmental degradation, usually combined with population pressure, that strains domestic resources until a nation's economic or political security is threatened. The country case studies in this book detail the ways in which resource degradation can clearly, albeit indirectly, affect the viability of states.

Development Costs of Environmental Degradation

The consequences of poor resource management manifest themselves differently in different countries. But whatever the variations, the impacts will eventually be economic. For example, demand for household fuel clearly threatens economic development. It has denuded forests near rural villages and around cities. With the loss of tree cover comes increased erosion and reduced crop yields. Where scarce fuelwood is replaced by dried dung—an estimated 400 million tons annually—the soil is robbed of natural replenishment. Soil fertility then falls, reducing harvests by an estimated 14 million tons of grain a year, more than all food aid from all donors to all developing nations. In China, as in other countries suffering acute energy shortages in the rural areas, 75 percent of the crop residues are burned for fuel, whereas in the United States, 70 percent are recycled.[14]

Throughout the developing world, deforestation proceeds apace. Some 80,000 square kilometers, an area roughly the size of Austria or of northern New England, is lost to nonforest uses each year. Another 120,000 square kilometers is damaged. Fuelwood shortages now affect an estimated 1.5 billion people in 63 countries. Of the 33 countries currently exporting industrial wood products, 23 will probably become importers of forest products by the year 2000. Commercial logging, land clearing to make way for cattle farms, and peasant use of the trees for fuel and fodder all eat away at remaining natural forest, which in tropical climates is highly susceptible to damage from human activities. Each year, runoff from 160 million hectares of degraded upland watersheds contributes to soil erosion, declines in agricultural productivity, downstream silting and flooding, and destruction of fishing grounds.[15]

For some countries with mounting oil-import bills, hydroelectricity is the most promising means of providing power for industrial and residential users, and often water for irrigation as well. But environmental neglect can stifle the promise through siltation. The loss of electric output from the silt behind hydroelectric installations runs into the billions of dollars. In the Dominican Republic, for example, siltation has already cost the large Tavera Dam, completed in 1973, 40 percent of its dead storage capacity and 10–14 percent of its active storage. In India, terrible deforestation in the Himalayan foothills has reduced the estimated life of the Tehri Dam from 100 years to 30 or 40. In Colombia, the Anchicaya Dam lost 25 percent of its storage capacity in just two years. In China, the Sanmenxia Dam silted up totally within four years of completion.[16]

The environmental, health, and other costs of hydroelectric dams can be high. The United Nations Food and Agriculture Organization (FAO) estimates that, worldwide, 20 percent of all irrigated lands are waterlogged, excessively saline, or both, which means additional costs in lowered agricultural productivity. In Egypt, 30–40 percent of the irrigated land is affected by salinization; in Syria, 30–35 percent; in India, 27 percent.[17] Health costs for treating malaria and schistosomiasis often climb drastically after dam construction because the mosquitos and snails that carry these diseases proliferate in the standing waters of irrigation canals. Egypt spends more than $500 million a year treating and preventing schistosomiasis. Harder to quantify, but nonetheless real, are the dislocation and losses to people (often tribal groups or extremely poor peasants) whose lands are flooded over, and of species that die out when tropical forests and free-flowing streams are submerged.

Clean drinking water is also in short supply, and shortages take a high toll in health costs. Throughout the developing world, water polluted by sewage and industrial wastes causes disease and death. In India, for example, 70 percent of all surface waters are polluted. As the Yamuna River flows through Delhi, it daily picks up a staggering 200 million liters of raw sewage and 20 million liters of industrial wastes, including 500,000 liters of "DDT wastes." Eighty percent of childhood deaths in developing countries are due to diarrhea, worm infestation, and other water-borne diseases. By 1985, despite the considerable efforts launched under the United Nations Decade of Water Supply and Sanitation, only about half of the urban populations had adequate water supplies and sanitation. Percentages for rural people were much lower.[18] Once groundwater is contaminated it can take decades, even centuries, before natural processes purify it. In a fundamental sense, health, too, is an environmental matter in developing countries.

World pesticide sales grew from $2.7 billion in 1970 to $11.6 billion in 1980. They are expected to reach $18.5 billion in 1990, with the most rapid growth occurring in developing countries, as consumption in the United States and other industrialized countries levels off.[19] Developing country use includes many compounds that have been banned in industrial countries. The costs in human life, health care, and agricultural losses due to pesticides and pest resistance are also rising. Some 10,000 people die each year and 400,000 suffer acute effects from pesticide poisoning, while the number of pesticide-resistant insect and mite species is growing (from 25 in 1974 to 432 in 1980).[20]

Soil loss everywhere undermines agricultural production, but the loss is especially worrisome in the developing countries, where food production often cannot keep up with population growth and food imports can drain national budgets. No part of the developing world has been spared. In Guatemala, 40 percent of the land's productive capacity has been lost to erosion, and some areas of the country have been abandoned because agriculture is no longer economic. In Turkey, an estimated 75 percent of the land is affected, 54 percent severely so. In India, 13 million hectares are eroded by wind and 74 million by water—equal to one-quarter of the country's land. Throughout Africa, overgrazing, overfarming, and overcutting—all pushed by rapidly growing populations—have so reduced land productivity that nearly a score of countries are prey to famine whenever the rains fail. In much of Haiti, topsoil is virtually gone. The costs, though enormous, are hard to calculate, partly because they occur so far from the eroding field or hillside. In the United States, though, the annual costs of off-site erosion from damage to marine resources, loss of hydroelectric capacity, and dredging requirements are estimated at $6 billion.[21]

Each year, 6 million hectares of drylands are added to the 1.3 billion hectares that by 1984 had already been severely degraded.[22] In 1984, the FAO predicted that, without conservation measures, the total area of rainfed cropland in developing countries will shrink by 18 percent (544 million hectares) because of soil erosion, salinization, depletion of nutrients and organic matter, pollution, and deterioration of soil structure.[23] In the same period, another billion people will be added to the world's population, more than 90 percent of whom will be born in developing countries.

Environmental degradation and growing populations together can undo the gains of national development, as a look at specific countries shows. Egypt, for instance, has already lost the struggle to meet its rapidly growing population's food needs. Despite substantial gains in food production over the last 20 years, per capita output has declined. The wildfire growth of Cairo (10 million residents, and still growing) and other urban areas, most of them along the fertile shores of the Nile River, encroaches steadily on farmland. New industries also take their share. Government policies favor cotton and other commercial export crops, and further reduce the areas left for growing food. At the same time, desert sand from the west encroaches on fertile soils at several places along the Nile valley. Soil along the Nile itself is eroding much faster than it did before the construction of the Aswan Dam. Increased soil salinity, the result of poor irrigation practices, threatens most of the irrigated lands and reduces productivity further. The charge for all this against Egypt's development hopes is staggering: wheat and flour imports cost the government $1 billion in 1986. Total annual earnings from Suez Canal fees barely pay for sugar imports.

In Central America, nations launched ambitious development programs in the 1960s and 1970s to raise their standard of living and bolster their economic independence. Although country-to-country differences were marked, all based their development strategies on agricultural exports and industrial development aimed at import substitution. Only a handful of industries have succeeded, and the debt assumed in the process is today the single largest impediment to growth. The production of export crops—principally coffee, bananas, sugar, cotton, and cattle—was modernized with deep-pocket investments in mechanization, pesticides and fertilizers. Throughout the region, farmers who rented or farmed small plots without title were divested of their land to make room for the export crops. For some years, these crops accounted for half to two-thirds of export earnings in El Salvador, Honduras, and Guatemala, but intensive monocultures have degraded the resource base, and the shift in land use caused a decline in food production. In the Costa Rican lowlands, for instance, small-scale agriculture virtually disappeared as a result of the banana plantations in the 1960s, while corn production declined 87 percent in six years. In Nicaragua in the same years, huge sales to Japan made cotton the leading export.[24]

Each of these agricultural activities has had its environmental costs, but deforestation for cattle ranching has caused the most destruction. From 1960 to

1980, Central American forests declined from 60 percent to 40 percent of the territory—with two-thirds of the cultivated land in livestock. Since 1963 the World Bank has lent funds for cattle ranching to every Central American country except El Salvador and has provided more credit for livestock than for any other kind of agricultural activity. The Inter-American Development Bank also recognized cattle production as "highly suited" to the region and looked to it as a promising earner of much-needed foreign exchange. But the planners did not understand that the luxuriance of the tropical forests is deceptive, hiding nutrient-poor soils unsuited to cattle raising. The amount of land needed to support one animal quickly rose from one hectare, in the first years of production, to five to seven hectares. After 10 years or less, cattle ranchers must often move on to new forest lands to support their herds.[25]

Today, the highest rate of deforestation in the hemisphere is in Central America. Fuelwood is already in short supply, and some countries will be forced to import lumber in a few years. Dams and rivers silt up faster than expected as soil is carried off.

Central America's development strategy exacted a high price: debt for the state, and concentration of agricultural land in fewer hands, and even greater poverty for the landless. And the land, the region's chief natural resource, has been used in a profligate manner without visible return. Far from fostering economic independence, the past generation's development strategy has left Central America more dependent than ever on the United States and the rest of the industrialized world.

The Population/Resources Connection

Even as land deteriorates, the world's population has doubled since World War II, growing from 2.5 billion to 5.2 billion. Most of this growth has occurred in the developing countries as health improvements have cut death rates sharply. Africa alone has 1 million more mouths to feed every three weeks, and food production, now increasing at a rate of 2 percent yearly, has failed to keep up with the 3 percent rate of population growth. Kenya, with the world's highest birth rate (54 per thousand population), will have to create almost 11 million jobs by 2000 just to accommodate those already born.

Barring unforeseen disasters or miracles, we will have another billion human beings on the planet before 2000. And United Nations "medium projections," based on fairly rapid but by no means certain declines in birth and death rates, project a further doubling of the population—95 percent of it in the developing world—by the time stabilization is reached, at about 10 billion, toward the end of the 21st century. A 1989 report by the United Nations Population Fund (UNPF) warns that 10 billion could be reached around 2025 and stabilization will come in 2100 at 14 rather than 10 billion unless the current rate of contraceptive use, by 45 percent of all women, is increased to 71 percent by 2025. Only China and a few industrialized countries now have such a high rate of use. The U.S. rate is about 65 percent.[26]

Mention of developing-country "population pressure" conjures up visions of too many people making claims on too few resources. In reality, population growth rates and peoples' effect on resources and the environment are both deeply affected by technology, social organization, cultural tradition, and national and international policy, so generalizations can be dangerous.

The surest and most direct impact of a larger population will be on agricultural resources. To feed that projected 10 billion adequately will require three times the calories consumed today, equivalent to about 10 billion tons of grain a year. To produce that much, all the world's current cropland would have to be farmed as productively as Iowa's best cornfields, or about three times the current world average. Recent developing-country achievements and emerging technologies suggest that the goal can, theoretically, be met. But the challenge is enormous, and population forecasts lend an undeniable urgency to food production efforts.[27]

Apart from the numbers, population distribution has important resource and environmental effects. In the Philippines, for example, wanton logging by favored concessionaires has pushed slash-and-burn cultivators onto steep, unstable hillsides, accelerating erosion. In the Amazon Basin, road-building and government incentives, along with extreme poverty, have propelled people farther and farther into the fragile rain forests. In Kenya, where nearly all arable land is now under cultivation, the rapidly growing rural population is being forced onto less viable, ecologically fragile areas, bringing desertification behind them.

A second inexorable population shift, to the cities, contributes to a different kind of environmental stress. In 1985, 28 cities in developing countries had over 4 million people each. By the late 1990s, there will be 50 such cities. According to United Nations projections to 2025, 85 percent of the population increase in the developing world will be in urban areas.[28]

The large cities of the developing world are growing so fast that water, waste, and power facilities cannot keep up. Vast squatter communities spring up on hillsides and gullies and in industrial areas. Often, such communities are gradually upgraded, only to be followed by further immigration from the countryside. The health problems in such instant cities are truly environmental in origin. They result from lack of clean water and sanitation, compounded by emissions from poorly maintained vehicles and uncontrolled industrial pollution. Indeed, the large cities of the developing world suffer from the worst of the "modern" sources of air and water pollution. Although the lack of waste treatment, regulations, and controls cannot be blamed wholly on population growth, spontaneous and uncontrolled urban growth makes dealing with these problems that much more difficult.

In the early 1970s, when population was growing worldwide at about 2 percent a year, the growth rate actually began to decline, and the rate seems now to have reached a plateau at 1.7 percent a year. Around the world, one country after another instituted policies to slow population growth. In Catholic, Hindu, and Moslem nations, birth rates fell in response to efforts to improve health, particularly that of mothers and children, and to increase life expectancy, raise the living standards and hopes of the poor, educate more people (especially women), and offer family planning services. In some countries, such policies had dramatic effects. In Mexico, for instance, a determined policy of public education and provision of family planning services through existing community health clinics brought the rates down from 3.5 percent to 2.2 percent in 14 years.[29] Unfortunately for Mexicans, the base of the population was already so large and the age profile so young that the government still has to find jobs every year for 700,000–800,000 young people joining the labor force. Even for countries that have developed policies to lick their population problem, a resource problem of how to meet the needs of people already born remains.

To understand the urgency of tapering off population growth rates, just look at the mathematics. Roughly 40 percent of the people in developing countries are under 15 years of age. Their fertility as adults will make an enormous difference in the size at which the world's population finally levels off. United Nations medium projections show world fertility reaching replacement level by 2035 and the world's population (now more than 5 billion) stabilizing at 10.2 billion late in the next century. A 30-year delay in bringing fertility rates down to replacement levels would mean an ultimate population that is 4 billion larger.[30]

The Poverty/Environment Connection

Our Common Future, the 1987 report of the World Commission on Environment and Development, underlines the connections among poverty, international policy, and environmental degradation. The report emphasizes that "poverty itself pollutes the environment... Those who are poor and hungry will often destroy their immediate environment in order to survive." They will cut forests, overgraze grasslands, overuse marginal land, and crowd into congested cities. "The cumulative effect of these changes is so far-reaching as to make poverty itself a major global scourge."[31]

Nowhere is this connection more graphically illustrated than among the famine-ravaged people of Africa who have grown so familiar on U.S. television screens in recent years. Their plight, to quote again from *Our Common Future*,

> ... tragically illustrates the ways in which economics and ecology can interact destructively and trip into disaster. Triggered by drought, its real causes lie deeper. They are found in part in national policies that gave too little attention, too late, to the needs of smallholder agriculture and to the threats posed by rapidly rising populations. Their roots extend also to a global economic system that takes more

out of a poor continent than it puts in. Debts that they cannot pay force African nations relying on commodity sales to overuse their fragile soils, thus turning good land to desert. Trade barriers in the wealthy nations—and in many developing ones—make it hard for Africans to sell their goods for reasonable returns, putting yet more pressure on ecological systems. Aid from donor nations has not only been inadequate in scale, but too often has reflected the priorities of the nations giving the aid, rather than the needs of the recipients.[32]

Throughout Latin America, Asia, and Africa, the worst poverty is found on the most degraded lands. And the worst rates of desertification, deforestation, and soil and water loss are found where human degradation is most severe. Achieving sustainable economic growth by curbing population growth and improving resource management requires an all-fronts attack on areas where poverty and environmental degradation exist together.

Four Countries—Unique but Representative

The following four chapters grew out of case studies commissioned by the World Resources Institute. The studies were undertaken by teams of U.S. and developing-country colleagues—political scientists, economists, and resource specialists—to analyze and document (in countries typical of important U.S. allies in Latin America, Asia, and Africa) how environmental degradation and population growth influence the economic and political viability of the state. One country at a time, the connections and the solutions are easier to see.

Many other countries fit well on the list, but these four firmly establish the thesis that unchecked environmental degradation can lead to economic hardship and political instability. In some countries, U.S. bases are an issue; in others it is access to resources and goods or key transportation routes. In the case of Mexico, the nation is an important trading partner and a source of oil, and it shares an oft-troubled and porous border. In all four, less tangible political factors are important to the United States: each has a relatively open and responsive government committed to democratic goals, each is a willing partner in the international system, and each admires American values and accomplishments and respects American interests.

None of these countries is at disaster's brink, and none is numbered among the poorest of the poor. Moreover, each has managed internal and external political problems astutely and with finesse; each has experienced significant economic growth and has improved its national standard of living. Compared with many of their neighbors in the developing world, these four are faring well.

Yet each country discussed in the following chapters is saddled with environmental and resource-management problems and varying degrees of population pressure. Current trends do not bode well for continued economic progress; if these patterns of resource use and growth remain unchanged, even competent, well-meaning, democratic governments will not be able to sustain economic growth and meet the basic needs of their peoples. Nor will the regimes that follow them, regardless of ideology.

Mexico had its revolution earlier than the other countries featured in this volume, and the one-party state engineered dramatic growth. Once population growth was recognized as a problem, decisive action brought the rate of increase down sharply. But the environmental consequences of revolutionary change— water shortages, air pollution, loss of forests, and agricultural productivity— went unnoticed and untended for too long. Richard Nuccio and Angelina Ornelas show how Mexico, having failed to deal adequately with its systemic economic, environmental, and resource problems during better times, is now forced to try to make fundamental changes in its model of development under conditions that make it extremely difficult to build support for further sacrifice. The debt crisis compounded by lower world oil prices has led to "austerity"—to acute suffering and to anger toward the ruling political party, as so clearly registered in the 1988 elections. Under these circumstances, what U.S. immigration law can be expected to stanch the flow of Mexicans across our common border?

In the *Philippines*, a former director of natural resources once prophesied, "if a revolution occurs it will start in the uplands" where the stripping of the forests, soil erosion, and unequal access to the nation's resources are most acutely felt. Gareth Porter, with assistance from Filipino colleague Delfin J. Ganapin, Jr., documents extensive logging (so wasteful and corrupt that it can only be described as rapacious), soil loss, sedimentation of streams, destruction of productive mangrove forests, dynamiting of coral reefs, and overfishing—all of which have become commonplace in spite of environmental laws. In no other country described in this book is political power and privilege so fully bound up with resource exploitation and the resulting inequity and environmental degradation. While the troubled Aquino government is a distinct improvement in many respects over its predecessor, it does not yet have high on its agenda either attention to better resource management or plans to relieve pressures exerted by a rapidly growing population.

It may be said that *Egypt*, though poor in natural resources (with only 4 percent of its land arable, limited water, and oil reserves that may be depleted within 15 years), is rich in human resources. Egypt's chief asset is a resilient, industrious, educated people, 3 million of whom work overseas and send remittances home, thereby fueling an informal economy that belies official statistics on the economy and foreign-exchange earnings. But the population pressures cannot be denied. If Egypt's population of 50 million continues to grow at current rates, it will double in 26 years. Nazli Choucri and her colleagues raise troubling questions: Can the country's limited and already severely strained resource base support twice as many people in another quarter-century? Will other Arab countries then be able to employ not 3 million but perhaps 6 million Egyptian workers, and will their remittances compensate for declining agricultural productivity at home? No development scenario yet proposed can keep pace with these population projections.

Kenya, the single most important country in East Africa from the U.S. point of view, is in many ways the most promising nation in sub-Saharan Africa. As Richard Ford makes clear, Kenya has managed well a variety of internal and international economic, political, and ethnic challenges. It has survived recent droughts without loss of life. Its economy, however, is vulnerable to fickle international prices for tea and coffee, as well as to the whims, fears, and fads of European tourists, the cost of imported oil, and the weather. And it faces a twofold population increase in 18–20 years (one of the world's fastest growth rates). Kenya's land—less than 20 percent of which is available for farming, pasture, and woodlands—is losing its productivity at an alarming rate. By one estimate, as much as 50–75 percent of total production potential for some crops will be lost by the year 2000. What will Kenya be like then? Still our promising model for East African development? Or yet another African state in economic chaos?

Despite the frightening statistics in the following chapters, few, if any, of the environmental and population problems highlighted are unsolvable. Just as some now-barren areas of the Middle East were once farms and pasture, some areas of Africa and elsewhere may be too degraded to ever again be productive agricultural land. For the most part, however, the know-how and the human resources to protect and restore resources exist, and examples of successful applications abound. But time is of the essence. Whereas a decade ago developing-country leaders viewed talk of environmental protection as part of a conspiracy to prevent their development, today many, if not most, would agree with Tanzania's former President Julius Nyerere that "environmental concern and development have to be linked together if the latter is to be real and permanent."

We have a little time, but only a little, to accelerate restoration and productivity of the land. The next decade is crucial. Recognition of the problems is growing in both the developing and industrialized worlds. Decisive action—development strategies that conserve vital resources and use them efficiently, achieving the highest productivity sustainable over time—are required to tip the global balance against disaster.

The United States has an ecological as well as an economic and political stake in the outcome, for our shared global resources are threatened. In none of these developing countries can U.S. policymakers dictate solutions. Policies as sensitive as education for women, the promotion of family planning, or land reform cannot be imposed from without. Often, models developed in the United States (highly mechanized agriculture, intensive pesticide use, and flood irrigation) are ill suited to the culture or the environment of a developing country, and U.S. research priorities are not those of less industrialized nations.

But the United States does have wealth, experience, knowledge and skills that should be put to work in our interest and theirs. The following chapters suggest some domains in which U.S. policies could make a big difference—trade, debt management and/or relief, bilateral and multilateral assistance, and domestic economic policies. The final chapter includes recommendations for U.S. policymakers, especially on cooperation for sustainable development. Whatever these nations' other political, ethnic, and racial problems are, economic growth and, therefore, political viability will ultimately rest on the availability and wise management of natural and human resources.

References

1. See, for instance, the annual issue reviewing the year's significant events, "America and the World, 1986," *Foreign Affairs,* Vol. 65, No. 3, 1987, where in more than 250 pages written by 11 illustrious scholars, news analysts, and world leaders, the words "environment" and "resources" appear not at all, and the term "development" is dropped casually, and only in passing, even in articles that analyze revolution in Central America, progress in the Philippines, and the world economy and the U.S. relation to it. In the comparable 1989 issue (Vol. 68, No. 1), global environmental issues do not appear, poverty and population growth are barely mentioned and never discussed.

2. David Rockefeller, "Help Waited: Apostles of Aid," speech presented to the American Bankers Association at the International Banking Policy Forum (Washington, D.C., September 22, 1984).

3. U.S. Department of State, Bureau of Public Affairs, *Gist*, April 1987.

4. From 1986 to 1988 imports from developing countries averaged 33.1 percent, exports 34.3 percent. Statistics provided by the Bureau of Census Merchandise Trade Data, Washington, D.C., July 15, 1989.

5. Ray Marshall, "Jobs: The Shifting Structure of Global Employment," in John W. Sewell, Stuart K. Tucker, et al., *Growth Exports and Jobs in a Changing World Economy, Agenda 1988* (New Brunswick, New Jersey: Transaction Books, 1988), 185–186. These export figures do not include jobs in related service industries, which Stuart Tucker of the Overseas Development Council, Washington, D.C., estimates at another billion dollars worth of employment annually (personal communication, July 5, 1989).

6. National Association of State Development Agencies, *State Export Program Data Base* (Washington, D.C.: March 1988).

7. John W. Suomela, *The Effects of Developing Countries' Debt Servicing Problems on U.S. Trade*, Washington, D.C.: The International Trade Commission, at the request of the U.S. House of Representatives, Ways and Means Committee, March 1987), 142.

8. Suomela, *The Effects of Developing Countries' Debt Servicing Problems on U.S. Trade*, 147.

9. See Arthur H. Westing, Ed., *Global Resources and International Conflict, Environmental Factors in Strategic Policy and Action* (New York: Oxford University Press, 1986) for numerous examples of conflicts involving resources, and Leonard Berry, *Land, People and Resources in Sudan*, a case study done for the World Resources Institute (Washington, D.C.: March 1987).

10. J.K. Cooley, "The War Over Water," *Foreign Policy*, Vol. 54 (1984), 3–26.

11. Wendy Grieder, U.S. Environmental Protection Agency, "Environmental Issues in the Bilateral Relationship," presentation at the Overseas Development Council, Washington, D.C., June 12, 1986.

12. Cited in Hobart Rowen, "Global Overpopulation," *Washington Post*, February 17, 1985, E1. CIA staff briefed Washington population organizations at the time.

13. See Ruth Leger Sivard, *World Military and Social Expenditures 1987–88* (Washington, D.C.: World Priorities, 1988), and James Everett Katz, ed., *The Implications of Third World Military Industrialization, Sowing the Serpent's Teeth*, (Lexington, Massachusetts: Lexington Books, DC Heath and Co., 1986), xv.

14. World Resources Institute and International Institute for Environment and Development, *World Resources 1986* (New York: Basic Books, 1986), 3, 54 (hereafter cited as WRI/IIED, *World Resources 1986*, citing V. Smil, "China's Food," *Scientific American*, December 1985, 125.

15. WRI/IIED, *World Resources 1986*, 2–4, 70–73.

16. Marc Reisner and Ronald H. McDonald, "The High Costs of High Dams," in Andrew Maguire and Janet Welsh Brown, ed., *Bordering on Trouble: Resources and Politics in Latin America* (Bethesda, Maryland: Adler and Adler, 1986), 270–307; Lester R. Brown and Edward C. Wolf, *Soil Erosion: Quiet Crisis in the World Economy*, Worldwatch Paper No. 60 (Washington, D.C.: Worldwatch Institute, September 1984); WRI/IIED, *World Resources 1986*, 3.

17. United Nations Food and Agriculture Organization, *Agriculture: Toward 2000* (Rome: July 1987), 24, and World Resources Institute and International Institute for Environment and Development, *World Resources 1987* (New York: Basic Books, 1987), 280 (hereafter cited as WRI/IIED, *World Resources 1987*).

18. Global Environmental Monitoring Systems (GEMS), *Assessment of Freshwater Quality*, Report on the results of the World Health Organization/ United Nations Environment Programme on health-related environmental monitoring (Geneva: World Health Organization, 1988), 29–31.

19. World Resources Institute and International Institute for Environment and Development, *World Resources 1988–89* (New York: Basic Books, 1988), 28–30 (hereafter cited as WRI/IIED, *World Resources 1988–89*).

20. World Commission on Environment and Development, *Our Common Future* (New York: Oxford University Press, 1987), 126. This volume is an indispensible primer on the relation between environment and development. See

also WRI/IIED, *World Resources 1986*, 48–49; Michael Dover and Brian Croft, *Getting Tough: Public Policy and the Management of Pesticide Resistance* (Washington, D.C.: World Resources Institute, 1984); and Charles Pearson, *Down to Business: Multinational Corporation, the Environment and Development* (Washington, D.C.: World Resources Institute, January 1985).

21. For illustration of the extent and cost of soil loss see WRI/IIED, *World Resources 1986*, 5–6, 52–55.

22. World Commission on Environment and Development, 1987, *Our Common Future*, 128; Edward C. Wolf, "Managing Rangelands," in Lester R. Brown et al., *State of the World 1986* (New York: W.W. Norton & Co., 1986), 72.

23. World Commission on Environment and Development, 1986, *Our Common Future*, 125.

24. James Nations and H. Jeffrey Leonard, "Grounds for Conflict in Central America," in Maguire and Brown, 1986, *Bordering on Trouble*, 55–98, especially 67–74. For an excellent in-depth analysis of the relation between Central American development strategies and natural resources depletion, see H. Jeffrey Leonard, *Natural Resources and Economic Development in Central America, A Regional Environmental Profile* (New Brunswick, New Jersey: Transaction Books, for the International Institute for Environment and Development, 1987).

25. Nations and Leonard, 1986, "Grounds for Conflict in Central America."

26. Nafis Sadik, *The State of World Population 1989* (New York: United Nations Population Fund, 1989), 2.

27. Robert Repetto, "Population, Resources, Environment: An Uncertain Future," *Population Bulletin*, Vol. 42, No. 2, July 1987, 34–35.

28. Repetto, 1987, "Population, Resources, Environment: An Uncertain Future," 11.

29. Francisco Alba and Joseph E. Potter, "Population and Development in Mexico Since 1940: An Interpretation," *Population and Development Review*, Vol. 12, No. 1, March 1986, 47–75.

30. Robert Repetto, "Population, Resources and Poverty," in Robert Repetto, Ed., *The Global Possible: Resources, Development and the New Century* (New Haven, Connecticut: Yale University Press, 1985), 131–169.

31. World Commission on Environment and Development, 1987, *Our Common Future*, 28.

32. World Commission on Environment and Development, 1987, *Our Common Future*, 6.

II

Mexico's Environment and the United States

Richard A. Nuccio and Angelina M. Ornelas
with Contributions by Ivan Restrepo

Like many other countries, Mexico long ago set out on a development path that has accumulated greater and greater environmental deficits each year, but pushed them off onto future generations in the hope that more wisdom (and more political will) would be available to those who followed. Washington has recognized—in its Treasury initiative to convert some of Mexico's debt into government bonds at a discounted rate—that rolling Mexico's $105 billion foreign debt into a large ball and suspending it over the heads of Mexicans in the 21st century is not a wise or even viable solution to the country's financial crisis. Similarly, the resumption of significant economic growth in Mexico—a desirable and urgent necessity—without a reexamination of the resource and environmental consequences of the style of past development may impose on future generations of Mexicans a burden too great to bear.

As Mexicans lament in a popular refrain, destiny has placed Mexico "so far from God and so near to the United States." This same geographic imperative means that the systematic erosion of Mexico's human and material resource base has profound implications for the United States. Because of the crushing international debt, official and unofficial sources in the United States and in multilateral institutions funded in part by the United States now have more influence over Mexico's policy choices than at any time in recent memory. If used appropriately, this degree of influence could help Mexico confront the difficult choices it faces. But U.S. understanding of Mexico's unique political system and its patience with Mexican leaders' search for politically sustainable solutions seem lower than ever in the 1980s. In the words of one perceptive analyst, Mexico often serves as a "lightning rod" for the multiple frustrations that many North Americans feel toward the Third World more generally.[1]

When looking through the lens of population, environmental, and resource issues, a different Mexico than that portrayed in even expert analyses of the country comes into view. During the 1980s, "Mexico bashing" became virtually a U.S. national pastime and, according to some, Mexico has been governed by a corrupt and inefficient elite, insensitive to the needs of the majority of Mexicans and inept in the management of the political and economic demands of a modern world economy. Indeed, public discontent boiled to the surface in 1988 and severely challenged the Partido Revolucionario Institucional (the PRI) for the first time. Yet, this same ruling group, so criticized in the United States, was responsible for astonishing growth after World War II and, more recently, adopted policies of encouraging birth control that produced one of the most rapid turnarounds in population growth rates seen in the Third World.

As in some other areas of foreign policy, the Bush Administration has brought a new tone to U.S.-Mexican relations. Mexico has been visited by the Secretaries of State and Treasury and by the U.S. Attorney General. In October 1989 President Salinas addressed a joint session of Congress and stressed his commitment to defense of the environment as a priority area for bilateral cooperation between the two countries. This new spirit of dialogue and respect, if it is to endure, must quickly address the momentous environmental dilemmas that Mexico now faces.

The U.S. Stake in Mexico

Of the many foreign policy concerns that compete for the attention of a U.S. public frequently preoccupied with domestic and "pocketbook" issues, Mexico is one of the easiest "sells." Although dramatically true in the parts of the United States closest to Mexico (parts that were once Mexico), there is a realization even at more distant points such as the Midwest or New England that what happens on the borders of the United States is of great significance to the health and well-being of the entire country. A survey of U.S. citizens conducted by *Public Opinion* magazine in the summer of 1986 demonstrated this fact. Asked when they could justify the use of U.S. forces to defend an ally or allies under attack, huge majorities of those polled looked to Mexico and Canada as places where they could most strongly justify such action.[2] The United States has long been recognized by Mexicans as crucial to their national future. The United States is finally acknowledging that the reverse is true as well.

There are many other ways to demonstrate the significance of developments in Mexico for the United States beyond these all-important public perceptions. Economically, Mexico and the United States are deeply intertwined. Commercial banks are owed about $76 billion by Mexico; 10 leading U.S. banks hold two-thirds of all public and private Mexican external debt. A Mexican default could severely affect U.S. banks and has been described by one former U.S. government official as a "time bomb" waiting to explode.[3]

The United States is Mexico's most important trading partner and is in turn the fourth most important partner for the United States. The decline in U.S. exports to the troubled Mexican economy has been estimated to have cost 200,000 actual and potential U.S. jobs.[4] In 1987, Mexico's total petroleum exports amounted to nearly 1.4 billion barrels per day of which roughly half went to the United States. Since 1986 Mexico has been the sole supplier of crude oil to the U.S. strategic petroleum reserve. Mexico is the fourth largest oil producer in the world and has the largest petroleum reserve in the Western Hemisphere outside of the United States.[5] There are approximately 2,900 U.S. companies operating in Mexico worth some $8 billion; they account for close to 65 percent of Mexico's total foreign investment.

Culturally, the two societies are deeply embedded in each other and a rich cultural diversity exists along the border region. According to 1986 census figures—probably understated—one out of every 14 U.S. citizens is a Latino, or 7.2 percent of the total population. At 10.3 million, Mexican-Americans constitute the largest single group within the Latino community. They are nearly five times the size of the next largest Latino group, Puerto Ricans. This Mexican-American community has the potential—so far unrealized—to become a significant domestic factor in U.S.-Mexican relations. By the year 2000, there may be 25 million Mexican-Americans living in the Southwest, a potential voting bloc courted by both 1988 presidential aspirants.

Of the 3 million to 6 million undocumented immigrants in the United States, an estimated 2.5 million are from Mexico. The number of illegal immigrants detained by U.S. authorities has doubled in the 1980s. Each year 90 percent of the Immigration and Naturalization Service detainees (or some 1.7 million people) are Mexicans attempting to cross the borders of the United States illegally.[6] The 11 million Mexican citizens residing legally and illegally in the United States send between $2.5 billion and $6 billion back home each year.[7]

U.S. tourism is a financial lifeline of the Mexican economy. Eighty-five percent of Mexico's tourists are U.S. citizens; more U.S. air passengers go to Mexico than to any other country. A less savory economic connection concerns drugs: some estimates are that up to 80 percent of the marijuana and heroin entering the United States passes through Mexico.[8]

Although U.S. citizens are less aware of them, there are already significant connections between resource and environmental issues in Mexico and the United States. The triggering of alarms at a U.S. nuclear facility in December of 1983 was the first step in the uncovering of the most significant nuclear accident ever to occur on the North American continent. The improper disposal of an antiquated X-ray machine (sold in Mexico after being replaced in the United States) led through a bizarre sequence of events to the incorporation of highly radioactive cobalt-60 pellets into steel made from scrap metal in Mexico. The scrap steel was in turn exported to the United States, where it would have emitted toxic doses of radiation if it had not been detected fortuitously when delivered to a construction site at the U.S. facility. Investigations led back to the Mexican scrap dealer who had removed the X-ray machine, and it was discovered that children from a poor neighborhood of Ciudad Juarez were still playing with the radioactive pellets from the machine left in the dealer's pickup truck. Radioactive steel from this accident was eventually traced to a pizza parlor in Chicago and to buildings in Hawaii and Kuwait.

Pesticides banned in the United States and the processes for producing them are routinely exported to Mexico. These banned chemicals continue to be used in Mexico and are exported to other countries. Significant amounts of Mexican fruits and vegetables exported to the United States are sprayed with toxic substances prohibited in this country and arrive on U.S. market shelves with residues.[9] Industrial wastes generated in Mexico's *maquiladora* (in-bond assembly) zone, which are supposed to be returned to the United States for proper disposal, are routinely flushed into sewer systems, improperly disposed of in remote areas, or stored on company back lots. Containers used to store hazardous and toxic chemicals imported from the United States to the *maquila* zone are not disposed of properly, and are often used by the poor to hold drinking water.[10]

Ties such as these between events in Mexico and the United States help to explain why Mexico has been called the most complicated foreign policy relationship that the United States has to manage. The local, regional and state interactions with Mexico also make the relationship more like a domestic policy problem than one of foreign policy. Virtually every agency of the U.S. government, from the Department of Transportation to the Environmental Protection Agency, and numerous state governments have offices devoted to some aspect of the myriad relations with Mexico.

Mexico in the Policy Spotlight

Mexico is experiencing some of the most far-reaching upheavals of its political and economic system in decades. The death knell of Mexico's oil-fed economic boom came in August of 1982, when external financing of the economy collapsed, and what has come to be known as the Latin American debt crisis spread from Mexico to the major economic powers in South America. Since then, Mexico has been engaged in a series of heroic holding operations to stabilize its stricken economy, satisfy the insistent demands of external lending institutions such as the International Monetary Fund (IMF) and the money-center banks for major restructuring of the Mexican economy, and negotiate new loans that go only to pay the interest on past debt—payments that amount to $60 billion over the past six years and consume 50 percent of Mexico's foreign earnings.

Mexico has made progress on each of these fronts—stabilization, restructuring, and new financing—but at enormous social cost. Per capita income fell by some 7 percent between 1980 and 1986; real wages declined by at least 20 percent during the same period. This in a country with few social "safety nets," where the wealthiest 10 percent of the population receives 41 percent of total income and the poorest one-fifth, less than 3 percent.

Politically, Mexico has had the dubious privilege of occupying more U.S. news column attention than at any point in recent memory. A pattern of fraudulently conducted elections has characterized Mexican politics for decades and helped to solidify the hold of the ruling PRI on national power.[11] These allegedly fraudulent practices became the object of organized protest and greater international scrutiny as the economic crisis of the 1980s deepened. The economic crisis encouraged the party of traditional middle-class protest, the PAN, or National Action Party, to question its role as a local party of meek and perpetual semiloyal opposition, and to debate whether it should attempt to acquire real national power. The PRI's imposition of orthodox stabilization policies that so pleased international bankers splintered the party's nationalist left wing and helped to forge the most successful challenge from the left in modern Mexican history. In July 1988 Cuauhtemoc Cardenas, son of a legendary PRI president, led a coalition of left-of-center parties to an electoral victory second only to the PRI's. By the PRI's own contested count, the Democratic Front won 30 percent of the popular vote and challenges continued months after the election.

The origins of Mexico's acute contemporary political and economic crises lie in the 1960s. It was during that decade that the economic model of import-substitution industrialization being followed by Mexico gave early indicators of having exhausted its usefulness. As discussed more fully in the section on agriculture and industry dealing with Mexico's rural problems, part of the inadequacy of the model lay in its neglect of the rural areas—where the majority of Mexicans at one point lived and where productive activities might have helped feed Mexico's increasing numbers and slowed the rush of population to the cities.

Another part lay in an intrinsic failure of the model everywhere it was applied in Latin America: the creation of an inefficient industrial structure that produced low-quality goods competitive only in an internal market protected by high tariffs. This model led to the dead end in Mexico, as in many countries, of substituting imports of even more expensive capital goods and, at times, raw materials for the earlier imports of finished and intermediate goods. Poor-quality products, desirable only in the protected domestic market, never earned the foreign exchange as exports to pay for the imports of capital goods. Foreign borrowing became the only way to fill the resulting foreign exchange gap.

Moreover, only the relatively privileged upper and middle classes could afford Mexican-produced, high-priced luxuries such as stoves, washers and dryers, and refrigerators. This small market of wealthier Mexicans, constituting perhaps 15 percent of the population, was to be found in the major cities. A vicious cycle began. Protected industries located close to their major markets in the cities drew labor from the countryside into increasingly crowded urban centers. Government policies kept agricultural prices low to supply inexpensive foodstuffs to the urban working class. Low agricultural prices drove even more peasants into urban areas and producers out of basic commodities such as beans and corn and into cash crops for exports.

The environmental consequences were equally grave. Guadalajara, Monterrey, Puebla, and, above all, Mexico City became the primary poles of economic growth, and of environmental deterioration. A macrocephalic development that outstripped urban services of housing, potable water, and sewage and other waste disposal became the rule. Industrial discharges and the overwhelming of dangerous but previously isolated sites of chemical production and energy distribution by residential areas contributed to truly horrific environmental conditions. It is this pattern of development that Mexico must now, in the midst of severe austerity, try to reorient.

The environmental and resource consequences of Mexico's development did not happen by accident. They flowed from a pattern of economic growth that was presented as being technically sound at the time—perhaps because it was politically acceptable to a growing middle class. But that model of development has already seriously eroded the human and material base upon which the future of Mexico will be built. In response to the economic and environmental failures of this import substitution model, a new model of export-led growth has been adopted by Mexico.[12] But the resumption of growth in Mexico without an examination of the style of development followed in the past and its environmental consequences may leave Mexico less equipped in the future to deal with the powerful social, economic, and political challenges it will face in the next century, little more than a decade away.

This chapter examines those key issues that are at once the most crucial for Mexico's future and, therefore, most likely to affect its national security if not addressed effectively. It then focuses on Mexico's responses to its environmental dilemmas and draws some policy conclusions about how the United States and Mexico can work more effectively together and separately to lift the unbearable burdens that environmental deterioration is imposing on Mexico's future generations. It does not pretend to be a comprehensive review of all the environmental challenges facing Mexico nor to necessarily reflect the priority that Mexicans would establish in dealing with them.

The State of the Mexican Environment

This section focuses on those environmental and resource issues that are the most basic to the structure of production in industry and the rural sector and to the provision of food and essential services to the poor majority of Mexicans. It begins with Mexico's natural resource endowment and the way it has been used and abused, particularly in the tropical zones. Part of the reason for abuse of natural resources is population pressure. While Mexico has made great strides recently in controlling population, the weight of past growth strains Mexico's ability to provide a decent standard of living for the majority of its people. Agriculture and industry are the sectors that must provide the employment and food to improve living standards, and the environmental consequences of past and present policies in those sectors are examined next. Finally, the situation in Mexico City is described as an extreme example of the consequences of overcentralization as pursued in Mexico's past development policies.

Natural Resources

Mexico has a rich natural endowment, but not necessarily one fully suited to the patterns of settlement and economic activity undertaken by modernizing Mexico. From the location of its principal rivers to the availability of land for distribution to landless peasants, Mexico faces a series of resource challenges that require wise management.

The distribution, availability, and quality of Mexico's water supply remains at the top of the country's resource dilemmas despite the fact that this precious liquid is renewable. Surface waters in Mexico are scarce. Those that do exist are far from the areas of major water demand or are located at elevations that require significant transport and/or pumping costs. All five of Mexico's major rivers—totalling more than 50 percent of the mean annual flow of all Mexican rivers—are located in the tropical, southeastern part of the country. Eighty-five percent of Mexico's water resources are located in areas of less than 500 meters in elevation, yet 70 percent of the population and 80 percent of the country's industry are in areas above that level. A disproportionate 55 percent of industrial activity is located in the Valley of Mexico at elevations of between 1,700 and 2,300 meters.[13]

As in most developing countries, this relatively poor geographic endowment is aggravated by an accelerated development process that has increased the extraction and consumption of water and produced discharges that are often dumped untreated into water supplies. This problem is particularly grave in Mexico City and the surrounding Valley of Mexico and is discussed more fully in the section on Mexico City.

Mexico is experiencing conflicts over water usage on regional and local levels. In Baja California, international agreements with the United States divert nearly 2 billion cubic meters of water annually to Mexico from the Colorado River. Mexico City, in turn, draws supplies from more and more distant points. Conflicts over water supplies or problems with water quality have led to calls for the diversion of water from agricultural production to urban use in cities such as Tampico, Coatzacoalcos, Merida, Torreon, Nogales, and Guadalajara.[14]

The pressures noted on Mexico's inland water supplies are unfortunately equally true for coastal zones. Mexico possesses some 10,000 kilometers of coastline, a wide continental shelf, and several hundred thousand acres of estuaries that are an incalculable source of food and economic activity. Rich and complex coastal ecosystems are in constant danger from the discharge of wastewaters from urban and industrial centers and ships, and from pesticide and fertilizer runoff. The impact of oil extraction and refining in the Southeast and Gulf has been documented as particularly alarming.[15]

Each year nearly a million acres of Mexican forests are lost due to human exploitation.[16] Figures vary as to the exact amount of forested land that remains (at least 100 million acres) and the degree of desertification.[17] But there is agreement that the over-exploitation of renewable resources, the extension of cattle grazing to vast new areas of the country, and the inappropriate application in tropical zones of techniques suited to temperate climates are producing grave losses in the quantity and quality of Mexico's land and forest resources.

The tropical areas of southeast Mexico have been particularly hardhit by "modern" techniques of land exploitation. Tropical silviculture requires a careful application of land-use techniques based on extensive studies of the existing flora and fauna. Yet these detailed investigations of field conditions in the Southeast do not yet exist.[18]

Development projects in the Southeast have too often ignored the special needs of the tropical areas. They have followed a pattern of razing the jungle with heavy earth-moving equipment and either planting monoculture crops such as sugarcane or rice that are not well suited to the climate and soil conditions of the region or establishing cattle-raising operations that damage the fragile ecosystem and actually increase unemployment in the area.[19] This has been the case in the ambitious development projects in the region of Uxpanapa in the state of Veracuz; those of Candelaria and Valle de Edzna in Campeche; and, in the state of Tabasco, of Balancan-Tenosique and La Chontalpa.

As one of the Mexican government's oldest development projects for the tropics, La Chontalpa merits special mention. Conceived in 1963, the Plan Chontalpa was designed to be a model of modern agricultural methods. It covers nearly 100,000 acres, includes almost 6,000 households, and represents an investment by the Mexican government and the Inter-American Development Bank of more than 3 billion pesos (or more than US$120 million at exchange rates prevailing during the years of the plan).[20]

Intended to focus the benefits of agricultural development on the local region, the Plan has suffered during its existence from political and technical confusion and produced mixed results. A backward and economically and culturally isolated region has become integrated into the national and even international market. But the clearing of large tracts of land for cattle raising and for sugarcane production has created new problems for La Chontalpa.

The tropical environment has been dramatically altered by the new agricultural and cattle-raising activities in ways not foreseen by the original developers of the Plan. The clearing of jungle forests and construction of dams to control floods and channel water has lowered the water table and reduced the soil's productivity by eliminating the nutrient-rich sediment that accompanied the floods. This has created a growing necessity for expensive artificial fertilizers to maintain an adequate return on investment. A dramatic decline has been noted in the number of species of plants and animals that traditionally served as an important component of local inhabitants' diets. Families eat more "modern" foods such as wheat bread and processed products, but their relatively high cost has actually lead to a reduction in nutritional levels. The destruction of forest cover has increased winds that damage crops and accelerate soil erosion. The relocation of peasant families to urban centers has given them greater access to health care facilities and certain diseases such as tuberculosis and malaria have decreased. But gastrointestinal parasites are more common among children living under the Plan.

The contradictions of modernization as revealed in the costs and benefits for the local population of the Chontalpa Plan are a warning sign of problems intrinsic to the current models of development being followed in the Mexican tropics. It is an example of massive investment being insufficient to consistently raise diet and nutrition in the countryside because of the Plan's unforeseen effects on the environment and on patterns of consumption and production.

Population

Until very recently, Mexico was not overly concerned about population growth at the national level. (See Table 1.) As late as 1970, Mexico's President Luis Echeverria endorsed a pro-natalist view with comments that, "To govern is to populate" and "I do not know whether Mexican mothers understand the effectiveness of the contraceptive pill. What I do know is that we need to populate our country...we do not want to control our population."[21]

In the late 1960s, the inability to meet rising economic demands despite impressive rates of economic advancement led the Mexican government to recognize that uncontrolled population growth threatened the Mexican economic "miracle," which had been central to the success of the PRI's dominance of the country.

Consequently, a revised General Law of Population was passed in 1973 and implemented in early 1974. Its key provision was Article 3, Part II, which stated the government's intention

to carry out programs of family planning through the educational and public health services of the public sector and to take care that these programs and those of private organizations be carried out with absolute respect for the fundamental rights

Table 1. Population of Mexico from 1519 to 2000

Date	Population	Date	Population
1519	25,200,000	1895	12,632,427
1532	16,800,000	1900	13,607,259
1548	6,300,000	1910	15,160,369
1568	1,900,000	1921	14,834,760
1595	1,375,000	1930	16,552,722
1605	1,075,000	1940	19,653,552
1650 (c.)	1,500,000	1950	25,791,017
1700	2,000,000	1960	34,923,129
1742	3,336,000	1970	48,313,438
1793	5,200,000	1980	66,843,833
1803	5,380,000	1985	78,996,000
1810	6,122,000	1986	79,914,000
1823	6,800,000	1987	81,521,000
1838	7,044,000	1988	83,061,000
1855	8,397,000	1990	86,018,000
1877	9,389,000	1995	93,120,000
1884	10,448,000	2000	104,000,000

Source: Ortiz Monasterio, F. et al., Tierra Profanada; Historia Ambiental de Mexico. INAH/SEDUE Mexico, 1987; Quote: Censos de Población. México.
Cited in Fernando Ortiz Monasterio, "Society and Nature in Contemporary Mexico." Paper delivered at the Conference on Environment and Development: The Outlook for U.S.-Mexican Relations, Racine, Wisconsin May 1–3, 1988.

of man and that they preserve the dignity of families, with the object of regulating rationally and stabilizing the growth of population, so as to achieve the best utilization of the human and natural resources of the country.[22]

In 1974, Article 4 of the 1917 Constitution was revised to guarantee equal rights for women, to bring about responsible parenthood, and to enable women to decide "in a free, responsible, and informed manner" on the size and spacing of their families.[23] Mexico thus became, with Yugoslavia and China, one of only three countries in the world to guarantee family planning as a constitutional right.

Under the banner of slogans such as "Vamonos haciendo menos" ("Let's become less"), the government mobilized considerable resources in its attempt to change public attitudes toward parenthood. In the field of the mass media, the government orchestrated planned population messages through radio and television stations, newspapers, and magazines. From a population growth rate as high as 3.5 percent as recently as 1973, Mexico decreased its rate of increase to 2.6 percent by 1986.[24] This dramatic turnaround is credited by population specialists to the effective measures taken by the government's often-criticized bureaucracy.[25]

But the damage had already been done. The base on which these lower rates will grow is already large. By the year 2010 Mexico's current population of 85 million is projected to reach nearly 200 million. Because of past population growth, Mexico is now a very youthful country. United Nations world population estimates show that in 1985, 42.2 percent of Mexicans were under the age of 15. This means that every year 700,000 to 800,000 young men and women enter the labor force. To reduce just the rate of open unemployment from its present level of 13–14 percent to 6 percent, Mexico will have to generate about a million new jobs per year through the end of this century.[26]

Unfortunately, forces have been set in motion that could reverse the important gains in controlling population made by Mexico in the last decades. A growing consensus among experts argues that three ingredients in modern developing economies produce declining birth rates: a growing degree of security in the society, based on security of land tenure or employment; a "rising opportunity cost for children" that encourages families to forgo additional children in favor of expenditures on goods and services; and the availability of easy and effective means of contraception.[27] The virtual abandonment of Mexico's fitful land reform programs, the transformation of the agricultural sector to export crops (detailed later), and the rapid decline of purchasing power for most Mexicans are putting pressure on the first two of these factors, affecting attitudes toward the costs and benefits of additional children. (See Table 2.) Indeed, as Angus Wright has pointed out,

> all of those things that provided a measure of security and rising opportunity costs for children during the high growth and relatively high social spending years of the seventies are being lost. The average Mexican is beginning to experience an increasingly insecure world in which the institutions of society other than the family are failing badly. If such trends continue long enough to constitute the main learning experience of a generation, there is every reason to believe that the rate of population growth will not decline further and that it might even begin to rise again.[28]

Mexico, like many developing countries, finds itself in the middle stage of a demographic transition marked by high fertility and low mortality that cannot continue indefinitely without exhausting Mexico's resource base. Yet Mexico has been trapped in this middle stage for nearly four decades. To exit from it, Mexico must be encouraged to develop a combination of economic policies and family planning programs capable of further reducing birth rates and increasing

**Table 2.   Changes in Population and Per Capita Income, Major
               Countries, 1980–86**

Country	Rate of Population Growth	Cumulative Change in Per Capita Income, 1980-86
Rising Incomes		
China	1.0	+58
South Korea	1.6	+34
Japan	0.7	+21
India	2.1	+14
West Germany	-0.2	+10
United States	0.7	+10
United Kingdom	0.2	+12
France	0.4	+ 3
Declining Incomes		
Nigeria	3.0	-28
Argentina	1.6	-21
Phillipines	2.5	-16
Peru	2.5	-11
Kenya	4.2	- 8
Mexico	2.6	- 7
Sudan	2.9	- 7
Brazil	2.3	- 6

Source: Lester Brown, et al., *State of the World 1987*, 28, citing population growth rates from
Population Reference Bureau, 1986 World Population Data Sheet (Washington D.C.:
1986); changes in per capita income for 1979–84 from B. Blazic-Metzner, and for
1985 from David Cieslikowski, Economic Analysis and Projections Department,
World Bank, Washington D.C., private communications, July 25 and October 22,
1986.

living standards. Otherwise, the logic of the ecological transition—rapid
population growth overwhelming natural support systems and environmental
deterioration reducing per capita food production and income—takes over.[29]

Agriculture and Industry

In 1942, after President Lazaro Cardenas' successful land and agricultural
reform of the 1930s, President Avila Camacho initiated the restructuring of

Mexico's agricultural sector to "serve as a basis for the founding of industrial greatness."[30]

Steven Sanderson, in his book, *The Transformation of Mexican Agriculture*, argues that

> public infrastructure investment centered on huge dams, irrigation canals, and federal districts for water control while private sector investment sought to modernize agricultural support industries such as fertilizer, farm machinery, seeds, and pesticides.[31]

Furthermore, continues Sanderson, "as the economy shifted from a rural to an urban setting and from agriculture to industry after World War II," the role of agriculture in the Mexican economy shifted to become the "adjunct of industrialization."[32]

Industrialization was intensified through public capital investments in industry and infrastructure programs and projects such as roads, electrification, telecommunications, and irrigation projects. These investments, combined with the Mexican government's ability to maintain political stability, increased confidence among the Mexican private sector and foreign (mainly U.S.) investors, promoting important infusions of private capital.

Under Mexico's import-substitution industrialization, the modernization of agriculture was sought through the investment of public funds in capital-intensive technologies suitable for good farmland or areas brought under cultivation by large irrigation projects. During 1941–52, "18 percent of Mexico's federal budget and 92 percent of its agricultural budget was spent on irrigation projects that created vast new stretches of rich farmland in the north of Mexico."[33] A pattern of inequality was established early in the irrigation programs that endures to the present day: of the more than 7 million acres of land that benefited from these public investments, only 400,000 belonged to small farmers or were part of the communal farm system known in Mexico as *ejidos*.

The End of Food Self-sufficiency. By the 1970s a new pattern of agricultural production in Mexico had emerged. As technology facilitated the exportation of manufacturing and of advanced labor processes worldwide, a "globalization" of production occurred. For Mexican agriculture, this meant a new mode of production characterized by the commercial contracting and technological packaging of whole-crops industries such as strawberries, asparagus, cucumbers, and tomatoes. Agribusiness giants like Del Monte, General Foods, and Campbell's, other "food brokers," and contracting supermarket chains such as Safeway brought Mexico into the "Global Supermarket." The shift in cultivation from local consumption to production for the U.S. market was dramatic. (See Tables 3 and 4.)

Table 3. Mexican Exports of Selected Irrigated Crops, 1950–1977 (tons)

	Cotton	Grapes	Garbanzos*	Strawberries
1950	162,637	75	11,639	1,632
1960	324,302	26	4,730	13,261
1970	222,681	4,965	8,492	81,990
1975	37,936	4,757	32,006	64,545
1976	179,099	7,625	28,450	38,100
1977	152,809	15,328	46,522	80,429

*Includes forage also.

Note: The viability of these data, along with other SARH figures, is thrown into question by the inconsistency of USDA, World Bank, SARH, and Bank of Mexico figures. All the sources do show similar trends.

Source: Mexico, SARH, Econotecnia agricola, 1980.
Steven E. Sanderson, *The Transformation of Mexican Agriculture.* Copyright © 1986 by Princeton University Press. Fig., p. 45, reprinted with permission of Princeton University Press.

- From 1960 to 1974, onion exports from Mexico to the United States increased over five times, to 95 million pounds.
- During the same period, cucumber exports soared from under 9 million to over 196 million pounds.
- Between 1960 and 1972, eggplant exports multiplied 10 times, and squash exports 43 times.
- By the late 1970s, frozen strawberries and cantaloupe from Mexico supplied more than a third of U.S. annual consumption.
- About half of all tomatoes sold in the wintertime in the United States (some two-thirds of a billion pounds by 1976) came from Mexico, or more precisely, from 50 growers in the state of Sinaloa, who in 1976 sold $100 million of tomatoes in the West and Midwest.[34]

The reduction of agriculture to the "adjunct of industry" and the internationalization of agribusiness to the production of exportable fruits and vegetables and of feed grains has contributed to Mexico's crisis of the 1980s. Despite the supposed benefits of comparative advantage theory, Mexico's agricultural exports have not kept pace with the costs of increasing imports of

Table 4. Mexican Exports of Selected Vegetables to the United States, 1971-1980 (metric tons)

	Asparagus	Cucumbers	Eggplant	Onions	Peppers	Tomatoes
1971	0	64,841	10,502	18,642	33,711	258,682
1972	0	69,884	13,066	25,993	27,646	264,124
1973	3,304	75,517	17,761	56,332	40,081	339,801
1974	4,132	76,143	11,885	40,982	39,274	267,897
1975	3,849	55,482	11,706	34,037	28,303	253,605
1976	3,739	89,004	13,480	33,754	40,106	294,198
1977	1,978	107,119	14,457	44,203	51,199	356,251
1978	2,271	129,223	18,942	53,857	65,598	369,283
1979	3,036	134,692	18,009	64,902	61,381	322,170
1980	3,267	135,785	16,443	57,108	75,610	294,601

Note: Includes fresh, chilled, and frozen vegetables.

Source: U.S. Department of Agriculture, Foreign Agriculture Circular. Fresh and Processed Vegetables, "Vegetables: Trade Statistics in Selected Countries," FVEG1-82, Foreign Agricultural Services, January 1982.
Steven E. Sanderson, *The Transformation of Mexican Agriculture.* Copyright © 1986 by Princeton University Press. Fig., p. 89, reprinted with permission of Princeton University Press.

other agricultural commodities made necessary by this very model of agricultural development. In a pattern not unlike that of manufactures, the prices of crops sold predominantly by industrial countries, crops like grains and soybeans, have risen faster than the prices of commodities exported by developing countries. In addition, agribusiness has failed to absorb rural labor displaced by modernization and industrialization and to improve the nutritional standards of the mass of the population.[35]

The Catch-22 of Mexico's current agricultural dilemma is well illustrated by the $5-billion program to spur food production announced in mid-1985 by President de la Madrid. The impetus for the program was a food import bill for 1985 of $1.5 billion—to be paid with scarce foreign exchange—to import corn and other daily dietary staples once grown in sufficient quantities in Mexico. Kenneth Shwedel, a senior economist at Banamex, a major Mexican bank, commented to the *Wall Street Journal* that, "Today's food problem comes, in part, from the success of the urbanization of the 1950s and 1960s. Real agricultural prices all reached a peak in 1950 and have been falling ever since."[36]

In making agriculture the "adjunct of industry," the Mexican government held down the price of tortillas to feed the thousands of people from the countryside drawn to industrial jobs in the cities. This depressed prices for corn, driving even more rural inhabitants off the land and into the cities, where industrial employment could not keep up with expanding demand for work.

While the government controlled the corn market, a private sorghum market sprouted. Land planted to sorghum (primarily used as feed grain for dairy cattle raised in Mexico) rose to 3.7 million acres from 2.5 million acres between 1970 and 1980. Corn cultivation, on the other hand, declined to 17 million acres from 18 million. From 1958 to 1980, the production of sorghum grew 2,772 percent and the amount of land sown in sorghum climbed 1,300 percent.[37]

At a time of heavy indebtedness, the last thing Mexico needs is a $5-billion program that will add to the public deficit because its product—corn—will be sold at controlled prices to lower the cost of tortillas. But any attempt to raise tortilla prices to provide greater incentives for corn producers could provoke urban protests of a kind Mexico must also seek to avoid.

Pesticides. Each year hundreds of millions of pounds of pesticides are used in developing countries. Unwise or unrestricted use of pesticides in Mexico has had truly disastrous consequences. In the Rio Grande Valley of Mexico cotton production virtually disappeared in 1970. Some 700,000 acres were abandoned. Cotton gins, compresses, and oil mills went out of business and farmworkers sought work elsewhere. A once prosperous community was plunged into social and economic depression.[38]

This disaster occurred when the tobacco budworm, an important cotton pest, became resistant to a wide range of pesticides. When the budworm's natural enemies were wiped out by pesticides, even levels of these chemicals that often made farmworkers ill were insufficient to defeat the budworm. In northwestern Mexico alone, the budworm wiped out, almost totally, cotton crops worth $135 million a year.

Unfortunately, crops are not the only casualties of indiscriminate pesticide use. The *Los Angeles Times,* as part of a 1980 investigative report on pesticides in Mexico, found that in Culiacan, Sinaloa, a state in northern Mexico, government doctors saw two or three pesticide poisonings every week on large plantations where tomatoes for American supermarkets are grown. Since they lack sick leave, stricken workers often returned to the fields immediately. The report also charged that some farmworkers died from aplastic anemia, a blood disease linked to organochlorine pesticides used in the area.[39]

Los Angeles Times reporters Laurie Becklund and Ron Taylor found that workers lived on small plots of land between the crops and irrigation canals that collected the pesticide runoff. In addition to washing their children, dishes, and clothes in the canals, the workers would fill discarded insecticide tubs with contaminated water from the canals for drinking purposes. Nearby, modern greenhouses were supplied with purified water to nurture tomato seedlings.[40]

Table 5. Pesticides Used in Foreign Countries on Food Exported to the United States

Commodity	Countries	Allowed or recommended in the U.S.	—Number of Pesticides— Any residue prohibited (no U.S. tolerance)	Not detectable with FDA test
Bananas	Colombia Costa Rica Ecuador Guatemala Mexico	45	25	37
Coffee	Brazil Colombia Costa Rica Ecuador Guatemala Mexico	94	76	64
Sugar	Brazil Colombia Costa Rica Ecuador Guatemala India Thailand	61	34	33
Tomatoes	Mexico Spain	53	21	28
Tea	India Sri Lanka	24	20	11
Cacao	Costa Rica Ecuador	14	7	7
Tapioca	Thailand	4	4	1
Strawberries	Mexico	13	—	5
Peppers	Mexico	12	—	4
Olives	Italy Spain	20	14	8
Totals		340	201 (59%)	198 (58%)

Source: General Accounting Office
Cited in David Weir and Mark Shapiro, *Circle of Poison: Pesticides and People in a Hungry World* (San Francisco, California: Institute for Food and Development Policy, 1981), 82.

Angus Wright has reported from his field experience in the Culiacan Valley that farmers apply toxic pesticides to their crops 25 to 50 times a season "in almost total disregard for elementary rules of human health protection and environmental safety." The result is that,

> with the new emphasis on and success of the winter vegetable crops sold in the United States, there are nearly a quarter of a million migrant farmworkers who live and work in an environment constantly sprayed with substances known to cause, in addition to immediate poisoning symptoms ranging from dermatitis to death, severe respiratory disease, long-term nerve damage, blindness, mental disturbances, birth defects, abortions, leukemia, aplastic anemia, liver cancer, kidney cancer, and a variety of other serious disease syndromes. Leukemia rates, for example, are three times as high in the agricultural areas of the state of Sinaloa as in non-agricultural areas.[41]

Although farmers, handlers, and fieldworkers suffer the most from pesticide exposure, consumers of fruits and vegetables on which pesticides are used are also potentially threatened. In the United States, shipments of imported raw agricultural commodities are regularly monitored, but authority for the control of pesticide residue in imported foodstuffs is divided between the Food and Drug Administration (FDA) and the Environmental Protection Agency (EPA). Critics charge that the monitoring program allows chemically contaminated food products to be sold to the U.S. consumer.[42]

There have been consistent problems with monitoring programs directed toward Mexico, the largest exporter of fresh fruits and vegetables to the United States. The EPA and FDA argue, for example, that because of climatic and biological differences between the United States and Mexico, pesticides permitted for use in Mexico may not always be approved for use in the United States. (See Table 5.) Residues of pesticides remaining on products grown in one country for export to the other are said to pose "legal" rather than "health" problems for consumers. U.S. government agencies have, therefore, granted Mexico numerous "emergency" exemptions to permit the importation of fruits and vegetables into the United States without established residue standards, examinations of dietary exposures, or regard for toxicological considerations.

In 1979, a special program of surveillance exclusively for Mexican produce imports was instituted by the FDA. (See Table 6.) Monitoring was stepped up by increasing the amount of "spot-check" sampling by 20 percent, so that by 1983 the Government Accounting Office found that the number of Mexican shipments sampled in monitoring programs equaled the total number of shipments sampled from all other countries combined.

But stepped-up monitoring has not actually prevented the entry of adulterated products into the United States. Almost one-third of the contaminated imports from Mexico are still sold in the United States as a result of the FDA's policy of

Table 6. Results of the FDA's Mexican Surveillance Program for the Years 1980 and 1981

	1980		1981	
Samples analyzed	1,917		1,687	
Commodity types analyzed	54		47	
Different pesticides detected	56		57	
Number of violative samples	90	(5.3%)	52	(2.7%)
Above EPA tol.	10	(0.6%)	14	(0.7%)
No EPA tol.	80	(4.7%)	38	(2.0%)

Source: Shelly A. Hearne, *Harvest of Unknowns: Pesticide Contamination in Imported Foods,* (New York, New York: Natural Resources Defense Council, 1984) p. 45.

allowing perishable goods to be marketed before completion of their analysis if the product has no previous history of residue violations.

Cooperative efforts between the United States and Mexico to reduce the misuse of pesticides apparently have been successful in the past. In 1981 an educational program on pesticide application and usage led to significant decreases in the percentage of contaminated samples. Yet because of Mexico's financial crisis and the lack of U.S. congressional funding, this cooperative program to prevent chemically contaminated foods from entering the United States was phased out.

Mexican growers have responded to these concerns about pesticide residues on their exports and the lobbying efforts of ever-watchful Florida growers to restrict Mexican imports on health grounds by changing the types of pesticides they use.[43] They have largely abandoned so-called persistent compounds banned in the United States (such as DDT) that have relatively low toxicity for workers applying them but that persist for long periods in the environment. Instead, they now employ non-persistents (such as parathion) that deteriorate rapidly and do not concentrate in animal and human tissue but that pose grave toxic risks to workers applying them, especially under the lax safety standards practiced in Mexico. Consumers and migrant workers who will suffer the illness and potential cancers associated with the use of these pesticides are arguably the most important interests at stake, and yet they are the least protected by the way in which Mexico and the United States are addressing this environmental problem.[44]

The Border and the Environment. In 1965, the Mexican government instituted the Border Industrialization Program—known as the *maquiladora* or in-bond industry in Mexico—to stimulate industrial development and provide employment on the Mexican side of the border and to help reduce illegal immigration to the United States. Taxed only on the value added to goods produced in the *maquiladora* program, numerous U.S. firms have been attracted to invest in border operations.

Particularly well-suited for the *maquiladora* program have been industries that combine three features: high labor intensity within an easily separable portion of the productive process; moderate transporation costs and easily transportable goods; and a need for fast turnover and rapid delivery to U.S. markets.[45] These include industries such as electronic and electric goods, machinery and transportation equipment, shoes and apparel, furniture, and nonelectric equipment.

Concern that flight from stricter pollution controls in the United States motivated some of these industries to participate in the *maquiladora* program was initially diminished by the fact that for many of the participating industries pollution control was not a major factor of production costs. However, because of the labor-intensive nature of their industrial processes, "there has been a growing focus in recent years on the workplace health dangers associated with some of the *maquiladora* industries."[46]

Because the electronic and electric industries represent close to half the *maquila* sector, recent pilot studies suggesting workplace hazards in their processes—once considered "clean"—are a special area for attention.[47] The manufacture and assembly of high-tech equipment and components requires the storage, use, and disposal of a wide range of hazardous materials. Accidents, faulty equipment, inadequate procedures, and routine releases all have the potential to expose substantial numbers of people in adjacent communities to chemical risks.[48] Studies documenting injury to workers in the electronic in-bond industries do not yet offer conclusive proof. But the indications of pilot studies in the United States that pregnant women (and their fetuses) may be especially susceptible to the health effects of solvents and chemicals used in these industries give cause for great caution. In 1983, Mexican women in the prime child-bearing age made up more than 60 percent of the blue collar jobs in the *maquila* sector.

Illegal Dumping and Transborder Flows. Despite the fact that there are few fully documented cases of illegal transboundary movement of toxic and hazardous waste from the United States and Mexico, the suspicion is that such movement is a growing problem with both national and international implications. Fear of an environmental and public health catastrophe abroad caused by waste from the United States reportedly helped to bring about a bilateral agreement between the United States and Mexico on the transboundary movement of hazardous waste and hazardous substances.[49]

On November 12, 1986, the Environmental Protection Agency and the Ministry of Urban Development and Ecology (SEDUE) agreed to take steps to regulate the export and import of hazardous substances in order to reduce or prevent risks to public health, property, and environmental quality. The agreement provides for "notification, and, in the case of hazardous waste, for prior written consent from a receiving country for a proposed export." Improperly shipped materials can be returned to their country of origin under the agreement. Finally, under its guidelines, it establishes "a program for the exchange of data and criteria regarding imminent and substantial endangerment and emergency responses."[50]

To encourage coordination between EPA and SEDUE in a number of areas including hazardous wastes, air quality, and water quality, this agreement was incorporated into an early framework agreement between the United States and Mexico, signed by Presidents Reagan and de la Madrid in 1983. At a time of generally poor relations between the two countries, the negotiation of this agreement was a significant step forward in addressing bilateral environmental dangers.

The March 1988 enactment of the General Law of Ecological Balance and Environmental Protection establishes much higher penalties for violations of Mexican environmental laws and devolves enforcement onto Mexican state and local governments. Environmentalists concerned about the lax enforcement of current laws believe that this new law may lead to stronger prosecution of violators and a cleaner *maquila* industry.[51]

Mexico City: Contamination Central

The Metropolitan Zone of Mexico City (MZMC) is the center of Mexico's most important economic, political, and cultural activities.[52] A product of unplanned urban growth, the city contains almost 25 percent of the national population, provides 42 percent of all jobs, generates 53 percent of wages and salaries in the country, includes 38 percent of the total value of industrial plant, accounts for 49 percent of sales of durable goods, and receives 55 percent of public investment in social welfare. The city and the metropolitan area consume 40 percent of the total food production, buy 90 percent of all electrical appliances, use 66 percent of the country's energy and telephones, and purchase 58 percent of the automobiles on the country's highways.[53]

Between 1970 and 1980, while the Federal District grew at a 4.5 percent annual rate, surrounding metropolitan municipalities grew at a rate of 10 percent. Over the last 10 years, 270,000 people arrived in the city annually, attracted by the hope of economic opportunity and driven from the countryside by declining employment in the agricultural sector. This population increase and natural growth have combined to produce one of the largest cities on earth: almost 19 million inhabitants by 1989 (over 10 million in the Federal District and another

7.7 in the State of Mexico) in an area of approximately 1,250 square kilometers (or 777 square miles).[54]

The outcome of a policy of centralized growth, Mexico City has become the place in which the majority of the natural and artificial sources of contamination are concentrated: erosion; exposed trash and feces; entry into the subsoil of untreated water; emissions from factories, workshops, thermoelectric plants, refineries, petrochemical plants, cement and fertilizer plants, iron and steel foundries, and a large quantity of industrial and domestic incinerators; and millions of internal combustion vehicles and airplanes. Together, these sources spew approximately 6,000 tons of contaminants into the atmosphere daily.

Indiscriminate dumping of domestic and industrial liquid waste into lakes and rivers and along shorelines has led to a significant contamination of above-ground and subterranean waters. Approximately 50 cubic meters per second of residual waters are dumped, and only 70 percent is filtered by the sewage system. In the past few years, the degradation of important ecosystems has worsened. For example, Lake Guadalupe (the closest lake to the Federal District) has become extremely polluted. Surrounded a few years ago by more than 7,000 acres of farmland, today this lake is considered one huge septic tank. It receives nearly 30 million cubic meters of residual waters annually, which come principally from industrial and residential areas close to the dam. These discharges contain garbage, grease, detergents, and phosphates. Almost all the wastewaters generated in neighboring residential areas enter the lake without any treatment.[55]

Excessive water consumption in the MZMC has already produced serious ecological imbalances in the water table of the region. Overuse of water has caused terrain in various zones of the Mexico Valley to sink. In Xochimilco-Tulyehualco, the land has sunk 13 feet in less than 20 years.[56]

To compensate for the indiscriminate extraction of drinkable water, one of the policies followed by the authorities is the substitution of treated residual water. Recycling of this water has been the only available alternative for area farmers to maintain the use of their lands. Unfortunately, studies have shown that the utilization of treated wastewater for cultivation eventually causes sterility of the soil because of the high concentration in the treated water of salts and heavy metals.[57] In addition, some agricultural products grown with this treated water are highly noxious because they contain toxic elements affecting human health. Several studies have confirmed that residual waters in the Mexico Valley contain some 40 pathogenic microorganisms that are very resistant to water treatment and to drugs taken by humans infected by them.[58]

The costs of expanding Mexico City's water supplies are becoming prohibitive. By the 1990s, increasing the supply will require bringing water from sources some 120 miles away and 6,500 feet lower than the altitude of the city. Such a feat would take nearly 125 trillion kilojoules of electrical energy each year and require construction of six 1,000-megawatt power plants, at a cost of

Table 7. Percentage of Pollutants in the Metropolitan Area of Mexico City by Source

Source	Carbon Monoxide (CO)	Hydro-Carbons (HC)	Oxides of Nitrogen (NOx)	Sulfur Dioxide (SO$_2$)	Particles
Industry	1.5%	30.7%	37.9%	97.0%	30.3%
Motor	98.5%	69.3%	62.1%	3.0%	9.8%
Natural	—	—	—	—	59.8%
Total	100%	100%	100%	100%	100%

Source: SEDUE: "La Contaminacion Atmosferica en el Valle de Mexico." Inuierno de 1987–1988, Mexico, 1988; "El Estado del Medio Ambiente en México," SEDUE, 198 .
Cited in Fernando Ortiz Monasterio, "Society and Nature in Contemporary Mexico." Paper delivered at the Conference on Environment and Development: The Outlook for U.S.-Mexican Relations, Racine, Wisconsin May 1–3, 1988.

some $6 billion. The city is thus faced with three rising costs in obtaining water: increasing distance of water transport, increasing height of water lift, and rising energy costs.[59] The new power plants, like all fossil-fueled ones, will contribute to the greenhouse warming effect and, depending on the technology, to other environmental effects downwind.

Atmospheric pollution in Mexico City is another grave problem. Industry contributes 20 percent of the annual total of atmospheric contaminants to the MZMC: approximately 393,000 tons of sulfur dioxide; 130,000 tons of hydrocarbons; 114,000 tons of carbon monoxide; 91,000 tons of nitric oxide; and 383,000 tons of diverse particulate matter. Of the total number of industries located in the MZMC, only 30 percent have antipollution equipment, equipment that in many cases is insufficient or inoperative.[60]

Automotive vehicles are, however, the main polluters. (See Table 7.) In 1983, the state-run oil company, PEMEX, based on its own studies, classified motor vehicles as the principal source of pollution, producing 85 percent of the tonnage emitted daily.[61]

The search for solutions is complicated by the explosive growth in the number of vehicles, the types of technology and fuels used in them, the lack of strict controls over the maintenance of motors, and the atmospheric conditions prevailing in the Valley of Mexico.

Between 1940 and 1980, the number of automotive vehicles in the Federal District grew six times as fast as the population.[62] This predominance of private over public transportation and the higher fuel consumption of private vehicles has increased atmospheric pollution. About 33 percent of the total annual national fuel consumption—some 3 million cubic meters of gasoline and 400,000 cubic meters of diesel fuel—is attributed to vehicles in the MZMC. Yet, of the almost 3 million motor vehicles that operate, 97 percent are private cars that transport only 19 percent of the trips per person per day. It is calculated that this private transportation consumes 15 times more fuel per person transported than the mass transit system.[63]

Poor motor maintenance and the advanced age of the vehicles also contribute to pollution. Devaluation and inflation, and the subsequent loss of buying power, have increased the number of run-down vehicles on the road and impeded government efforts to replace older, polluting buses.[64]

The relationship between vehicle speed and air pollution contributes to the city's pollution dilemma. As the number of vehicles increases and average speeds decline on the Federal District's principal roadways, the situation becomes more grave. During peak hours (7:00–9:00 A.M., 2:00–4:00 P.M., and 6:00–9:00 P.M.), when 60 percent of the vehicles are in transit, the use of gasoline increases 1.5 times and exhaust emissions double the average.[65]

The geographic location of the MZMC further complicates the pollution problems of vehicles. At Mexico City's altitude (7,800 feet above sea level), internal combustion engines produce more contaminants than at lower elevations. Calculations indicate that altitude-induced inefficiencies mean the 3 million vehicles in the MZMC produce as much pollution as 6.3 million vehicles operating at sea level.

A second disadvantage of the MZMC's location is its low wind velocity. The high mountains surrounding the city effectively reduce ventilation of the city's polluted atmosphere. This lack of wind turbulence combines with seasonal drops in temperature to produce thermic inversions that trap life-threatening levels of pollution in the city.

Photochemical smog is now a normal component of the atmospheric pollution in the Mexican capital. High levels of sulfur dioxide have been detected in the MZMC, emitted principally by diesel traffic, electric power plants, and industry, even in apparently uncontaminated zones, such as the south of the city, where it is blown by the wind.

In spite of the efforts of PEMEX to reduce contaminant particles in fuel, almost all private automotive transport continues to use gasoline with high tetraethyl lead compound content and only a minimal proportion of public transportation (between 1.2 and 1.5 percent) employs diesel fuel with low sulfur content. Leaded gasoline is a particular concern because of recent studies documenting high levels of lead in newborns. In a sample of 102 Mexican newborns conducted by Dr. Stephen Rothenberg, 50 percent of those studied between March 1987 and the end of July 1988 had lead levels above the 10.5 microgam per deciliter (mcg/dl) of blood. Based on research in other countries, children with levels above 10 micrograms at birth tend to have slower rates of mental development.[66]

Recent steps by PEMEX to reduce lead in gasoline have had the the paradoxical effect of raising ozone levels in the capital. In the absence of catalytic converters on most Mexican cars, the unleaded gasoline introduced by PEMEX in 1986 caused ozone levels to shoot up. SEDUE's relatively modest ozone standard of 0.11 ppm is exceeded on more than 300 days each year, more than twice as often as in Los Angeles.[67]

The Government Response

Developments in the last few years have placed increasing pressure on the federal government to take more direct and immediate action against environmental dangers, especially in Mexico City. A series of thermal inversions in the winters of 1985, 1986, and 1987 dramatically increased pollution levels in the metropolitan area.[68] The catastrophic explosion of the PEMEX gas distribution facility at San Juan Ixhuatepec, a Mexico City suburb, in November 1984 that killed more than 500 people, injured some 5,000 and forced the evacuation of 100,000, also provoked public and media outcries for government action.[69]

Numerous government programs and agencies are attempting to address environmental problems in Mexico. At the federal level, the agency charged with prevention and control of atmospheric as well as soil and water pollution is the Ministry of Urban Development and Ecology, and, more specifically, the Subsecretariat of Ecology.[70] Within the Federal Government there is the Ecology Commission, which also has lower-level offices charged with responsibility for the state of Mexico. In addition, the Senate and Chamber of Deputies have several committees concerned with environmental problems, including a National Ecology Commission.

One significant response of the de la Madrid government to increasing public concern for the environment was the issuing of the so-called 21 Points in February 1986—a series of decrees that included reforestation projects, regulation of automotive pollution, relocation of especially dangerous or toxic industries in residential areas, innovative pilot projects to use gas and energy sources more efficiently, water purification projects, and public education programs promoting environmental awareness. Significantly, the government promised (and delivered) a report on its progress in implementing each of these points eight months after they were issued.

The increasing gravity of the pollution situation in the capital and continuing public protests led to a new series of 100 Actions by the federal government. Announced in a January 13, 1987, meeting of the National Ecology Commission (created in 1986 and chaired by President de la Madrid), the "Program of 100 Necessary Ecological Actions" includes a number of emergency provisions for responding to grave pollution levels in the capital. These include forced closings of schools and of selected, highly polluting industries during severe thermic inversions, compulsory inspection of motor vehicles, relocation of polluting and/or dangerous industries, prohibition of parking on important arteries in the city, and reforms of the laws regulating forests.

The 100 Actions were put into force during 1987 and 1988 and have a special focus on air pollution generated by automobiles and industry, both because of the gravity of the air quality situation in Mexico City and because of the visible nature of the pollution. They encourage relocation of schoolchildren and teachers and of industrial workers to avoid long commutes, prohibit the location of new factories in areas that already suffer high pollution levels and water shortages, and subsidize the installation of pollution control equipment in existing factories. Although the program has a particular focus on the metropolitan area, there are steps planned for a number of Mexico's most threatened rivers, reservoirs, and shorelines.

It is too early to judge the effectiveness of the "100 Actions." Skepticism among Mexican environmentalists runs high, however. Manuel Fernandez, president of the Mexican Conservationist Federation, has criticized the program as having "no timetable, no system of accountability, no enforcement mechanism." Others have pointed out the lack of a specific budget for the program, estimated to cost $100 million.[71]

On March 1, 1988, a new General Law of Ecological Balance and Environmental Protection (Ley General del Equilibrio Ecologico y la Proteccion al Ambiente) replaced the earlier Federal Law of Environmental Protection (Ley Federal de Proteccion al Ambiente). Among the main features of the new law are regulation of natural resource use as well as of pollution; the decentralization to state and municipal authorities of a wide range of policy development, regulations, and enforcement; a focus on the causes of pollution rather than just attending to its effects; and encouragement of the participation of nongovernmental actors in the environmental policy process.[72] Because of the new law's emphasis on enforcement and decentralization of important powers to local authorities, initial reactions to the new law by environmentalists have been positive.

Environmental Policymaking in Mexico

As recently as the mid-1970s, environmental problems in Mexico, as in much of the rest of the world, commanded only limited public attention. Under Presidents Luis Echeverria (1970–76) and Jose Lopez Portillo (1976–82), concerns about environmental issues had a low priority. When the environment did reach the presidents' policy agenda, it came as the result of agitation by middle-level government planners, university researchers, and professional organizations, generally located in Mexico City. Even though it was included in the global planning documents favored by the Lopez Portillo administration, "environmental policy as such was never mentioned in the President's major policy speeches, nor actively promoted as a major policy initiative at the national level."[73]

This changed with the beginning of Miguel de la Madrid's presidential campaign in 1982. De la Madrid pursued a three-pronged strategy to push environmental issues up the agenda of Mexican politics: a program of popular mobilization; a strengthening of environmental statutes and better coordination of administrative responsibilities in the environmental area; and improved regulatory performance.

In a searching evaluation of environmental policymaking in Mexico, Stephen Mumme gives de la Madrid's administration the highest marks for its program of popular mobilizations. Perhaps spurred by the PRI's assessment of the likelihood of a Green Party-like movement emerging in Mexico,[74] de la Madrid's government set up a series of impressive "consultative mechanisms" to arouse and channel awareness of environmental issues among the population. State and regional conferences brought together local political leaders from the PRI's sectors, government officials, scholars in the state universities, and citizen groups to discuss a new environmental program being proposed by the government and to identify environmental problems. These efforts appear to have succeeded in placing the issue of the environment permanently on Mexico's domestic political agenda, and in uniting urban and rural, middle and lower classes in common cause.[75]

With his "consultative mechanisms" to arouse and channel popular concern for the environment, de la Madrid has made a clear contribution to focusing greater attention on the need for government action on the environment. But Mumme's assessment of two other areas—statutory reform and regulatory performance—is less sanguine. Despite SEDUE officials' protest that de la Madrid's measures are more than symbolic reform and represent a serious commitment to environmental improvement in the long run, Mumme concludes that, "Unfortunately, the government's record fails to bear them out."[76] Mumme attributes this weak performance to both what he calls "circumstantial problems" and "actual priorities." Mexico's economic crisis and the crushing burden of the foreign debt are among the principal "circumstantial problems" hindering the fulfillment of commitments to environmental programs.

"Actual priorities" refer, however, to aspects of environmental policymaking that are intrinsic to the nature of the Mexican political system. Mumme points out that rather than relying on sanctions and making the initial investments in costly abatement programs, the government has opted for an approach to abatement that stresses moral suasion, planning, bargaining, education, data collection, and incentives. The activities of environmental interest groups are dealt with in the classic petitionary pattern of supplication and persuasion that often characterizes legitimate interest articulation in Mexico.[77]

It may seem at first glance that this is precisely the kind of strategy that Mexico should pursue under the prevailing conditions of extreme fiscal austerity. By relying on the traditional mechanisms employed by the state to encourage compliance by the private sector and interest groups, the government avoids difficult political confrontations and costly expenditures that would be necessary to strictly enforce regulations and punish violators.

But as Mumme points out, this approach rests on the plans under way for conversion and decentralization of industrial activities that will require decades to take full effect. In response to increasingly grave environmental deterioration, the Mexican government appears to have retreated into more of a hortatory and less of an enforcement role with regard to pollution.

Moreover, the success of any decentralization strategy will require that new areas of industrial growth be under the same environmental restrictions to prevent pollution problems from merely being transferred elsewhere. Although the evidence so far is anecdotal, some observers of Mexican environmental policy are concerned that in some officials' desire to stimulate growth outside Mexico City they may loosen environmental standards in the new industrial growth areas. One senior U.S. business executive was quoted as saying that government officials "don't care [about pollution] so long as a plant is going to be built away from Mexico City and will create a lot of jobs."[78]

A hortatory approach to environmental enforcement may in the long run strain Mexico's limited financial resources more rather than less. The explosion of the PEMEX gas plant in November 1984 may ultimately cost the government dozens of times the entire 1983 environmental budget. Yet, according to Mumme, only this "planning by disaster" was sufficient to spur the government to begin to relocate hazardous industries outside the immediate metropolitan area.[79]

Clearly, Mexico cannot do everything at once. It cannot open its political system, dramatically restructure the economy, and spend unlimited sums of political and financial capital on environmental enforcement. Yet it is important to heed the judgments of experts such as Mumme that the Mexican government's record on environmental policy regulation has sought to defer high costs by responding to demands primarily through symbolic reform and by opting for low-cost, future-oriented solutions in the planning and development realm.[80]

The steps taken by the de la Madrid government are obviously welcome. The early returns on the environment from the 1988 presidential elections are that the focus on this issue will continue. Carlos Salinas de Gortari, the declared winner of the 1988 elections, is a brilliant and technically sophisticated leader who counts the former minister of SEDUE (and current Mayor of Mexico City) among his closest personal advisers. The new environmental law of March 1988 gives important new powers to the federal government and to local authorities, which, if exercised, could break with the hortatory tradition of Mexico's regulatory past.

But any meaningful assessment of the status of the environment as a policy concern in Mexico in 1988 must also confront the fact that decades of neglect have brought the nation to the brink of environmental disaster in key sectors such as the urban problems of Mexico City or land use in the tropical areas of the southeast. The scale of these problems and the difficulties Mexico's authoritarian political system will have in addressing them caution against easy optimism that an environmental corner has been turned in Mexico.

Perhaps the most sobering aspect of Mexico's economic and environmental dilemma is that the strain on the country's urban services, the destruction of forests and rural habitat, and the pollution of crucial water resources are the unintended but nevertheless inevitable consequences of a style of development pursued by Mexico since World War II. This import substitution model of development no longer serves Mexico as an engine of growth and an alternative path of export promotion is being sought. But the model's heritage of overcentralized production, protected and polluting industries, and distortions between the rural and urban sectors will be the central concerns of Mexico's economic and environmental actions in the coming decades.

Powerful alliances of political and economic groups were forged in the creation of the import substitution model. Those alliances are already being challenged in Mexico's search for a new model of economic development capable of overcoming the external financial constraints and excessive dependence on foreign capital and technology that ended Mexico's unprecedented growth since World War II. The journey to a new and less environmentally damaging pattern of development has barely begun. Tragically, this search comes at a time of economic travail—when public sector spending is being slashed, when wages cannot keep up with triple-digit inflation, and when businesses are being driven into bankruptcy.

A strong but perceptive critic of the official approaches to environmental protection in Mexico ended a recent review of the prospects for environmental improvement in this context on this somber note:

The present development model, which privileges large-scale export manufacture at the expense of all else, provides no effective means to reverse the tendency toward environmental decay. Industry will not, unless obliged by government regulation, integrate a social conscience into its calculus of profit and loss. In Mexico, the state has shown itself unwilling to impose the costs of environmental controls on production, lest the drive for successful export promotion be thwarted. Some people argue that small scale industry and agricultural production may be more consistent with an environmentally sound pattern of development, but such considerations seem beside the point at a moment when macroeconomic policy has decimated small industrial firms and converted the country into a net importer of food, leaving millions of hectares of land and millions of people idle. Official policy offers no solace in this regard: in place of a concrete set of policies to deal with the impending environmental crisis, the candidate of the ruling party for the presidency only implores the "civil society" to raise its level of collective conscience. And what shall we ask of the producers?[81]

How Can the United States Help?

Given the political and economic constraints under which Mexico must operate and the importance of Mexico's decisions on the management of its resource base for both the United States and Mexico, it is vital to ask whether the United States can play a positive role in helping Mexico meet its environmental challenges. The first point to be made is that there is virtually unanimous agreement among those who have studied Mexico that expressions of concern by the United States about conditions there are often interpreted as intervention in Mexico's internal affairs, and that actual attempts at pressure will be totally counterproductive.[82]

A recent interaction between these two neighbors gives a negative example of how environmental issues work themselves out in the bilateral relationship. The debate over regulation of the use of the fumigant ethylene dibromide (EDB) on mangos exported from Mexico is a classic study in bureaucratic politics and of the blurred lines between international and domestic politics in U.S.-Mexican relations.

In the wake of a 1983 court decision, the Environmental Protection Agency banned EDB, commonly used as a fumigant on mangos grown worldwide, because of its cancer-causing potential. State Department concern with efforts to encourage export agriculture through President Reagan's Caribbean Basin Initiative and protests from growers in the producing countries led EPA to give Mexico, Haiti, Belize, and Guatemala a two-year grace period. That deadline has since been extended, protested, reversed in law suits, and extended again in a mixture of interagency disputes, foreign policy, and domestic politics.[83]

Three competing interests clash in the case. The State Department, the Mexican government, and Mexican growers have as their primary interest the maintenance of an export market for Mexican goods and the flow of foreign exchange to Mexico at a time when it is sorely needed. Environmental groups and some officials at EPA see the protection of the U.S. consumer as the highest priority. Domestic suppliers of mangos, such as those in Florida, see the pesticide issue as a way to combat foreign competition and have joined with environmental groups in suits to guard the health of consumers that, not coincidentally, have the effect of protecting their markets from Mexican competition.

Two other interests are not as well represented in this regulatory merry-go-round. One is the Mexican workers exposed to the hazardous chemicals used on the produce. The second is the U.S. consumer, who is blithely unaware that his or her well-being is a bargaining chip in bilateral relations.

Addressing conflicts between the United States and Mexico in the largely uncoordinated fashion that characterizes current relations can have its successes and failures. In the case of the series of border agreements signed by the United States and Mexico since 1983 on hazardous wastes, sewage, and air quality, negotiations at relatively high levels on each side—mostly uncomplicated by local politics—produced success at a time when other Mexican-American relations were acrimonious. On the issue of pesticides, enmeshed as it is in a web of foreign policy concerns and domestic politics, agreement has been elusive and the environmental consequences more damaging.

Abraham Lowenthal has described this issue-by-issue, "muddling through" approach to U.S.-Mexican relations as but one of four ways in which contacts between the two countries could be organized. Others include: a *unilateralist and nationalist stance* on the part of the United States that attempts to subordinate Mexican interests to U.S. ones; a *"special relationship"* approach that seeks to build the two countries' mutual dependence into preferential policies and procedures on energy, tourism, migration, markets, capital, and technology; and *a more generalized positive response* by the United States to Third World concerns that gives an advantage to Mexico because of the especially close ties between the two countries.[84]

Which of these approaches to Mexico will contribute most to protecting the resource base upon which future development and stability depend? The most severe environmental threats facing Mexico today flow from the style of development pursued since World War II. That Mexico must now reorient its developmental approach is plain from the exhaustion of the prior model and its inability to provide a future engine of growth for the economy. Government proposals to relocate and decentralize productive activities and the modest steps taken so far to implement these proposals indicate recognition in official circles of the connection between environmental deterioration and the economic patterns established in the country over the last several decades.

It would be foolish, however, to underestimate the immensity of the task facing Mexico. The current economy and environment are the results of complex political arrangements worked out between powerful actors such as business, labor, the peasantry, foreign investors, the state, and the party apparatus. These arrangements and the economic benefits created by them have favored a relatively small group within Mexican society, referred to repeatedly here as the middle class or middle sector. Those advantaged by this distribution of burdens and benefits will be reluctant to see them changed significantly. Nothing less than the consensus underlying Mexican stability for the last 60 years is at stake.

Of the four options for approaching U.S.-Mexican relations just outlined, it is easy to reject two as being inadequate to the enormous challenge before Mexico. A unilateral, nationalist approach on the part of the United States that tries to bully Mexico into "recognizing" that its interests are best served by subordinating them to those of the United States is bound to increase the already formidable pressures on Mexico to the point of explosion. The issue-by-issue "muddling through" that has mostly prevailed in U.S.-Mexican relations can perhaps patch up oil spills, salinity problems, and pesticide dangers, but it will not produce the positive context needed for the system-wide changes required.

What Mexico needs from the United States are actions that help to depressurize the situation, to open up more political and economic space, and to encourage the use of this breathing room to take some difficult decisions. U.S. initiatives in three interrelated areas are vital.

First would be strong efforts to relieve Mexico's debt burden. Analysts have argued for some time that this would include combinations of measures to limit interest payments; convert some part of the debt to long-term, fixed rate securities; and confer greater accounting flexibility on creditors.[85] An initial step toward such debt relief was taken in the agreement to a partial write-down of Mexico's debt through the issuance of Mexican bonds backed by U.S. Treasury paper, announced in December 1987 with much fanfare.[86] The plan proved to be far less than a breakthrough for Mexico on debt reduction.

It was followed by a new debt accord reached in mid-1989 between Mexico and the more than 500 commercial banks that have lent money to Mexico. This agreement is hailed as the first success story of the new policy initiatives undertaken by Treasury Secretary Nicholas Brady and known as the Brady Plan. It allows banks to choose among three basic options in restructuring $53 billion in foreign debt owed by Mexico to the commercial banks: reduction of outstanding principal by 35 percent, reduction of the interest rates Mexico pays, or providing new loans that could be used, in part, to help pay off old ones.[87] President Salinas has celebrated the accord as an historic breakthrough in Mexico's international relations, but it is still too early to tell if the promise of this most recent agreement will prove as much a disappointment as previous attempts to ease the debt burden.[88]

Given the close connection between Mexico's economy and that of the United States, better economic policies in Washington, especially reduction of the public sector deficit, would also help to reduce pressures on real interest rates for Mexico.

West German Chancellor Helmut Kohl has called on the United States and other creditor countries to link debt relief more closely to ecological requirements. In a speech at the September 1988 Annual Meeting of the International Monetary Fund and the World Bank, he stressed the need for total cooperation in making environmental protection a focal point of future development policy for both developed and developing countries. Innovative proposals by private organizations to swap outstanding debt for the establishment of conservation preserves, sites of "ecological tourism," and transfers of pollution control technology need to be explored with Mexico.

A second priority is increased development funding to come primarily from international financial institutions such as the regional development banks, the International Monetary Fund, and the World Bank. This will help to end the dangerous anomaly of Mexico exporting capital to the United States when it needs to be importing funds for future growth. The increased sensitivity of these international institutions to criticism of the environmental impacts of past projects may allow the targeting of new capital flows on environmental problems.

A third area for U.S. action is the avoidance of protectionist legislation that affects Mexican exports. Demands for trade reciprocity between industrialized countries such as Japan and the United States are understandable and necessary, but the same standards will not be productive if applied to Mexico. The removal of existing barriers to trade between Mexico and the United States and the prevention of new forms of protection can, however, be part of a bilateral process of negotiation.[89]

Steps such as these, difficult as they will be to take, could help to open up political and economic space in Mexico and avoid immediate disasters or the adoption of extreme solutions. A more subtle dilemma for U.S. policy is how to encourage Mexico to use this space to take hard decisions on the reorientation of its development strategy, the revival of the agricultural sector, and the enforcement of environmental regulations. As a Mexican analyst has put it with regard to pressures for greater democratization in Mexico, there are trade-offs between economic breathing space and political change:

> Concessions are easier when cushioned by prosperity; the country's rulers will not loosen their grip on power unless they can make the process relatively painless through economic growth. Yet, if such growth were possible, the need for political change would not be so acute.[90]

How to lessen economic pressure on Mexico while encouraging the government to use the political space created to protect that country's environment and resource base brings us back to a consideration of Lowenthal's last two approaches: whether the United States should seek a "special relationship" with Mexico or address Mexico as a component of a more general policy toward Latin America and the Third World.

Each appproach has its advantages and disadvantages as judged from the perspective of what will most support positive change in Mexico. The "special relationship" has much to recommend it because it offers the possibility of rallying the U.S. domestic support necessary for such an initiative. Constituencies in both Mexico and the United States have long argued for greater recognition of the unique relationship between the two countries, even to the point of arguing for a "North American Common Market" that would actively promote greater integration of Mexico, Canada, and the United States.[91]

The "special relationship" would, however, require an immense amount of coordination among the myriad agencies concerned and would go against some of the United States' broader international commitments. Most importantly, such a direct focus would raise Mexican fears of being overwhelmed culturally, economically, and politically by the United States.

Because it avoids a direct focus on Mexico and, hence, may lessen such concerns about U.S. interference, Lowenthal believes that a more general set of policies designed to address Latin America's problems of debt and development is the most desirable approach. Because of its close ties to the United States, Mexico would benefit differentially from this overall policy initiative toward the developing world. Specific issues such as migration, the border, energy, and the environment could be the subject of special bilateral arrangements and procedures.[92]

The central defect in this proposal is precisely its advantage. By deflecting attention from the bilateral relationship it mutes Mexican sensitivities, but it also loses a coherence and immediacy that would allow the policy to be explained and justified to a U.S. public already skeptical of the value of foreign aid programs.

This analysis of the problems Mexico faces and the approaches by the United States that are most likely to be effective in encouraging Mexico to take the hard decisions necessary to address them ends with a dilemma. The United States must proceed with the day-to-day business of the bilateral relationship with Mexico and utilize the mechanisms already in place as a result of border agreements on environmental cooperation to address environmental concerns between the two countries. By protecting its own environment, policing the export of hazardous substances and industrial processes to Mexico, and making available training and technical assistance, the United States will contribute to the solution of the current manifestations of the style of development pursued by Mexico.

The larger challenge the United States must face, however, is that these kinds of efforts will ultimately be inadequate to the task that Mexico must undertake. That task is no less than a fundamental restructuring of the prevailing development model and an acceptance by a majority of Mexicans of the political changes required to support such a restructuring. The emergence of strong challenges to the PRI from Cardenas on the left and the PAN on the right will force a public dialogue about the different directions that Mexico's future might take. Contrasting proposals on a range of issues from debt repayment to the agricultural sector will be offered by opposition parties whose combined votes (by official count) nearly equalled those of the PRI in the recent election.

If the United States is to be more than a mere bystander in this process of debate and change it must develop both a far more sophisticated approach to Mexico than it now has and a greatly strengthened political will to ease Mexico's unbearable burden. The coincidence of new presidents in Mexico and the United

States in 1988—and the inevitable policy reviews of the bilateral relationship that attend this simultaneous succession—can offer just such an opportunity.

References

1. "Statement of Richard E. Feinberg," in U.S. Senate, Subcommittees on Western Hemisphere Affairs and International Economic Policy, Oceans, and Environment, *United States Policy Toward Mexico, Hearings,* June 10, 1986.

2. "Opinion Roundup," *Public Opinion,* Vol. 2, Summer 1986, 29.

3. Norman A. Bailey and Richard Cohen, *The Mexican Timebomb* (New York: Priority Press, 1987).

4. Abraham F. Lowenthal, *Partners in Conflict, The United States and Latin America* (Baltimore, Maryland: The Johns Hopkins University Press, 1987), 66.

5. *Meoria de Labores* (Mexico: Pemex, 1987).

6. Lowenthal, 1987, *Partners in Conflict,* 95.

7. Banco de Mexico Figures reported by *Latin America Regional Report: Mexico and Central America,* 1988.

8. Lowenthal, 1987, *Partners in Conflict,* 87.

9. Shelley A. Hearne, *Harvest of Unknowns: Pesticide Contamination in Imported Foods* (New York, New York: Natural Resources Defense Council, 1984), 8.

10. James Pinkerton, "Chemicals Catastrophe Lurking Behind Border," *Austin American Statesman* (March 27, 1988).

11. Peter H. Smith, *Labyrinths of Power, Political Recruitment in Twentieth-Century Mexico* (Princeton, New Jersey: Princeton University Press, 1979), 251; Lorenzo Meyer, "Historical Roots of the Authoritarian State in Mexico," in Josá Luis Reyna and Richard S. Weinert, Eds., *Authoritarianism in Mexico* (Philadelphia, Pennsylvania: Institute for the Study of Human Issues, 1977, 11; and, Susan Kaufman Purcell, Ed., *Mexico in Transition, Implications for U.S. Policy* (New York, New York: Council on Foreign Relations, 1988).

12. Mauricio de Maria y Campos, "Mexico's New Industrial Development Strategy," in Cathryn L. Thorup, ed., *The United States and Mexico: Face to Face with New Technology* (Washington, D.C.: Overseas Development Council, 1987), 67–81.

13. Ronald G. Cummings, et al., *Improving Water Management in Mexico's Irrigated Agricultural Sector* (Washington, D.C.: World Resources Institute, 1989), 30–33.

14. Secretaria de Agricultura y Recursos Hidraulicos, *Plan Nacional Hidraulico, 1989,* March 1981.

15. Alejandro Toledo, *Petroleo y ecodesarrollo en el sureste de Mexico* (Mexico City: Centro Ecodesarrollo, 1982).

16. Figure cited by Jose Sarukhan Kermez, President of the Academy of Scientific Research, in a speech given at El Colegio de Mexico, June 26, 1987.

17. For estimates on desertification see Comision Nacional de Zonas Aridas, diversos documentos, 1976–1984; Bassols Batalla A., *Geografia Economia de Mexico* (Mexico: Editorial Trillas, 1984); Consejo Nacional de Ciencia y Technologia (CONACYT), *Programa Nacional de Desarrollo Agropecuario y Forestal* (Mexico: CONACYT, 1981). Estimates on forested lands come from Ivan Restrepo of the Centro Ecodesarrollo and are based on studies from the Subsecretaria Forestal of the SAHR and from the Instituto Nacional de Recursos Bioticos (INIREB).

18. For indictments of the lack of adequate research on the tropical ecosystem see Toledo, *Petroleo y ecodesarrollo*; David Barkin, *Desarrollo regional y reorganizacion campesina* (Mexico: Centro de Ecodesarrollo/Nueva Imagen, 1978); and Ivan Restrepo, "El estado del medio ambiente en Mexico: una vision de conjunto" (Mexico: Centro de Ecodesarrollo, 1986), 37.

19. Discussions of the dangers of planting crops such as rice in areas with tropical conditions of thin topsoil can be found in Ana Maria Ortiz, *El cultivo del arroz en el sureste de Mexico* (Mexico: Centro de Ecodesarrollo, 1987). The environmental and employment effects of cattle-raising are discussed in Barkin, *Desarrollo regional y reoganizacion campesina*.

20. This section on the Plan Chontalpa is drawn from Barkin, *Desarrollo regional y reorganizacion campesina*, 131, 134, and 35.

21. John Nagel, "Mexico's Population Policy Turnaround," *Population Bulletin*, Vol. 33, No. 5, (December 1978) 18.

22. Cited in John Nagel, "Mexico's Population Policy Turnaround," 20.

23. Nagel, "Mexico's Population Policy Turnaround," 20, 21.

24. Nagel, "Mexico's Population Policy Turnaround," 34; and Lester R. Brown, et al., *State of the World 1987* (New York: W.W. Norton and Company, 1987), 23.

25. Francisco Alba and Joseph E. Potter, "Population and Development in Mexico Since 1940: An Interpretation," *Population and Development Review*, Vol. 12, No. 1, March 1986.

26. Victor Urquidi, "Population and Employment at the end of the Century," speech presented at the First Seminar on "Projections on Mexico's Population," Colegio de Mexico, 6–7. By way of comparison, the U.S. economy during the Reagan administration generated less than 2 million new jobs per year.

27. Angus Wright, "Agricultural Policy and the Future of the Meso-American Environment," paper prepared for the XIV International Congress of the Latin American Studies Association, New Orleans, Louisiana, March 17–19, 1988, 9.

28. Wright, "Agricultural Policy and the Future of the Meso-American Environment," 13.

29. Brown, et al., 1987, *State of the World 1987*, 36.

30. Frances Moore Lappe and Joseph Collins, *Food First: Beyond The Myth of Scarcity* (Toronto: Houghton Mifflin Company, 1978), 125.

31. Steven E. Sanderson, *The Transformation of Mexican Agriculture: International Structure and The Politics of Rural Change* (Princeton, New Jersey: Princeton University Press, 1986), 38.

32. Sanderson, *The Transformation of Mexican Agriculture*, 38, 39.

33. Lappe and Collins, 1978. *Food First*, 126.

34. Lappe and Collins, 1978, *Food First*, 281–282.

35. Sanderson, 1986, *Transformation of Mexican Agriculture*, 40.

36. Walsh, "Sorghum Creates Joy and Trouble in Mexico as Corn is Supplanted," *Wall Street Journal*, July 31, 1985.

37. Walsh, "Sorghum Creates Joy and Trouble in Mexico as Corn is Supplanted."

38. David Bull, *A Growing Problem: Pesticides and the Third World*, (Oxford: OXFAM, 1982), 16.

39. Cited in David Weir and Mark Shapiro, *Circle of Poison: Pesticides and People in a Hungry World* (San Francisco: Institute for Food and Development Policy, 1981), 12.

40. Weir and Shapiro, 1981, *Circle of Poison: Pesticides and People in a Hungry World*, 12.

41. Wright, "Agricultural Policy," 14.

42. The following discussion of monitoring problems in imports of Mexican fruits and vegetables is based on Shelley A. Hearne, *Harvest of Unknowns: Pesticide Contamination in Imported Foods* (New York, New York: Natural Resources Defense Council, 1984), especially 25–46.

43. Angus Wright, "Pesticides in Mexico: The Culiacan Valley Farmers," *Catholic Rural Life*, Vol. 35, February 1986: 15–18.

44. A recent study by the Board of Agriculture of the National Research Council concluded that up to 20,000 cancer tumors may be caused annually in the United States by insecticide residues on imported and domestic fruits and vegetables. See *Regulating Pesticides in Food, The Delaney Paradox* (Washington, D.C.: National Academy Press, 1987).

45. H. Jeffrey Leonard, *Pollution and the Struggle for the World Product, Multinational Corporations, Envirnoment and International Comparative Advantage* (London: Cambridge University Press, 1988), 195.

46. Leonard, *Pollution and the Struggle for the World Product*, passim. Certain firms do appear to have been attracted to Mexico for reasons related to environmental issues such as the production of hazardous chemicals (lead, zinc, and arsenic trioxide) for export to the Untied States, smelting of copper (a potential source of "acid rain" problems for the United States), and the production of banned or highly regulated chemicals such as pesticides.

A more recent study produced by the AFL-CIO asserts that

One of the big attractions that the *maquiladoras* hold for American industry is the Mexican government's hands-off attitude toward environmental protection and worker health and safety laws.

—Leslie Kochan, *The Maquiladoras and Toxics, The Hidden Costs of Production South of the Border*, Publication No. 16 (February 1989), 2.

47. Harris Pastides, "Digital Equipment Corporation Pilot Study," unpublished article, University of Massachusetts, Amherst: School of Public Health, 1986.

48. Susan Sherry, *High Tech and Toxics: A Guide for Local Communities* (Sacramento, California: Golden Empire Planning Center, 1985), 2.

49. Janny Scott and Patrick McDonnell, "U.S. Toxic Waste Shipments to Mexico on Rise, EPA Says," *The Los Angeles Times*, February 12, 1986.

50. U.S. Environmental Protection Agency, International Division, and Mexican Secretary of Urban Development and Ecology (SEDUE), "Joint Communique," November 12, 1986, 1.

51. James Pinkerton, "Chemicals Catastrophe Lurking Behind Border," *Austin American Statesman* (March 27, 1988).

52. The MZMC includes the Federal District of Mexico City and the surrounding metropolitan area of the state of Mexico.

53. Instituto Nacional de Estadistica, Geografia e Informatica, Secretaria de Programacion y Presupuesto (SPP), various documents, 1981–1986.

54. Jorge Legorreta, Centro Eco-desaretto, personal communication, May 1989.

55. Gobierno Federal, *Programa de Desarrollo de la Zona Metropolitana de la Ciudad de Mexico y de la Region Centro*, 1985, 12–13.

56. Gobierno Federal, *Programa de Desarrollo de la Zona Metropolitana de la Ciudad de Mexico y de la Region Centro*, 1985, 12.

57. *Uno Mas Uno*, March 6, 1985 (Mexico City).

58. Studies by Dr. Armando Baez of the Centro de Ciencias de la Atmosfera of the National Autonomous University and Professor Eduardo Rodriguez Mestre of the Autonomous Metropolitan University have identified various contaminants and heavy metals in the treated water of Mexico City. Because these materials combine with sulfuric acid also present in the wastewaters to form insoluble compounds, the metals do not present a danger to human health in the concentrations and forms in which they arrive in the fields. The microorganisms carried by the water, however, are very dangerous for humans consuming irrigated crops. *Uno Mas Uno*, April 2, 1985.

59. Brown, et al., *State of the World 1987*, 52.

59. Brown, et al., *State of the World 1987*, 52.

60. Comision de Ecologia del D.D.F., *Informe de Labores*, 1983.

61. Figures provided by the Camara Nacional de Comercio (CANACO), *Punto*, November 12, 1984.

62. Statement by engineer Gerardo Cruickshank, spokesperson of the Comision del lago de Texcoco, *Uno Mas Uno*, January 13, 1985.

63. *La Jornada*, November 23, 1984.

64. Rachel Sternberg, "Mexico City: The Politics of Pollution," *In These Times* (October 7–13, 1987), 13.

65. *Programa de Desarrollo*, 51.

66. William Branigan, "Bracing for Pollution Disaster," *The Washington Post* (November 28, 1988), A14.

67. Branigan, "Bracing for Pollution Disaster," A14.

68. In the thermal inversion of January 1987, songbirds literally dropped from the trees because of pollution levels. In the inversion of 1989, visits of a few days by those unaccustomed to the pollution levels produced bleeding in nasal passages.

69. Jonathan Kandell, *La Capital, The Biography of Mexico City* (New York: Random House, 1988), 565. Sixty-six acres were razed by the explosions and fire.

70. The predecessors of this agency are: from 1972 to 1976, the Subsecretariat of Environmental Improvement, a department of the Secretariat of Public Health and Assistance, and from 1977 to 1982, the Directorate of Ecology, a department of the Secretariat of Human Settlements and Public Works.

71. Sternberg, "Mexico City: The Politics of Pollution," 12–13.

72. *General Law of Ecological Balance and Environmental Protection* (Mexico, 1988), Chapter II, Article 6.

73. Stephen P. Mumme, "The Evolution of Mexican Environmental Policy," presented to the XII International Congress of the Latin American Studies Association, Albuquerque, New Mexico, April 18–20, 1984, 17.

74. H. Jeffrey Leonard, "Confronting Industrial Pollution in Rapidly Industrializing Countries: Myths, Pitfalls, and Opportunities," *Ecology Law Quarterly*, 1985, Vol. 12, No. 4, 799.

75. Mumme, "The Evolution of Mexican Environmental Policy," 18, 35.

76. Mumme, "The Evolution of Mexican Environmental Policy," 26.

77. Mumme, "The Evolution of Mexican Environmental Policy," 29, 32.

78. Interview with Edward Wyegard, Director, Arthur D. Little (Mexico), quoted in Leonard, "Confronting Industrial Pollution," 791.

79. Mumme, "The Evolution of Mexican Environmental Policy," 31.

80. Mumme, "The Evolution of Mexican Environmental Policy," 32–33.

81. David Barkin, "Environmental Degradation and Productive Transformation in Mexico: The Contradictions of Crisis Management," paper presented at the XIV International Congress of the Latin American Studies Association, New Orleans, Louisiana, March 17–19, 1988, 12.

82. This is the conclusion of experts with such disparate viewpoints as Bailey and Cohen, 1987, *Mexican Timebomb*; Jorge G. Castaneda, "Mexico at the Brink," *Foreign Affairs*, Winter 1985/1986, Vol. 64, No. 2; Lowenthal, 1987, *Partners in Conflict*; and Sol Sanders, *Mexico: Chaos on Our Doorstep* (Lanham, Maryland: Madison Books, 1986).

83. National Coalition Against the Misuse of Pesticides, "Last Mango with EDB," *Pesticides and You*, March 1987, Vol. 7, No. 1, 1; and "Mango is example of legal legerdemain," *Arizona Daily Star*, April 8, 1987.

84. Lowenthal, 1987, *Partners in Conflict*, 96–102. The last of these four items is favored by Lowenthal.

85. Bailey and Cohen, 1987, *Mexican Timebomb*, 48.

86. Details of the plan are discussed in Peter Truell and Alan Murray, "Debt Breakthrough," *Wall Street Journal*, December 30, 1987.

87. John Berry and William Branigan, "Opinion Mixed to Deal to Reduce Mexican Debt," *The Washington Post*, July 25, 1989.

88. Larry Rohter, "Salinas and Business Leaders Hail Debt Accord," *The New York Times*, July 25, 1989. For criticism of the limitations of the Brady Plan see, Peter Hakim, "How to improve on the Brady Plan," *Chicago Tribune*, July 17, 1989.

89. Bailey and Cohen, 1987, *Mexican Timebomb*, 50.

90. Castaneda, "Mexico at the Brink," 294.

91. President Reagan raised this idea explicitly in his 1980 presidential campaign, but did not pursue it while in office. Henry Kissinger also suggested that some form of association of Mexico with the U.S.-Canada free trade area, spaced over a period of years, would be a desirable element of future U.S.-Mexican negotiations. See Henry Kissinger, "The Rise of Mexico," *The Washington Post* (August 17, 1988).

92. Lowenthal, 1987, *Partners in Conflict*, 101.

III

Resources, Population and the Future of the Philippines*

Gareth Porter with Delfin J. Ganapin, Jr.

During the next two decades, the Philippines will face a subsistence crisis involving the ability to meet the minimum human needs of close to half its people. The country's politics will be stalked by the lengthening shadow of a huge rural stratum of landless, underemployed laborers whose families are hungry and many millions of upland farmers who are equally poor. This subsistence crisis will unfold, moreover, while the Philippine government is struggling with a powerful armed insurgency by the Communist Party of the Philippines and its military arm, the New People's Army (NPA), which has attracted the support of enough of the rural population to defy military suppression.[1] Even if this insurgency could be repressed by military force over the next few years, the survival of the democratic system in the Philippines is uncertain at best as long as a large proportion of the population lives below the subsistence level.

This socioeconomic and political crisis is related to a larger ecological crisis: the erosion of the country's natural resource base, which has suffered stress as a result of environmental mismanagement and population pressures. Rapid population growth has overwhelmed the agricultural land base. An increasingly large proportion of the rural population has been forced into upland areas, where land is easily eroded and degraded. Irresponsible logging and overpopulation of these areas have caused massive deforestation, which has in turn destroyed watersheds, washed away hillsides, caused serious flooding, and reduced the productivity of lowland agriculture. Siltation, pollution, the destruction of mangroves, and other environmentally unsound practices have seriously affected

---

This chapter is based on a case study of the same title published by the World Resources Institute in Washington, D.C., in October 1988.

the productivity of Philippine fisheries, reducing both the incomes of subsistence fishers and overall protein availability.

The ability of the Philippines to avoid a long-term collapse of liberal institutions will depend in large part on its will and capacity to provide access to productive resources to those who now lack it. That goal will require, in turn, an orientation to sustainable use and, in some cases, the rehabilitation of the country's natural resource base. Without major institutional and policy changes in these directions, the processes of environmental degradation and resource depletion can only worsen, and the possibility of a democratic system surviving in the Philippines will be greatly diminished.

Overwhelming the Agricultural Land Base

The country's topography, climate and soil characteristics make the Philippine land base extremely vulnerable to degradation. The archipelago contains approximately 30 million hectares of land area, of which 59 percent (17.6 million hectares) has a slope of 18 percent or greater, making it extremely susceptible to soil erosion.[2] But even more gently sloping lands (on an incline from 3 to 15 percent) require careful management to prevent erosion. In centuries past, when the population was thinly dispersed across the hilly land, farmers simply moved on to virgin areas when the soil's productivity waned. But in the 20th century, population pressures have forced them to remain in the same place, further eroding and depleting the soil.[3] Nearly half the arable land in the Philippines must be cultivated with soil conservation techniques to avoid serious reduction of its long-term productivity.[4]

The impact of soil erosion and nutrient depletion on productivity can be measured by comparing yields of upland rice among similiar soils, both eroded and non-eroded. The provinces of Batangas, Iloilo, Lanao, and Cavite were the most important in the country for upland rice cultivation in the 1960s. They all had roughly similar soil types and thus might have been expected to have roughly similar yields. Yet the soils of three of these—Batangas, Iloilo, and Cavite—suffered fertility depletion and erosion because of intensive cultivation, without conservation techniques and over a prolonged period of time, and had yields only 22 to 40 percent of those of Lanao, which had not yet been depleted and eroded.[5]

In the context of the country's vulnerable land base, continued high population growth has introduced an important new element into the Philippine ecosystem. The population has more than tripled in four decades, from 19.2 million in 1948 to 63.1 million in 1988.[6] It grew at an average annual rate of more than 3 percent during the 1950s and 1960s, fell to an average of 2.7 percent during the early 1970s, but crept up again in the late 1970s and early 1980s. For 1975–85, according to data from the most recent National Demographic Survey, the average annual rate remained virtually stable at 2.7–2.8, which would make it the highest growth rate in East Asia.[7] The 1983–87 development plan of the Philippine government, which assumed an annual population growth rate of only 2 percent, anticipated 4 million to 6 million fewer people than the best estimate for the current population.[8]

During the 1960s, population growth for the first time exceeded the growth in cultivated land. While cultivated land was estimated to have grown at a rate of 3.8 percent annually during 1948–59, it grew only 1.4 percent a year on the average in the 1957–72 period.[9] By the late 1960s, the Philippines confronted a serious food shortage. In response, high-yielding varieties of rice were introduced in the late 1960s, supported by major loans for increased irrigation projects from the World Bank. The government encouraged greater use of chemical fertilizers and pesticides needed by the new varieties, by providing cheap credit and by subsidizing their purchase through the Masagana 99 program beginning in 1975. Consumption of fertilizer increased from around 200,000 metric tons in 1960 to 878,000 metric tons in 1983 (see Figure 1), increasing yields and contributing to the pollution of lakes, rivers, and the near-shore environment.[10] The result was that rice yields on irrigated lowland farms increased from an average of two metric tons per hectare in 1970 to three metric tons per hectare in 1983.[11] The Philippines was transformed from a rice importer to a rice exporter by the end of the 1970s.

Poorest of the Poor: Landless Laborers and Upland Farmers

Increasing yields did not, however, solve the problem of those who could find no land to cultivate in the lowlands. They had three choices: to search for work in the cities, to join the swelling ranks of the landless agricultural laborers, or to move to the uplands in search of land. Most followed the second course, becoming agricultural workers who have no ownership or other legally recognized rights to cultivate farmland and who earn most of their income from wages. The total number of unemployed and underemployed rural laborers in 1987 has been estimated by the Philippine government's National Economic and Development Authority (NEDA) at nearly 50 percent of a rural labor force of 13.7 million, or 6.8 million people.[12] It should be noted, however, that this estimate is based on an assumed total population that is 4 million fewer than the best recent estimate. The actual number of unemployed and underemployed may be substantially greater.

Agricultural workers, along with upland farmers and small-scale fishers, are the poorest of the poor in the Philippines. With no economic security, they must struggle to survive day by day. They live, as one of them has described it, "like frail little birds, each day waking at dawn to look for grains of rice and flitting here and there all day searching for ways to feed their families."[13] Real wages of agricultural workers fell by as much as 50 percent from the late 1960s to the late

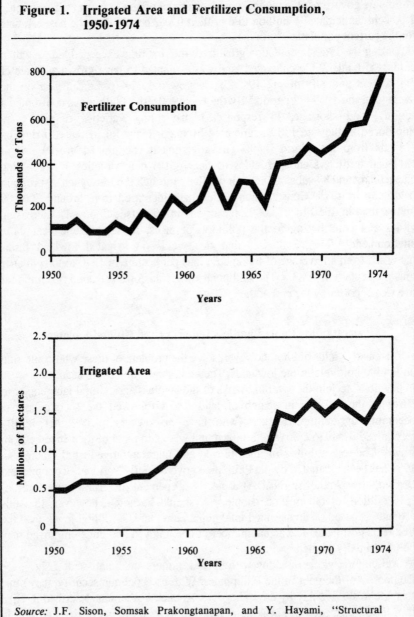

Figure 1.   Irrigated Area and Fertilizer Consumption, 1950-1974

Source: J.F. Sison, Somsak Prakongtanapan, and Y. Hayami, "Structural Changes in Rice Supply Relations: Philippines and Thailand," International Rice Research Institute, *Economic Consequences of the New Rice Technology,* (Los Banos, Philippines, IRRI, 1978): 35

1970s. A World Bank study in 1980 concluded that "labor supply pressure" had been a major cause of this precipitate drop in real earning power.[14]

The number of landless workers will continue to grow in the next two decades. The only question is by how much. The Philippine government's draft five-year plan projects a net addition of 800,000 job-seekers to the market during 1991 and nearly 900,000 more in 1992.[15] At that rate of increase, the annual increment to the labor force would go over 1 million new entrants a year by 1994. The socioeconomic tensions inherent in that intense competition for limited industrial and agricultural employment is one of the Philippines' most critical problems.

Population pressures on the land, combined with the continuing maldistribution of landownership and increased dependence on expensive agricultural inputs, have reduced the security of a large proportion of the tenant farmers as well. Tenants who have been able to obtain cheap credit have been able to reap the benefits from higher yields. But those who have lost the patronage of their landowner by shifting to leasehold or who lack management skills have become less economically secure. Even weak tenants are, however, generally better off than the landless agricultural workers and the upland population.[16]

The global boom in commodity export prices in 1973–74 exacerbated the subsistence crisis of the landless by providing incentives for agricultural corporations, both domestic and foreign, to invest in or expand their holdings in pineapples, bananas, palm oil, and rubber for export. Because much of the land was acquired by putting pressure on smallholders, by ignoring long-standing claims to the land by the cultivators, or by arranging leases that resulted in indebtedness to the company on the part of the farmers, many former smallholders lost their land.[17] There was also a significant expansion nationwide of the production of sugar and coconuts—the two major traditional export crops. Landowners increased planting coconuts from 2.1 million hectares in 1972 to 3.1 million hectares in 1980, and expanded sugarlands from 440,000 hectares in 1972 to 540,000 hectares in 1976.[18] By 1980, agribusiness firms were estimated to be planting up to 52 percent of all of Mindanao's arable land.[19]

Laborers in the coconut and sugar industries and on banana plantations are among the poorest of the landless laborers in the Philippines. They normally get only two or three days of work each week.[20] Wages in these sectors are set well below the minimum necessary to support a family. Companies involved in banana plantations do not expect their workers to be able to live on the wages from plantation labor. Instead they recruit the poorer tenants and agricultural workers from local rural villages, pay them far less than subsistence, and expect them to supplement their wages by farming and raising animals.[21] For example, one of the leading multinational firms involved in growing oil palms pays wages that in 1983 were only 36 percent of the estimated requirement for a family of six to stay above the poverty line.[22] The families of sugar workers suffered from serious malnutrition long before the world market for sugar collapsed in the mid-1980s. A 1975 survey of sugar workers' families revealed that, on the average, each family had lost at least one child to disease because the child had been weakened by malnutrition, and 29 percent had lost two or more children.[23]

Notwithstanding these low wages, plantation crops such as coconut, rubber, pineapple, and oil palm are not efficient in providing employment to the landless agricultural laborer. They are capital-intensive rather than labor-intensive, requiring less labor than mixed crop farming geared toward family subsistence. It has been estimated that plantation crops require an average of about one person for three to five hectares, far less than on a subsistence crop farm.[24] Coconut requires the least labor of all these crops: an average of only 30 person-days per hectare for maintenance, harvesting, and copra processing for an entire year. Even so, almost as much land is planted to coconut as to rice.[25] Former landless lowland migrants have been driven into the uplands by population pressures and the dearth of employment opportunities. The once sparsely scattered population of the uplands has been swollen with migrants. No one really knows how many people now live on the more steeply sloped land. Estimates range from a low of 4 million to a high of 14.4 million people—about 25 percent of the total population—living on land categorized as forestland because of its slope.[26]

Unable to practice ecologically sound traditional agricultural techniques because of growing population density and lacking secure ownership status, cultivators plant the area for three or four successive crop years with annual crops—rice and corn—before moving onto another area. This depletes the fertility of the soil by exposing the topsoil to heavy runoff and continuous erosion. Primarily because the soils on which they live have lost productivity, upland farmers are among the poorest of the poor in the Philippines. The average annual household income in the uplands has been estimated at about 2,500 pesos, or only about one-third of the commonly used "food threshold income" of about 7,500 pesos.[27]

The Destruction of Philippine Forests

Forests are a key resource for the Philippines, not only as a major source of income and fuel for the poor, but also because they are vital to the functioning of the watersheds—drainage basins of river systems that flow to the sea—that are necessary for the viability of agriculture as well as near-shore fishery production systems. They serve to hold the topsoil and store water that is slowly released into the lowlands, where it is used for irrigation, industrial uses, and hydroelectric power. These precious resources are threatened by two converging social and economic problems: a corrupt and wasteful system of commercial logging, and the destruction of forests by the upland population under the pressure of overpopulation. Most observers agree, however, that the primary cause of deforestation in the Philippines is a highly politicized system of commercial logging. Access to natural resources, like other economic privileges in Philippine society, has long been allocated on the basis of political influence. Both during the U.S. colonial period and since, the Philippines has been a "rent-seeking" state—one in which a dominant elite uses state power to redistribute income in favor of itself.[28] In the Philippines, one of the most important forms of rent-seeking behavior has been the continuing appropriation of Philippine forest resources for the personal profit of a small minority at the expense of the sustainability of those resources.

During the U.S. colonial era, the elected Filipino legislature, which represented the interests of the land-owning class, succeeded in frustrating any real regulation of logging by denying the Bureau of Forestry sufficient funds.[29] Only in 1955 did the government introduce the policy of selective logging and sustained yield, requiring that forest be cut so that it could regenerate itself in a few decades. Because of poorly researched regulations, however, loggers were allowed legally to cut faster than the forests could renew themselves.[30]

The 1960s saw a rush to get in on logging in response to the explosion in Japanese demand for wood. Logging concessions were allocated on the basis of political favoritism and corruption, as timber licenses were granted for short terms varying between one, two, four, and 10 years.[31] It became necessary for companies to have an influential politician—usually a member of Congress—on the board of directors to ensure that leases got renewed. By the late 1960s companies were being pressured by political figures to make them major stockholders in return for protecting their concessions. Often political cronies of President Ferdinand Marcos and other political leaders got their own license and then rented it to a legitimate logging company in return for a share of the profits.[32]

As competition for timber concessions increased, the attitude of most logging companies was "cut and get out."[33] There were enormous profits in the first cut, but no incentive for most companies to use sustained-yield methods of logging. Concessions were granted for periods from one to 10 years, and no assurances were made that it would be renewed, while it took at least 35 years before the stand would be ready for harvesting again. So most companies simply maximized their revenues on the first cut and ignored the second.[34]

In part because of its chronic balance-of-payments problems, logging became a central element in Philippine national economic strategy. In 1969 forest products, primarily logs, were the largest single category of Philippine exports, representing 33 percent of total export earnings. Between 1961 and 1972, the government increased the area of forestland leased for logging concessions from 4.48 million to 10.6 million. (See Figure 2.) A gradual reduction in log exports was ordered by the Bureau of Forestry in 1967, but it was suspended two years later in order to alleviate the balance of payments problem.[35] Instead, log

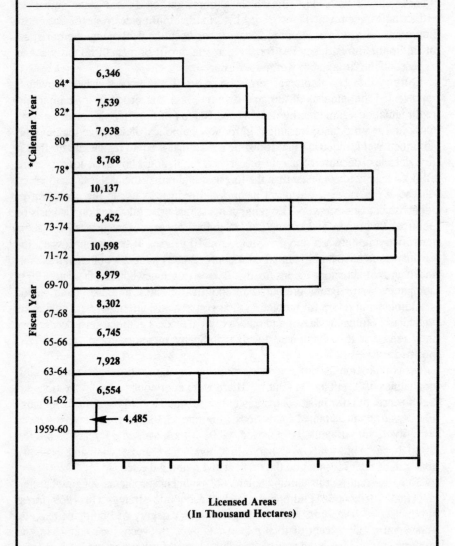

Figure 2. Forest Area Under License, 1960-1984 (In Thousand Hectares)

Calendar Year / Fiscal Year	Value
84*	6,346
82*	7,539
80*	7,938
78*	8,768
75-76	10,137
73-74	8,452
71-72	10,598
69-70	8,979
67-68	8,302
65-66	6,745
63-64	7,928
61-62	6,554
1959-60	4,485

Licensed Areas
(In Thousand Hectares)

Source: Cited in Repetto and Gillis, eds., *Public Policies and the Misuse of Forest Resources,* (Cambridge University Press): 174

production and exports rose to their highest point historically in the 1967–71 period, during Marcos' first and second presidencies. (See Table 1.)

As Marcos began to go more heavily into debt, the pressures to use forest resources for export earnings intensified. Only a slowdown in Japanese market growth appears to have prevented a much higher level of log exports in the late 1970s and early 1980s.[36] The Minister of Natural Resources said in 1983 that a log export ban was desirable, but could not yet be implemented because of the need for foreign exchange.[37]

Meanwhile, many established concessionaires were losing their licenses to cronies of Marcos.[38] Concessionaires closest to Marcos obtained control over the bulk of the forest area under concession. In 1977, one-third of the 250 companies with leases had nearly 90 percent of the allowable cut.[39] The average size of a concession was 30,000 hectares in 1977 and 36,000 by 1982, but logging companies controlled by Minister of Defense Juan Ponce Enrile obtained four or five leases, each with 80,000 to 90,000 hectares.[40]

The martial law regime's authoritarian political structure created both incentives and opportunities for military and civilian officials to take advantage of their position to participate in the illegal exploitation of natural resources. The fact that mayors were stripped, in effect, of their political power and became merely distributors of largesse from the central government left little reason for loyalty to that government except for opportunities for corruption. Military officials acquired extraordinary power over all activities within their areas of responsibility. As one scholar has observed, the military commanders replaced traditional politicians as "dispensers of political privilege."[41] They helped protect the interests of wealthy businessmen in their regions in return for a percentage of profits. A confidential report of the Natural Resources Management Center cited the protection and even ownership of logging companies by military officials as well as politicians as an obstacle to strict implementation of rules on forestry management.[42]

Because of cozy relations between the political elite and the logging industry, the government captured only a very small percentage of the value of the resources being exported. The system of fixed "forest charges," first adopted more than 70 years ago, valued timber resources at such an artificially low level (only 1 to 3 percent of real market value in log form) that the logging industry was given no incentive to produce logs efficiently.[43] During the late 1970s and 1980s, moreover, an increasing proportion of forest destruction was due to illegal logging, primarily for export, either through smuggling or underinvoicing. The value of illegal exports of logs to the Republic of Korea, Japan, and Taiwan during 1978–82 has been estimated at about $60 million annually.[44]

The restoration of democratic institutions by the "snap revolution" of 1986 has not ended the mismanagement of Philippine forests. The Department of Environment and Natural Resources (DENR) has initiated some new policies that eliminate the former disincentives for efficiency in logging concessions, by

Table 1. Log Production and Export FY 1960–CY 1981 (in cubic meters)

Fiscal Year	Production	Exported	% of Production
1960–61	6,596,458	3,028,020	45.9
1961–62	6,771,781	3,749,087	55.4
1962–63	7,668,078	4,593,485	69.9
1963–64	6,536,115	4,542,505	69.5
1964–65	6,175,142	3,486,646	56.5
1965–66	8,047,148	5,534,375	68.8
1966–67	7,843,283	5,648,531	84.8
1967–68	11,113,650	7,510,956	67.6
1968–69	11,583,713	8,649,021	71.3
1969–70	11,004,564	8,616,078	78.3
1970–71	10,679,519	8,443,256	79.1
1971–72	8,416,099	7,018,218	83.4
1972–73	10,445,620	6,949,312	66.5
1973–74	10,189,898	5,434,217	53.3
1974–75	7,331,898	4,579,225	62.5
1975–76	8,440,691	3,050,262	36.1

Calendar Year	Production	Exported	% of Production
1976	8,645,835	2,331,297	26.9
1977	7,873,490	2,046,735	25.9
1978	7,168,549	2,210,463	30.8
1979	6,577,864	1,248,153	19.0
1980	6,400,000	714,885	11.0
1981	5,399,523	706,399	13.0
1982	4,514,000	1,590,000	35.2
1983	4,430,000	1,017,000	23.0
1984	3,849,000	1,323,000	34.4
1985	3,285,000	679,000	21.3
1986	3,078,000	427,000	13.9
1987	3,412,000	200,000	5.9

Source: Adapted from *FAO Forest Products Yearbook 1987* (Rome: 1989), 56; and National Environmental Protection Council, *The Philippines Environment 1982* (Quezon City: NEPC, 1983).

increasing stumpage fees dramatically and capturing the full economic rent on the concessions. It has also required a deposit from logging concessionaires to ensure that reforestation would be carried out.[45] However, illegal logging has apparently not been reduced. In the Central Luzon province of Tarlac it was reportedly more rampant in 1987 than it was under Marcos, and some military men were said to be involved.[46] Moreover, political considerations have sometimes intruded upon decisions on forest management. Although President Corazon Aquino's Ministry of Natural Resources acted to strip Defense Minister Enrile of his logging interests in 1986, the government also ensured the support of one important general's loyalty in the November 1986 political crisis by giving him logging rights in a military forest reserve. Logging companies who continue to violate the forestry code have escaped penalty because of connections with highly placed military or civilian officials.[47] It will take the achievement of political stability and civilian control of the military, as well as a redistribution of political power to those more concerned about environmental security, to end the waste of Philippine forests.

The second cause of deforestation in the Philippines has been the massive movement of landless workers into the uplands. The upland population, increasingly unable to carry on environmentally sound cultivation techniques because of population density and driven by subsistence needs, is believed to be responsible for as much 25 percent of the destruction of Philippine forests and the consequent erosion of upland soils.[48] The Philippine government recognized in the late 1970s that it could not evict the upland population from forest areas and has since tried to involve them in tree plantations and other reforestation schemes while recognizing their rights to access to the land. But obtaining their cooperation has been impeded by the refusal of the government to grant secure tenure on the land to those living in forestlands, and by the upland population's massive mistrust of government intentions.[49]

The combination of rent-seeking state behavior and the relentless pressure of landlessness and unemployment has brought about perhaps the fastest process of destruction of forest reserves in world history. Some 16.6 million hectares—over half the land area of the Philippines—were once covered with forest. But those forests have disappeared at a steadily increasing rate throughout the post-World War II period. Statistics on deforestation from the Bureau of Forest Development, which have long been suspect as too conservative by most forestry specialists in the Philippines, showed that between 1971 and 1980 alone 1.7 million hectares of forest were lost (1.1 million of which were converted permanently to nonforest uses) leaving 11.2 million hectares of forest area, of which only 7.6 million hectares were adequately stocked.[50] By others' reckoning, however, the present level of adequately stocked forests would be between 6.8 and 7.3 million hectares.[51]

The World Bank estimated in January 1989 that only about 1 million hectares of old-growth dipterocarp (hardwood) forest remain, mainly in northeastern

Luzon, Mindanao and Palawan. If the recent "implied harvesting rate" of about 200,000 hectares per year continues, the World Bank warns, this natural resource will disappear completely within five years.[52] It is expected that in the first quarter of the next century, little timber will be harvested from natural forests and that the forestry industry will focus on establishing and maintaining tree plantations.[53]

The most serious environmental and economic impact of the removal of forest cover is on the watershed system. Of 5 million hectares of denuded land that were already in need of reforestation by the late 1970s, at least 2 million were in critical watershed areas.[54] The Agno River Basin in Luzon provides a good case study of the costs of denuding forestlands. The river has silted up so much that in some areas it is higher than the surrounding ricefields. In the rainy season, the Agno River becomes a raging flood; in the dry season it has too little current. A survey of the river basin in the mid-1970s showed that 58,415 hectares within five different watersheds had become severely eroded, with the topsoil completely swept away and 50 percent of the subsoil eroded. In another 125,000 hectares in the same watersheds, 75 percent of the topsoil had been carried away.[55]

The increased sediment load of rivers and streams has greatly increased the severity of floods. A study of watershed management by United Nations organizations in 1982 reported that the magnitude of floods in the typhoon belt (from northern Luzon to southern Samar) had "increased greatly" due to watershed degradation.[56] Entire villages, or *barangays*, in the Cagayan Valley of northern Luzon have been washed into the rivers during some typhoons, a catastrophe people in the valley said had never happened before the loggers came to the mountains.[57]

The sedimentation of rivers and streams has also affected the operation of irrigation facilities, reducing the amount of water for cultivation in Luzon and Mindanao. In Luzon, it has been estimated that the three most important reservoirs have lost half their life spans due to excessive silt and sediment.[58]

A study done for the U.S. Agency for International Development (AID) in the mid-1970s also revealed that deforestation in northwestern Luzon had reduced rainfall, which thus negatively affected both quality and quantity of crops.[59]

Degrading the Marine Environment

The ability of the Philippines to feed its population depends heavily on fish and other seafood, which provide 54 percent of the protein for the average Filipino household and an even higher percentage for poor households. Fishing also provides a livelihood for 4.3 percent of the total labor force.[60] Thus far, however, the fisheries sector has failed to play its potential role in meeting the basic needs of the poor.

Table 2. Fish Production by Sector (1973–86) ('000 metric tons)

Year	Aquaculture[a]	Municipal[b]	Commercial	Total
1973	100	640	465	1205
1974	113	684	471	1268
1975	106	732	499	1337
1976	159	726	508	1393
1977	164	827	518	1509
1978	217	858	506	1581
1979	241	839	501	1581
1980	289	895	488	1672
1981	340	939	495	1774
1982	392	978	526	1896
1983	445	1146	519	2110
1984	479	1089	513	2081
1985	495	1045	512	2052
1986[c]	471	1072	546	2089

a. Aquaculture includes its three subsectors, namely mariculture for oyster, mussel and seaweeds; brackishwater culture for fishpond; and freshwater culture for fishpen, fish cage and fishpond.

b. Municipal includes fishing done in coastal and inland waters with or without boats of three gross tonnage or less.

c. Preliminary data.

Source: Bureau of Fisheries and Aquatic Resources, Fisheries Statistics Section, *1986 Philippine Fisheries Profile.* Adjustments/revisions were made from 1976–1986 based on the new classification of Fisheries Sector.

While fisheries production increased from 1970 to 1980, the growth was not enough to meet rapidly rising domestic demand. The target for per capita fish consumption was 40 kilos a year. In fact, despite increased fish production (see Table 2), per capita supply of fish declined from 25.6 kilograms in 1976 to 22.7 kilograms in 1980—the same level as in 1970. By 1986, fish consumption was still only 35 kilograms per capita. The result was that a sizable proportion of the population has suffered from protein deficiency.[61]

A major reason for the failure of the fisheries sector to provide sufficient supplies has been the failure of government and other social institutions to ensure the sustainability of fishery resources. Overfishing and other forms of degradation of coastal and marine ecosystems have caused decreases in fish catch for the small fisherman and affected his future yields. Fisheries policy has also benefited larger commercial fishing operations at the expense of poor fishers.

Some 574,000 small-scale or "municipal" fishers (those who use boats of less than three gross tons operating in shallow water up to three kilometers from shore) contribute about 63 percent of the total fish catch. But most of them are very poor, with incomes averaging only one-fourth the national average.[62] Their livelihood has been severely undermined in the past two decades by the pollution of the marine environment, the absence of employment opportunities outside the fisheries sector, the intrusion of commercial fishery operations, and the proliferation of commercial fishponds. All these factors have contributed to reductions in catch per unit of effort for municipal fishermen, as well as in the size and quality of the fish.[63] Ten of the 50 major fishing grounds for municipal fishers are believed to have been overfished.[64]

Trawlers, using a net that is dragged along the sea bottom, disrupt marine life there and destroy corals and other marine habitats. Commercial fishing boats also use the purse seine, a net with an incandescent light to attract fish near the surface. The intrusion on municipal fishing grounds of these larger commercial boats with higher technology equipment causes massive waste and depletion of fishery resources. Fine nets take virtually every living thing from the water, including the larvae of many fishes and even microplankton.[65] In a number of areas, the maximum biologically sustainable levels of production have been exceeded, meaning that fishing stocks in coastal fishing areas cannot regenerate themselves.[66]

The intrusion of commercial fishing boats has also led to a starkly unequal distribution of the fish catch in near-shore fishing areas. A study of fishing in San Miguel Bay, for example, showed that large-scale trawlers got 31 percent of the total catch with only 95 vessels, half of which were owned by only five families, while the rest of the catch was shared by 2,300 small-scale fishing boats.[67]

The government, with the aim of boosting exports, promoted the rise of high-technology fishing by providing generous loans to larger commercial fisheries to purchase advanced equipment and larger boats. In 1980–81, for example, the municipal fishing sector received only $500,000 in loans from government institutions, while commercial operations received $17.6 million.[68]

Another major cause of the decline of traditional small-scale fishing has been the expansion of aquaculture—the growing of fish in fishponds or pens—at the expense of the degradation of the coastal zone environment. Mangrove forests, found along the coasts of almost all the near-shore fisheries of the Philippines, serve to stabilize the shoreline, protect the marine system from sedimentation, enhance the near-shore nutrient supply, and provide breeding, feeding, and nursery grounds for marine life. Converting the mangroves to fishponds lowers radically the number of living organisms on which the surrounding seas depend for nourishment, seriously reducing both the fish catch and fry population.[69]

Mangrove forests in the Philippines declined from 448,000 hectares in 1967 to 254,000 hectares in 1976, an annual rate of decrease of 4 percent.[70] Mangrove destruction has also been caused by heavy siltation due to soil erosion in upland areas, removal of mangrove trees for commercial, industrial, and human settlement purposes, and conversion to charcoal for export. The construction of fishponds was a major contributing factor, however, and the one most directly affected by government policy. During this period, influential individuals were granted outright ownership of 124,000 hectares of coastal swampland for conversion into fishponds, which would account for half the destruction of mangroves forests during that decade.[71]

After 1975, the rate of conversion slowed temporarily to 2,439 hectares annually, as the environmental and economic consequences of destroying mangrove forests were brought to light.[72] But the association of fishpond owners mounted a powerful campaign of pressure to have the remaining mangrove area released for conversion, and in 1984, an additional 28,000 hectares of mangroves were released for fishpond development, including 846 hectares of old-growth mangrove forest.[73] The total mangrove forest area was reduced to only 56,000 hectares by 1984, most of which were young-growth stands.[74]

The coastal zone environment is also menaced by pollution from mining discharges and from manufacturing wastes, sewage, and chemicals used in farming. Much of the country's mineral deposits are located in or near the coastal zone area, and dumping of mine tailings has upset the coastal ecosystems. At Calangcan Bay in Santa Cruz, Marinduque, some 12,000 fishermen have lost their livelihood because of the dumping of mine tailings into the bay by Marcopper Mining Corporation. The catch has been reduced to only 8 percent of what it had been before the copper mine began to pollute the bay in 1975.[75]

Coral reefs, which provide spawning, feeding, and nursery grounds for as much as one-fourth of the total fish catch, have been destroyed at an alarming rate in recent years by heavy siltation from deforestation, mine tailings, and other sources, as well as by illegal collection for export and destructive fishing methods. Harvesting coral for commercial purposes has been stimulated by increased demand for ornamental corals in the industrialized countries, which constitute 90 percent of the total market (more than half this market is located in the United States).[76] Illegal fishing methods that destroy coral reefs have been carried out in a highly organized manner under the protection of powerful local political and military figures.[77]

The productivity of inland lakes has also been seriously affected by environmental mismanagement, mainly by the dumping of organic and chemical wastes. Laguna Lake, located near Metro Manila, receives the wastes of approximately 900 factories as well as the wastes of the heaviest concentration of population in the country. It receives heavy deposits of nitrogen and phosphorous, which stimulate algae and thus kill fish, and heavy siltation, which destroys the plankton on which fish feed. The total annual fish catch on Laguna Lake dropped from 320,000 metric tons in 1964 to only 163,000 in 1968; by 1982, it had fallen to 126,000 metric tons.[78]

Economic and Political Implications of Environmental Degradation

The pressure of population on land and the depletion of forest and marine resources will have a grave impact on the country's economic and political future. The most direct impact is the support that the Communist insurgency has gained among landless laborers, insecure tenant farmers, and upland communities—particularly ethnic minorities whose livelihood and way of life have been imperiled by the incursion of logging operations on their traditional lands.

The potential for revolutionary mobilization of the Philippine rural poor is greater today than ever. Peasant protest movements in the past, particularly the ones in central Luzon in the 1930s and 1940s that culminated in the Huk movement, were reformist rather than revolutionary in character, since they did not aim at overthrowing the entire agrarian structure and were dissipated with relative ease.[79] The rural poor in a subsistence crisis today, unlike the tenant farmers of earlier agrarian conflicts, are more likely to support radical socioeconomic and political change. Their survival depends not on a wealthy landowner but on supplementing what little income they earn from wage labor with other low productivity pursuits, such as crafts, services, or gathering.[80]

Tenant farmers as well as agricultural laborers have become the most active supporters of the New People's Army (NPA), which endorses more favorable economic arrangements with landlords and agricultural capitalists.[81]

The NPA has also gained the support of communities by leading or supporting their struggles against unpopular logging concessionaires. In the Cordillera region of northern Luzon, the NPA launched "Operation Lapat" in 1986 to stop the operations of logging companies who do not comply with forestry laws. A key feature of the campaign is that logging trucks are not allowed to enter the concession area unless they carry seedlings for replanting.[82]

The NPA's stance as protector of forest resources has been the important factor in gaining the sympathy of several ethnic minorities to the Communist movement. The best example concerns the Cellophil Resources Corporation (CRC), a subsidiary of Marcos crony Herminio Disini's Herdis conglomerate, which received, along with a sister company, nearly 200,000 hectares of timberland extending across the mountains of five Cordillera provinces. The concession embraced the lands of five tribal minority groups, but the most seriously affected were the Tinggians, most of whose lands were within the concession.

The Tinggians depended primarily on irrigated terraced rice farms, which are supplemented by shifting cultivation and cattle raising. But they also depended on the forests for timber, fuel and game and on the rivers for fish. They were apprehensive that the CRC would deny them the use of their communal forests and pastures and threaten the rivers, since the logging would be carried out in coniferous forests on very steep terrain, resulting in massive erosion and damage to Tinggian fields.[83] Tinggian nonviolent resistance to CRC's plans brought troops from the Marcos regime. By 1980, the Tinggians allied themselves with the NPA, and some leaders of the movement to stop CRC, including Father Conrado Balweg and two other Catholic priests, became local NPA leaders.[84]

The Tinggian experience illustrates what has been happening elsewhere in the Cordillera in other regions. The Communist insurgents convinced many tribal minorities threatened by logging operations that the only way to resist the plundering of their land by "imperialist companies" allied with Marcos was to take up arms with the NPA.[85] In Augusan del Norte, Mindanao, a large proportion of the 200,000 Higaonons joined or supported the NPA in response to the U.S.-owned Nasipit Lumber Company's destruction of traditional Higaonon forests.[86] Thirty-six logging operations in Luzon and 49 in Mindanao affect the land, forests, and rivers traditionally used by national minorities as well. (See Figure 3.)

Forest destruction also has indirect but potentially serious impacts on social stability. An estimated 70 percent of the poorest households in the Philippines have traditionally depended on plentiful supplies of wood from the forests for cooking fuel. But as the forests have been destroyed, shrinking the supply of fuelwood, it has cost the poor household an increasing share of its income to have sufficient cooking fuel.[87] The further reduction of fuelwood will mean that the poor will have less money left over for other essentials, including food.

The process of deforestation has already reduced the productivity of lowland agriculture by an unknown factor. It has also made the irrigation of additional agricultural land more expensive and less effective. To sustain a population of roughly twice the present size, irrigated ricelands would have to be increased from the present level of 1.5 million hectares to 3.1 million—the estimated maximum area of irrigable land.[88] But to successfully irrigate all this land, the Philippines will need forested watersheds capable of holding and slowly releasing water. And much of the watershed system has already been degraded. As of 1981, nearly 30 percent of the 5.1 million hectares of forestlands regarded as needing immediate reforestation were within critical watersheds.[89] Less irrigation will mean a shortfall in food, which will have to be covered by imports paid for in scarce foreign exchange.

A recent study provides some long-range calculations regarding the island of Palawan that convey the magnitude of the impact that deforestation may have on lowland agriculture. The study estimates that, within 20 years, irrigation will no longer be feasible on about half the island's projected total irrigated area of

Figure 3. Major Mining and Logging Operations Affecting National Minorities

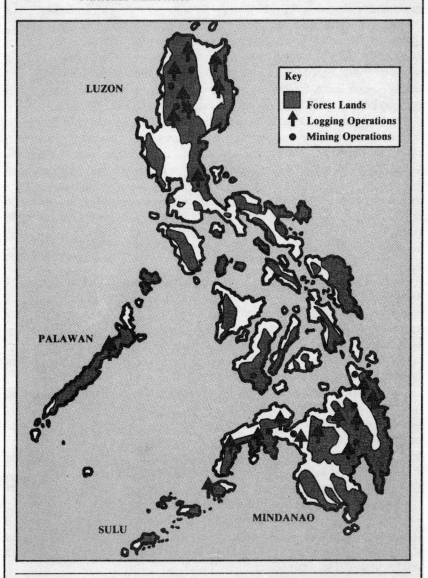

Key

Forest Lands

↑ **Logging Operations**

● **Mining Operations**

LUZON

PALAWAN

SULU

MINDANAO

Source: Anti-Slavery Society, Indigenous Peoples and Development Series, Report #1, 1983, "The Philippines: Authoritarian Government, Multi-Nationals, and Ancestral Lands

36,000 hectares, because of the hydrological effects of the loss of forest cover expected by then.[90] The Palawan case suggests that efforts to increase production per hectare through increased irrigation may be frustrated by past and continuing removal of forest cover.

In short, the destruction of forest resources exacerbates the subsistence crisis created by the pressures of population growth on a limited agricultural land base, access to which is inequitably distributed. It weakens the ability of the economy to provide sufficient food, reduces the incomes of small farmers by increasing floods and reducing the availability of irrigation water, and increases the cost of one of the basic necessities of life for the poorest of the poor.

Both socioeconomic equity and productivity have been diminished by a fisheries policy that has overemphasized high technology and capital-intensive investment and has failed to stem environmental threats to marine ecosystems. Because of overfishing and environmental stresses, the poor have had greater difficulty finding adequate food, and small-scale fishers have suffered declining income. The fisheries sector has thus failed to mitigate the pressure of population on a limited and fragile land base.

Policy Implications

Resource and environmental problems should no longer be viewed by the Philippine and U.S. governments as secondary to economic, social, and political problems. As the discussion in this chapter has shown, environmental destruction and the waste of resources are of the essence in the Philippine socioeconomic crisis and a primary factor in its political future. If there is to be any hope of saving the country's watersheds, providing a livelihood for the rural poor, and halting the deterioration of the marine environment, the Philippine government must set some priorities.

First, to protect what is left of Philippine forests and assure a sustainable yield, the government must put an end to the system of corruption and political favoritism that has facilitated illegal logging and exporting—a task that will require a strong political will as well as strong popular support. The requirement that logging companies must carry out large-scale reforestation should be rigorously enforced, and the ownership rights of 3.4 million tribal people as well as the rest of the upland population should be recognized. A land reform program that reaches at least all the current tenant population would help provide more incentives to protect the resource base. High-technology fishing should be more closely regulated and further destruction of mangroves prohibited.

The Philippine government will have to devote greater budgetary resources to the task of saving the country's resources and environment. Its ability to implement policy reforms will depend in part on whether peasants' and fishers' organizations emerge that can defend natural resources against abuse by both outsiders and the local population itself. One priority for the government is to encourage community and nongovernmental organizations (NGOs) as vehicles for restoration of degraded lands and protection of resources. The government's ability to support resource and environmental conservation with additional budgetary resources will also depend on obtaining relief from its crushing debt burden, which is expected to reach $33.5 billion in 1992. Debt repayments were already consuming 37 percent of the country's export earnings in 1987.[91]

Finally, the Philippines must have a clear national policy aimed at slowing population growth, embracing both family planning services and education and a concerted effort to improve maternal and child health. Such a policy would aim at providing basic educational, health, and nutritional services to the poor through community health workers and paramedical personnel in an effort to bring down fertility rates.

The Philippine government's response to environmental and resources issues should be a matter of urgent concern to Washington. After years of accepting the imposition of Marcos' authoritarian martial law regime, both the U.S. Administration and Congress now seem determined to help the resuscitated Philippine democracy survive.[92] U.S. press and political attention to the Philippines in the aftermath of their dramatic democratic revolution has reawakened American awareness of genuine long-term interests in the Philippines. During a period of transitions from authoritarianism to democracy in Latin America and Asia, the Philippines has come to be widely perceived as a reflection of U.S. commitment to support for democratic institutions in the developing world.

The United States has long had an interest in an open economy in the Philippines. As late as 1972, U.S. investments in the Philippines constituted 65 percent of all such investments in the noncommunist Southeast Asian states.[93] U.S.-based corporations have had a significant presence in the Philippines for some time. They played an important role, for instance, in the expansion of logging in the 1960s and 1970s, either alone or with Filipino partners. Five of the major logging firms in the Philippines have been subsidiaries of American companies: Lianga Bay, owned by Georgia Pacific Corporation; Findlay Millar Company, Zamboanga Wood Products, owned by Boise Cascade; Basilan Lumber Company, owned by Weyerhaeuser Corporation; and Paper and Industrial Corporation of the Philippines and Bislig Bay Lumber Company, owned by Andres Soriano and Associated Companies.

Over the past two decades, U.S. economic interests have been in relative decline, because of the martial law regime's failure to maintain a favorable climate for investment and the emergence of more favorable opportunities for U.S. investment elsewhere in the Association of Southeast Asian Nations (ASEAN) and East Asia. Between 1972 and 1984, U.S. investment in the Philippines grew less rapidly than in any other state in East Asia. In fact, when deflated in terms of the 1980 consumer price index, U.S. investment actually fell during that 12-year period by nearly 25 percent, from $1.3 billion to $940 million. Meanwhile, investments in the ASEAN region increased from $2 billion to nearly $7 billion, and those in Asia as a whole went from $9.1 billion to $18.2 billion.[94]

U.S. trade with the Philippines in 1986 amounted to about $3.5 billion, less than trade with Singapore ($8.1 billion), Indonesia ($4.6 billion), or Malaysia ($4.3 billion).[95] As U.S. investments and trade relations in Southeast Asia have shifted increasingly to other East Asian states, however, a new economic stake in the Philippines has emerged over the past 15 years: the exposure of U.S. commercial banks to loans to the Philippines. United States banks hold more than $5 billion in outstanding loans to the Philippines, out of a total of $92.5 billion in loans to developing countries.[96]

U.S. interests in the Philippines during the past decade have centered increasingly on the continued use of military facilities at Subic Bay Naval Base and Clark Airbase. After the Vietnam War, the bases were viewed by Washington as a symbol of U.S. determination to maintain its role as a Pacific power. Since 1979, they have taken on two new rationales: first, they are part of the support system for the deployment of U.S. forces in Indian Ocean/Persian Gulf region; second, they are presented as a counterweight to Soviet bases in Vietnam.

During the late 1970s and early 1980s the U.S. Embassy in Manila was geared primarily toward getting the Marcos regime's cooperation in negotiating a new agreement on the bases. There was a strong desire to keep any other problems from interfering with the 1983 base negotiations. As a result, critical socioeconomic issues were not raised with Marcos, according to former embassy officials.[97] Meanwhile, something as minor as a bus drivers' strike at Subic Bay was the subject of long discussion at Mission Council meetings. As one U.S. official stationed in the Philippines observed of the embassy's preoccupation with the military bases, "It took me a year or two after I got there to realize that it completely dominates U.S. interpretations of Philippine events."[98]

This obsession with assuring access to military bases has tended to obscure more important U.S. interests. Given the fact that even the conservative Philippine opposition is only supporting a phaseout of the bases before the end of the 1990s, it is clear that the U.S. tenure there is only temporary. The United States should face the fact that its more fundamental interest in the Philippines is the survival of democracy and an open economy. That interest depends, in turn, on the ability of the Philippines to achieve greater equity and to stem environmental degradation and rapid population growth. Washington must be engaged in a deliberate and sustained way in support of sound environmental and resource policies in the Philippines. Such an effort requires a commitment of high-level U.S. official energies, diplomatic influence, and budgetary support.

Since the early 1980s, the U.S. Agency for International Development (AID) has been sensitive to the need for innovative approaches to these problems. In 1983, AID began supporting a rainfed resources development project to raise incomes of coastal zone residents and upland farmers through encouraging soil conservation techniques, diversified farming systems, forest protection, and reforestation. This and similar programs should receive increased funding along with programs of research on appropriate technology for agroforestry in the upland areas, the training of specialists in environmental economics and for agricultural extension agents for those areas; technical assistance for upland farmers in yield improvement, and support for enhanced enforcement of environmental protection laws.

Nongovernmental organizations involved in environmental programs in the Philippines also deserve support. The leading Philippine environmental organization, Haribon, is engaged in a wide variety of activities, including promotion of implementation of the Strategic Environmental Plan for Palawan province, public education, and legal and community action work. With their strong commitment to saving the environment, Haribon and other NGOs have an important role to play in raising consciousness and organizing communities for political and economic actions that can halt environmental degradation. They should be an essential part of U.S. policy toward environment and natural resources.

Similarly, the United States should bring its influence to bear on behalf of a Philippine family planning program as part of a broader effort to reduce fertility. The United States has long been involved in Philippine population programs. It was the outreach program funded by the Agency for International Development that increased contraceptive usage in the 1970s. AID provided $50 million up to 1980, when a new project agreement was reached that provided about $8 million per year for support of population programs.[99] When the momentum dissipated in the early 1980s and demographic targets were eliminated from the five-year development plan, the AID mission in Manila expressed its concern.[100]

The strong bias of the Catholic hierarchy and, apparently President Aquino herself, against effective means of contraception represents a serious obstacle to progress on this vital issue. The next U.S. administration may be tempted to let the issue slide while the United States works to help the Philippines avert short-term economic and political disaster. It is important, however, that the United States support the revival of a strong family planning program of education, information and services, along with a renewed commitment to community health, nutrition and education programs aimed at reducing child and infant mortality rates.

AID already recognizes the crucial importance to the socioeconomic future of the Philippines of restoring an active family planning program, as suggested by its strategy of promoting "a policy dialogue leading to national consensus on the need for a strong population program."[101] That policy dialogue should be pursued by strongly supporting the call by a group of Filipino development experts in 1986 for new national consensus on establishing the two-child family.[102] The United States should also support the efforts of Philippine and international NGOs to educate Filipinos about the use of birth control measures and to provide family planning services.

The so-called "Marshall Plan" for the Philippines, or Multilateral Assistance Initiative, now being negotiated with the Philippines government by the United States, the World Bank, Japan and other donors, is aimed at increasing international assistance to as well as private investment in the Philippines. It should have as two of its central principles environmental protection and sustainable development. The United States should ensure that a large percentage of the new United States assistance supports programs to strengthen the institutional capacity of the Department of Environment and Natural Resources, national capabilities for enforcing environmental protection laws, reforestation, and augmentation of family planning and health services.

The United States can use its influence to alter the system of external pressures and incentives that inhibit the capacity of the Philippine government to implement policies aimed at long-term sustainability of and equitable access to natural resources. The single most important external pressure, of course, is the burden of external debt. The U.S. named the Philippines one of the 15 most troubled debtor nations to receive substantial new lending under the Baker Plan, but the reality has been that sufficient money has not been available to help reduce the Philippine debt problem.[103] The U.S. executive branch should continue to take the lead in multilateral efforts to reduce dramatically the financial resources drained from the Philippines annually, based on the principle of ability to pay and contingent on a development strategy that can sustain and rebuild the resource base.[104] Also worth support are Philippine efforts to eliminate protectionism by industrialized countries against Philippine exports and to expand the markets, especially for processed and manufactured goods.

The combination of a young democracy in Manila and a new administration in Washington provide an opportunity for a fresh look at how best to further U.S. and Philippine interests. The Philippines cannot afford to slip back into the familiar way of dealing with social, economic, and political problems, as it has led to the present subsistence crisis, massive political unrest, and a dwindling resource base. It must place the sustainability of its most fundamental resources as a nation at the center of its planning, and then readjust economic and political strategies accordingly.

References

1. For an analysis of the insurgency's political and military strengths and vulnerabilities, see Gareth Porter, "Philippine Communism After Marcos," *Problems of Communism*, December 1987, 14–35.

2. National Environmental Protection Council, *Executive Summary of the Report on the State of the Philippine Environment, 1982*, July 1983, 2.

3. J.E. Spencer, *Land and People in the Phlippines: Geographic Problems in Rural Economy* (Berkeley and Los Angeles: University of California Press, 1954), 52.

4. A. Barrera, "Classification and Utilization of Some Philippine Soils," *The Journal of Tropical Geography,* Vol. 18, August 1964, 28.

5. R. E. Huke, *Shadows on the Land: An Economic Geography of the Philippines* (Manila: Bookmark, 1963), 65.

6. The 1948 figure is from Republic of the Philippines, National Economic and Development Authority, *1983 Philippine Statistical Yearbook* (Quezon City, 1984), 38; the current estimate is from U.S. Bureau of the Census, Philippine Total Population Medium Series, Revised December 1985.

7. United Nations Fund for Population Activities, *Draft Report of the Mission on Needs Assessment for Population Assistance. Republic of the Philippines,* Manila, November 1985, first draft, p. 36. (Hereinafter cited as *Draft Report.*); Agency for International Development, Congressional Presentation, FY 1988, Annex II, Asia and the Far East, 253.

8. For the projection as of 1983, see *1983 Philippine Statistical Yearbook,* 50, 58, 66.

9. Mahar Mangahas and Raymunda Rimando, "The Philippine Food Problem," in Jose Encarnacion, Jr. et al., *Philippine Economic Problems in Perspective* (Quezon City: Institute of Economic Development and Research, School of Economics, University of the Philippines, 1976), table 4.1, 108.

10. International Rice Research Institute, *Economic Consequences of the New Rice Technology* (Manila: IRRI, 1978), 35; The World Bank, East Asia and Pacific Regional Office, *The Philippines: An Agenda for Adjustment and Growth,* Report Nl. 5258-PH, November 30, 1984, table 7.17, 142.

11. *Statistical Handbook on Agriculture,* table 3, 372.

12. Republic of the Philippines, National Economic and Development Authority, *Draft Medium-Term Development Plan, 1987–1992* (Quezon City: 1986), table 2, 8 and figure 2.

13. Benedict J. Kerkvliet, "Peasants and Agricultural Workers: Implications for United States Policy," presentation to Conference on the Philippines, Washington Institute for Values in Public Policy, Washington, D.C., April 30, 1986, 2.

14. The World Bank, *Philippine Poverty Report,* (Washington, D.C.: The World Bank, 1980 draft), tables 4.3, 4.4 and 4.19, and 114–130.

15. *Draft Medium-Term Development Plan,* 8, table 2.

16. Jean G. Rosenberg and David A. Rosenberg, *Landless Peasants and Rural Poverty in Indonesia and the Philippines,* Rural Development Committee, Center for International Studies, Cornell University, 1980, 82–91.

17. See Gary Hawes, *The Philippine State and the Marcos Regime: The Politics of Export* (Ithaca, New York: Cornell University Press, 1987), 115, 121, 123; Gary Hawes, "Southeast Asia Agribusiness: The New International

Division of Labor," *Bulletin of Concerned Asian Scholars*, Vol. XI, No. 4, October–December 1982, 24; Ecumenical Center for Development (ECD), *Philippine Regional Profiles* (Quezon City: ECD, n.d.), 351; Paul Freese and Thomas J. O'Brien, *Forests, Trees and People* (Davao City: Alternative Resource Center, 1983), 73.

18. The World Bank, East Asia and Pacific Regional Office, *An Agenda for Adjustment and Growth*, Report No. 5258 PH, November 30, 1984, Tables 7.1 and 7.2, 126–127.

19. Agricultural Policy and Strategy Team, University of the Philippines at Los Banos, Agriculture Policy Research Program, and the Philippines Institute for Development study, in *Agenda for Action*, August 1986 (preliminary version), 17. (Hereafter cited as *Agenda for Action*.)

20. Hawes, "Southeast Asian Agribusiness," 24; Linda Susan Magno, "Harvest for a Few: Profits and Poverty in the Mindanao Export Fruits Industry," in Eduardo C. Tadem et al., *Showcases of Underdevelopment in Mindanel: Fishes, Forests and Fruits* (Daval City: Alternate Resource Center, 1984), 206.

21. Robert A. Hackenberg and Beverly H. Hackenberg, "The Urban Working Class in the Philippines," presented to the Conference on Philippines and U.S. Policy, Washington, D.C., April 30, 1986, 15.

22. "Palm Oil Industry," *Mindanao Focus*, October 1983, 20.

23. United Nations Children's Fund, *Project: Rehabilitation and Development Program in the Province of Negros*, E/ICEF/624, 4; Alfred W. McCoy, *Priests on Trial* (New York: Penguin Books, 1984), 108. McCoy indicates that parish records in Kabankalan parish of Negros Occidental in the early 1970s showed that half the burials in parish were of children under the age of one.

24. Hawes, "Southeast Asian Agribusiness," 23. This generalization does not apply, however, to the comparison between sugar, the most labor intensive of the export crops, and corn, which is far less labor intensive than rice. The labor inputs for these two crops are roughly equal. See Howarth E. Bouis and Lawrence J. Haddad, "A Case Study of Commercialization of Agriculture in the Southern Philippines: The Production, Consumption, and Nutrition Effects of a Switch from Corn to Sugar Production in Bukidnon," Draft Final Report to U.S. Agency for International Development, January 1987, 10.4.

25. The World Bank, *Philippine Poverty Report*, 95.

26. "Agro-Forestation Improvement," Project Identification Document, USAID/Manila, January 1982, 1; Aguilar, 1; Ma. Concepcion J. Cruz, "Integrated Summary Report: Population Pressure and Migration: Implications for Upland Development," Philippine Institute for Development Studies Working Paper 86-07, August 1986, 3; *Philippines Forestry, Fisheries, and Agricultural Resource Management Study* (ffARM Study), Report No. 7388-PH (Washington, D.C.: World Bank, January 17, 1989), 20.

27. Delfin J. Ganapin, Jr., "Tropical Deforestation: Philippine Report," presented to "Forest Resource Crisis in the World Conference," Penang, Malaysia, September 6–8, 1986, 17.

28. On the concept of the "rent-seeking" behavior in Third World states, see Myron Weiner, "Asia, Africa and the Middle East," in Myron Weiner and Samuel P. Huntington, eds., *Understanding Political Development* (Boston: Little, Brown, 1987), 54–55.

29. Richard Tucker, "Forest Exploitation in the Philippines, 1900–1950," presented to the Conference, "Rethinking Development in Southeast Asia," University of California, Berkeley, March 15, 1987, 1–13.

30. Martin Reyes, "Intensifying Conservation of the Philippine Dipterocarp Forest," *The Philippine Lumberman*, January 1982, 51; Telephone interview with Patrick Dugan, now consultant to the Ministry of Natural Resources, January 26, 1987.

31. Eufresina L. Boado, "Incentive Policies and Forest Use in the Philippines," in Robert Repetto and Malcolm Gillis (eds)., *Public Policies and the Misuse of Forest Resources* (New York: Cambridge University Press, 1988), 177.

32. Interview with Patrick Dugan, January 26, 1987.

33. As early as 1965 one specialist projected, on the basis of estimates of previous rates of deforestation, that the growth of log exports would begin to tail off by the mid-1970s and probably contract by the 1975–85 period. See J.D. Farquhar, *Demonstration and Training in Forest, Forest Range and Watershed Management* (Manila: United Nations Development Programme, 1967), 43–44.

34. *Agenda for Action*, III.123. The only exceptions to this generalization appear to have been those companies with large requirements for particle wood. See Woell, 8.

35. Boado, "Incentive Policies and Forest Use in the Philippines," in Repetto and Gillis (eds.), *Public Policies and the Misuse of Forest Resources*, 188.

36. Martin R. Reyes, "Intensifying Conservation of the Philippine Dipterocarp Forest," *The Philippine Lumberman*, January 1982, 47.

37. *Ibon Facts and Figures*, January 15, 1984, 4.

38. Interview with Dugan. For other ways that favored loggers used their Marcos regime connections, see Benjie Guevarra, " 'Favored' Loggers Assisted by MAR," *Malaya*, June 5, 1986.

39. *Agenda for Action*, III.122.

40. *Agenda for Action*, III.122; interview with Dugan. Enrile's extensive interests in logging, as well as other sectors of the economy, are discussed in Fred Poole and Max Vanzi, *Revolution in the Philippines: The United States in a Hall of Cracked Mirrors* (New York: McGraw-Hill, 1984), 253; and *Philippine-American News*, June 16–31, 1986.

41. Carolina G. Hernandez, "The Role of the Military in Contemporary Philippine Society," *The Diliman Review*, Vol. 32, No. 1, January–February 1984, 21.

42. "BFD Replanting Program Flawed," *Malaya,* July 10, 1985, 12.

43. A. V. Revilla, "A Critical Review of Philippine Forestry Policies," Forestry Development Center, UPLB College of Forestry, Policy Paper no. 19, August 1986, 9. Revilla estimates that as much as 70 to 90 percent of the timber resources in the concessions have been wasted in logging and processing.

44. Ganapin, "Tropical Deforestation: Philippine Report," 17.

45. *Philippines Forestry, Fisheries, and Agricultural Resource Management Study* (ffARM Study), Report No. 7388-PH (Washington, D.C.: World Bank, January 17, 1989), 20

46. *Malaya,* June 3, 1987.

47. *Manila Chronicle* (FOCUS Supplement), July 5, 1987, 4.

48. Florentino Librero, "Land Use Management in Hilly Areas of the Philippines," Paper for International Workshop on Hilly Land Development, Legaspi City, Philippines, August 1977.

49. Frances Seymour, "Ten Lessons Learned from Agroforestry Projects in the Philippines," unpublished paper, May 30, 1985, 3–5; comment by Mariflor P. Pagsura, in "Native Title: Its Potential for Social Forestry," *Lakas-Yaman,* Vol. IV, No. 1, 29–36.

50. Boado, "Incentive Policies and Forest Use in the Philippines," in Repetto and Gillis (eds.), *Public Policies and the Misuse of Forest Resources*, 1.

51. Ganapin, "Tropical Deforestation: Philippine Report," 6.

52. The World Bank, ffARM Study, 11.

53. A. V. Revilla, Jr. "Framework of a Comprehensive Forestry Development Program for the Philippines," Forestry Development Center, University of the Philippines, Los Banos, College of Forestry, Policy Paper, no. 3, August 1980, 2; Boado, "Incentive Policies and Forest Use in the Philippines," in Repetto and Gillis, *Public Policies and the Misuse of Forest Resources*, 80–81.

54. Patrick Durst, "Problems Facing Reforestation in the Philippines." *Journal of Forestry*, October 1982, 86.

55. Anacleto C.. Duldulao, "Kaingin Erosion and Kaingin Management," *Forestry Digest*, Vol. 5, No. 2, 1978, 55–56.

56. Food and Agriculture Organization and United Nations Development Program, *Watershed Problems and Status of Watershed Management, Country Brief, Philippines,* FAO:RAS/81/053, Working Paper no. 7, June 1982, 10.

57. Interview with Chip Fay, former Peace Corps Volunteer in Northern Luzon, Washington, D.C., January 8, 1987.

58. The World Bank, ffARM Study, 3.

59. Gerald Hickey and Robert A. Flammang, "The Rural Poor Majority in the Philippines: Their Present and Future Status as Benefactors of AID Programs," AID Contract ASIA-C-1251, 1977, 54.

60. Hickey and Flammang, "The Rural Poor Majority in the Philippines," 56.

61. Jesse M. Floyd, "The Political Economy of Fisheries Development in Indonesia, Malaysia, the Philippines and Thailand," unpublished Ph.D. dissertation, University of Hawaii, 1985, 213; Tito Giron, "Fish Supply Dwindling," *Manila Chronicle*, July 4, 1988.

62. Eduardo C. Tadem, "Modernization and Depletion: The Case of the Fishing Industry in Mindanao-Sulu," in *Showcases of Underdevelopment*, 15; Floyd, "The Political Economy of Fisheries Development in Indonesia, Malaysia, the Philippines and Thailand"; Coastal Zone Management Workshop, November 5–6, 1981, Annex D to "Natural Resource Management," Project Identification Document, USAID/Manila, January 1982, 1.

63. The World Bank, ffARM Study, 44–45.

64. *Agenda for Action*, III. 109–110; Jesse M. Floyd, private communication to the author, May 7, 1987.

65. R. B. Gonzales, F. Vande Vusse, and A. C. Alcala, "Coastal Biological Resources: Problems and Prospects," paper provided by Natural Resources Management Center, Ministry of Natural Resources, 185.

66. Floyd, "The Political Economy of Fisheries Development in Indonesia, Malaysia, the Philippines and Thailand," 56, 152.

67. *Agenda for Action*, III.112.

68. "Coastal Zone Management Workshop," 1.

69. Prescillano M. Zamora, "Conservation and Management of Philippine Mangroves," First National Conservation Conference on Natural Resources, December 9–12, 1981, co-sponsored by the Resource Policy and Strategy Research Division, National Resources Management Center and The National Environmental Protection Council, 85–89.

70. Adelina G. Cortiguerra, "Mangrove and Estuarine Ecology in the Philippines," *CANOPY International*, October 1979, 9.

71. Benjamin R. De Jesus and Dexter M. Cabahug, Jr. "Mangrove Resources in the Philippines: Status, Land Uses, Policy and Management Strategy," unpublished paper, 1986, 9–10.

72. Feurdeliz M. Lauricio, "Mangroves in the Philippines," *CANOPY International*, January 1981, 13.

73. David Wurfel, *Philippine Agrarian Policy Today* (Singapore: Institute of Southeast Asian Studies, 1977), 159; De Jesus and Cabahug, "Mangrove Resources in the Philippines," 5.

74. *Philippine Environmental Report, 1984–85*, 138.

75. Lingkod Tao-Kalikasan for the Philippine Federation for Environmental Concern, *Coral Reefs and Mangrove Forests*, Primer Series, No. 5, n.d., 20; Domingo C. Abadilla, "It is Cheaper to Pollute," *Philippine Daily Inquirer*, December 21, 1986.

76. *MNR Newsletter*, September 1981, 11.

77. During the Marcos regime, the Bureau of Fisheries and Aquatic Resources (BFAR) and the military, who were jointly responsible for catching illegal fishermen and coral poachers, were constrained by political pressures, according to the to the BFAR's conservation and law enforcement division. "Coral Destruction Blamed on BFAR," *Malaya*, June 13, 1986.

78. Edward Ma. U. Coronel, "Laguna Lake: Lake of Ignorance," *Enviroscope*, Vol. VI, Nos. 1 and 2, January–June 1986, 2–6; Celso Roque, "A Loch Ness Monster in Laguna lake," *Business Day*, May 13, 1986.

79. Benedict J. Kerkvliet, *The Huk Rebellion* (Berkeley: University of California Press, 1977), 23–30.

80. Rosenberg and Rosenberg, *Landless Peasants and Rural Poverty in Indonesia and the Philippines*, 84–85.

81. See Porter, "Philippine Communism after Marcos," 18.

82. Michael D. Marasigan, "Liberating the Land," *Business Day*, February 13, 1987, 7.

83. Filemon V. Aguilar, Jr., *Social Forestry for Upland Development: Lessons from Four Case Studies*, Quezon City Institute of Philippine Culture, Ateneo de Manila University, 1982, 156; Anti-Slavery Society, *The Philippines: Authoritarian Government, Multinationals and Ancestral Lands* (London Anti-Slavery Society, 1983), 79–85; interview with Bion Griffin, Department of Anthropology, University of Hawaii, January 7, 1987. Prof. Griffin has done research in upland areas of northeast Luzon for several years.

84. Anti-Slavery Society, *The Philippines: Authoritarian Government, Multinationals and Ancestral Lands*, 86–90; *Veritas*, June 2, 1985.

85. See the special issue of *Tribal Forum* (Manila), Vol. VI, No. 5, September–October 1985, devoted to "Land: Our Lost Heritage. How Do We Regain It?", especially 43–45.

86. Romi Gatusao, "The Higaonon's Fight for Ancestral Land," *Mr. & Ms.* (Special Edition), November 7–13, 1986, 17–20.

87. George Carner, "Survival, Interdependence and Competition among the Philippine Rural Poor," *Asian Survey*, Vol. XXII, No. 4, April 1982, 378.

88. Martin R. Reyes, "Intensifying Conservation of the Philippine Dipterocarp Forest," *The Philippine Lumberman*, January 1982, 46. An earlier study had estimated that the maximium irrigated area was 2.5 million hectares, but admitted that there was no detailed soil data or feasibility studies on which to base an estimate. The World Bank, *Philippine Poverty Report* (Washington, D.C.: 1980), 96.

89. R.Z. Callaham and Robert E. Buckham, "Some Perspectives of Forestry in the Philippines, Indonesia, Malaysia and Thailand," unpublished paper, U.S. Forest Service, December 1981, 3.

90. Christopher E. Finney and Stanley Western, "An Economic Analysis of Environmental Protection and Management: An Example from the Philippines," *The Environmentalist*, Vol. 6, No. 1 (1986), 56.

91. *Philippine Daily Inquirer*, October 31, 1987; AID Congressional Presentation Fiscal Year 1986, Annex II, 250.

92. For a detailed account of U.S. relations with the Marcos regime, see Raymond Bonner, *Waltzing with a Dictator* (New York: Times Books, 1987).

93. Data provided by U.S. Embassy, Manila.

94. Data supplied by U.S. Embassy, Manila.

95. Data supplied by the Office of Economic Analysis, Bureau of Intelligence and Research, U.S. Department of State.

96. Data supplied by the International Banking section, Federal Reserve Board, April 1, 1987.

97. Interviews with two U.S. officials stationed in Manila during this period, both of whom request anonymity, Washington, D.C., February 15 and 24, 1987.

98. Interview with former U.S. diplomat in the Philippines who requests anonymity, Washington, D.C., January 15, 1987.

99. "Philippines: Population Program/Progress," information supplied by AID, *Foreign Assistance Legislation for Fiscal Year 1985 (part 5)*, Hearings and Markup before the Subcommittee on Asian and Pacific Affairs of the Committee on Foreign Affairs, House of Respresentatives, 98th Cong., 2nd Session, 1984, 215.

100. See "Country Development Strategy Statement, FY 1984: Philippines," AID, Washington, D.C., January 1982, 9.

101. Agency for International Development, Congressional Presentation FY 1988, Annex II, Asia and the Far East, 253.

102. *Agenda for Action*, 150.

103. For a critique of the Baker Plan by a former Treasury Department official involved in its planning, see Robin Broad, "How About a Real Solution to Third World Debt?" *The New York Times*, September 28, 1987.

104. See John Cavanagh et al., *From Debt to Development* (Washington, D.C.: Institute for Policy Studies, 1985), 49–50.

IV

Dimensions of National Security: The Case of Egypt*

Nazli Choucri, Janet Welsh Brown, and Peter M. Haas

In ancient times Egypt was referred to as the "gift of the Nile"; its rich alluvial soil and reliable waters fostered one of the greatest ancient civilizations, and the coastal plain was productive through the 11th century. Today, however, 96 percent of Egypt's territory is uninhabitable desert. Most of Egypt's 50 million people live on a ribbon of land along the Nile and in its delta. Serious problems of degradation and pollution throw into question the valley's ability to support its population and to sustain agricultural growth equal to Egypt's rapidly increasing numbers. Two mutually reinforcing trends, high population growth and strong pressures on the resource base, raise urgent questions for Egypt—and for United States interests in Egypt and the Middle East.

Although scientists and experts agree that these pressures are serious, they are not yet a priority for the government of Egypt, which is well aware of the need to expand cultivated areas, to increase productivity, and to create jobs and income for those who no longer live off the land. Active attention is given by the government of Egypt, U.S. policymakers, and academics to energy, agriculture, industrial development, education, health, and population growth. But rarely do any of these people deal with the mutually reinforcing and dislocating forces working together. The Mubarak government's concerns are with energy, the military, the political opposition and the survival of new institutions in relative freedom. United States policymakers still think primarily in terms of military

This chapter is based largely on a case study by Dr. Nazli Choucri, "Challenges to Security: Population and Political Economy in Egypt," prepared for the World Resources Institute in 1988. The collaboration of Parichat Chotiya in the preparation of this chapter is gratefully acknowledged.

security against Soviet inroads in the Middle East and Egypt's role in U.S. regional defense strategies.

Historical Context

Since the decline of the ancient civilization, Egypt has been ruled mostly by foreigners. Conquered by Greeks, Romans, Phoenicians, and, centuries later, Arabs and Turks, Egyptians were alienated from their leaders.[1] The revolution of 1952 for the first time brought in an Egyptian as leader. Under President Nasser, Egypt was noted in the West primarily for its claim to leadership of the Arab world and for the revolution's concerns for social equity and economic development. The nation embarked on industrialization, the modernization of agriculture (with special attention to cotton for export), and the construction of the Aswan Dam to control the Nile, generate electricity, and increase irrigation.

In the early 1960s, commercial banks and most medium-sized and heavy industries were nationalized, and measures were instituted to expand employment and redistribute income. Considerable investments were made in social services, especially in education, and public jobs were guaranteed to college and secondary-school graduates (and later to military conscripts dismissed from the services between 1973 and 1976), making the public sector the largest employer except in agriculture. Private-sector small manufacturing firms employing up to 10 workers—shoemakers, tailors, carpenters—enjoyed a great boom between 1967 and 1974, stimulated by favorable export terms with Eastern bloc countries.

Until they were expelled by President Sadat in 1974 and Egyptian policy shifted toward the West, the Soviets and Eastern bloc countries provided the bulk of foreign investment, markets, and technical aid—as well as military assistance. Now, however, Egypt is squarely in the Western camp.

After Sadat's economic liberalization in 1974, Egypt experienced phenomenal growth. Private and international capital poured in, stimulating growth and employment in the nonagricultural sector. The government encouraged overseas employment, with important results: now 15 percent of the labor force is employed outside of Egypt, mostly in the oil-rich Arab states. Though opportunities rise and fall with the price of oil, the remittances of these workers are Egypt's single most important source of foreign exchange and, when they reach home villages, a boost to the standard of living in rural areas. During this time rising urban demand increased profits on the sales of crops whose prices were not controlled by the government (fruits, vegetables, and birseem). Tourism rose. Oil became the most valuable visible export, as Egypt came into the world market just as the Organization of Petroleum Exporting Countries (OPEC) embargo took hold and world oil prices skyrocketed. And after the peace treaty with Israel, U.S. assistance, both military and economic, multiplied.

Population doubled between 1952 and 1980, but the economy kept pace in most respects. Because of Egypt's social policies, and despite mistakes and mismanagement, opportunities expanded, incomes increased, and distortions between rich and poor were largely avoided. The extremes of rich and poor found in Latin America, the Philippines, and elsewhere were not evident in Egypt.

By the late 1980s things became more difficult for Egypt. Oil prices were down, debt payments were up, and remittances were not growing as fast. Mubarak's government undertook some experiments with a more politically liberal constitution and a freer press—and with sometimes too-close-for-comfort relations with the United States.

Underneath the ups and downs of post-revolutionary governments, two trends climbed steadily: population and natural resource problems. And Egypt's long-term security and U.S. interests therein are held hostage to these fundamental underlying trends.

U.S. Interests in Egypt

United States interests in Egypt are dominated by straightforward political and military concerns, though the articulation of those interests is argued usually only with reference to military or political security, and rarely with respect to Egypt's population/resource balance. Egypt is the largest nation in the Middle East (in terms of population size); its integrity is least questioned (in terms of historical continuity); its identity is established and stable (Egyptians have little difficulty defining themselves as such); and it is the most developed of the Arab states (in terms of literacy, education level, institutional capabilities, and all other indicators of "development" aside from oil wealth). Egypt's strategic location is critical geopolitically, and, having discarded the Soviet links and rejected the "socialist ideology," it is a key nation in the Western alliance.

The military interests of the United States in Egypt are considerable. A viable United States military posture in the Middle East depends significantly on the capabilities of its allies and their general support for U.S. priorities in the region. An integrated military stance with Egypt enhances U.S. capabilities to pursue United States objectives in the region. In the last analysis, Middle East defense policies for the United States continue to involve the capacity to contain Soviet pressure, to assure access to oil supply, to keep the Gulf and the Suez Canal safe for international shipping, and to contain regional conflicts and turmoil. United States military assistance to Egypt—now running at $1.25 billion per annum—is a reflection of this importance.[2]

The United States is involved in supplying, training, monitoring, and managing Egyptian military capabilities. The logic of the United States rearming Egypt following the Camp David accord in March 1979 was based on establishing a leaner, more effective Egyptian military, capable of responding to a variety of scenarios relevant to U.S. concerns. For example, the United States expects Egypt to provide support for U.S. military activities, to serve as a surrogate and covert instrument of U.S. military policy, and on all issues involving U.S. strategic concern to provide logistical support.[3]

In entering into a military assistance treaty with Egypt, the United States assumed that Egyptian political and security interests were identical to those of the United States, that U.S. priorities would supercede those of the Egyptian leadership, and that the imperatives of the alliance would override those of the junior partner. These assumptions emerged as flawed, and U.S. expectations unrealistic. Nonetheless, the military link remains strong, and is a relationship essential to the posture of both the United States and Egypt. On the Egyptian side, there is some disenchantment among segments of the professional military who perceive that the alliance engenders costs that exceed the benefits.

Such assumptions and assessments may erode U.S. military security in the region. But far more serious, from the U.S. perspective, are any threats to Egypt's stability and overall security. An "insecure" Egypt, for whatever reason, remains antithetical to U.S. interests. With considerable turmoil in the region—in Iran, Iraq, Lebanon, Libya, Sudan, Ethiopia, Mauritania, Somalia, and Israel—"losing" Egypt remains a risk no U.S. administration wishes to run.

In dealing with Egypt, the United States is dealing invariably with the Arab world as a whole. The events of the past decade have illustrated the robustness of the Egyptian role in the Arab world. Even a treaty with Israel could not break Egypt's many ties with the Arab countries. And while, as has been well put, "the Arab state that did most of the fighting decided to change its profession," the interdependence with the Arab world has emerged mostly unaffected by this dramatic diplomatic move.[4] Egypt's attendance at the Fifth Islamic Conference in Kuwait, in January 1987, is testimony to the influence of an Islamic state whose population of 50 million is regarded in the region and elsewhere as a factor of nontrivial proportions.

U.S. economic interests in Egypt are less pressing than the political or military concerns, but relevant nonetheless. During the past decade, Egypt has become an oil-exporter. Increasing petroleum and natural gas revenues have contributed in part to the expansion of imports from the United States in recent years, as has a huge increase in U.S. economic support funds. Between 1978 and 1986, U.S. exports to Egypt more than doubled, from $1,134 million to $2,704 million, whereas Egyptian imports to the United States rose only slightly, from $105 million to $170 million. Compared with U.S economic ties with Saudi Arabia, the U.S. trade balance is always positive. Indeed, the United States is Egypt's most important trading partner, a source of foodstuffs, machinery, and equipment and fertilizers.[5] The trade balance improved (from a U.S. point of view) to $51,385 million in 1985.

Clearly, Egypt's imports of U.S. goods and services would not have been possible without U.S. economic assistance. Over the past decade U.S. aid to

Egypt for development and civilian purposes amounted to more than $10 billion. In 1989 Egypt received 11.3 percent of all food aid given by the United States and about 23 percent of the total budget of the U.S. Economic Support Fund.[6] In fact, Egypt received roughly 16 percent of the total U.S. Agency for International Development (AID) budget in FY 1989. (Only Israel received more aid, and in cash—a bone of continuing contention in Egypt.) The total figure for assistance from 1977 to 1989, including military aid, is about $33 billion.[7] For the United States, however, Egypt's importance cannot be counted in dollars. Egypt is literally the gateway to the Arab world. The most important of Egyptian assets to the United States for the decades to come is the nation's geopolitical position—as it was to Britain and other European countries in the last century. As long as U.S.-Soviet competition in the region continues, Egypt is an invaluable ally to the United States. U.S. strategic interests in the Middle East are therefore best served by a secure Egypt—a nation threatened neither by erosion of its military capability and sovereignty, nor by challenges to its governance or by undue pressures on its resources and environment.

Egypt's National Security

To get a balanced picture of Egypt's security, three critical dimensions must be considered. The conventional view of security is that of the state against external aggression and the capacity of the state to exert its sovereignty and its control over its territory. Egypt's military security is thought to be enhanced primarily by its manpower, weapon systems, and performance. With one of the largest armies in the Middle East, modern weapons and equipment, and backing by the United States, Egypt is clearly secure, despite the hostility of its western neighbor, Libya.

A second essential dimension of national security, concerns political stability, or governance. This is the security of government against pressures from society; it refers to the capacity to ensure legitimacy for the regime in power, to guarantee domestic support for government policies, and to assure that government policies will effectively deal with challenges to authority created by perceived threats, whether internal or external. Political security is not independent of military security: to the extent that a country's borders and its sovereignty are ensured, a prerequisite for political security is met; this condition is necessary, however, but not sufficient. Though the Mubarak regime is often referred to as a weak government that shares its power with a large independent military and is challenged by a politically and economically significant religious fundamentalist movement, it is nevertheless the legitimate government in the eyes of the Egyptian people.

The essential and necessary condition for the security of any state is the third dimension of the security complex—the sustainability of the resource base in light of the pressures and "demands" of the population and the level of technology of the society. Resource security refers to the broad socioeconomic framework supporting the state, in terms of overall contextual and structural viability. The absence of this type of security will be manifested in trouble and disorder in political security due to the internal pressures and the inability of the government to contain, manage, regulate, diffuse, or export the pressures on its resource base. To the extent that internal pressures are greater than the state's capacity to contain them, threats generated by the absence of resource security can strain the Mubarak or any other regime and translate attendant pressures into threats to political security. In simple parlance, political security can be eroded from "above" (by threats of a military nature or transgressions on sovereignty) or from "below" (from pressures of population demands given prevailing capabilities to meet them). The former seems not likely now in Egypt; the latter bears further examination.

The elements of this third type of security include, first, human resources—in Egypt, a population of 50 million in 1986, growing at a rate that translates into a doubling time of 26 years. This is a prodigious number of people to feed and put to work. But to consider Egypt's population only in a negative way, simply as a load or source of pressure, is misleading. People embody technology (education and management), can become an important economic resource (due to billions in foreign exchange remitted by Egyptian emigres), and are generally considered as the single most critical element of Egypt's national power.

The second element is education and technology—found in Egypt's highly literate public, 11.5 percent of whom have higher, and often highly technical, training. The Ministry of Agriculture, for instance, is said to have more than 400 Ph.D.s with credentials not only from Egyptian institutions, but from the "best" of the West as well.[8] The skill and experience with which a people "convert" and otherwise manage resources to meet demand is a key element in the population/resource balance—and Egypt has a wide lead over most other Arab countries.

The third element is the natural resources of the nation—land, water, and oil being Egypt's primary ones. Land and water, properly husbanded, are renewable; the extent of oil is uncertain. At current rates of production, known petroleum resources will surely last until the turn of the century; beyond that there are major uncertainties, despite possible deposits in the western desert.

Policies and practices that pollute essential resources like water and air, that degrade the land base, or that squander the mineral resources, destroy the continuing capacity of a nation to support its human resources. Good management of resources makes development and growth sustainable. Policy can mediate, intervene, influence, and shape the disposition and distribution of human and natural resources, even when it cannot fundamentally transform critical parameters.

In sum, a state is secure to the degree that all three dimensions of security are under control. Because the security of states is the single most important priority for national policy (everything else is derivative), it is essential to understand the entire security matrix—its military, political, and resource dimensions. The interconnections among the three dimensions will define the nature and extent of a state's true security at any point in time.

Population

Most analysts agree that "population pressure, especially on land and water resources" is labeled "Egypt's principal economic problem," to quote one AID environmental report.[9] However, population is not often mentioned as priority by either Egyptian or U.S. policymakers concerned with Egypt's security. The population of Egypt in 1897 is estimated to have been 9.7 million. At the time of the revolution in 1952 it was approximately 20 million. By 1982 it had more than doubled once again. There are negative as well as positive sides to these numbers.

Birth rates have declined from 44.3 per 1,000 population in 1927 to 34 in 1986, while death rates plummeted in the same period from 27.1 per 1,000 to 10. Average annual growth rose from 1.51 percent in 1907 to a high of 2.7 percent in 1986. It has since declined to 2.31 percent—which translates into 1.7 million additional Egyptians each year. Forty percent of the population is under 15, 4 percent is over 65. Life expectancy at birth is 58.3 years, up from 46.7 in 1970.[10]

According to the United Nations medium-case scenario, Egypt's population is projected to be 65.2 million in 2000. It will double today's total, to approximately 100 million, in the year 2012.

In 1985, 46.5 percent of the population was urban, up from 37.9 percent in 1960. The rate of urbanization appears now to be a steady 3.3 percent per annum.[11] One-third of the nation's people are concentrated in cities of over 100,000. Cairo, with over 10 million people, is one of the most densely populated cities in the world.

The labor force in 1983 was 12.75 million, with approximately 400,000 workers joining annually, making job creation critical to political security. The labor force grew annually at 2.2 percent in 1965–73, at 2.4 percent over the following decade, and is estimated to grow at 2.3 percent a year through the year 2000.[12]

Each year less of the work force is employed in agriculture, even in the rural areas, and more in industry. On the basis of 1983 International Labour Organization (ILO) statistics, 56.6 percent of the labor force was in non-agricultural occupations and 41 percent in agriculture.[13] And even in rural areas, 28 percent of the labor force works in non-agricultural jobs. Labor surveys in 1983 placed unemployment at 6.6 percent,[14] though it is probably higher now given the drop in oil prices and levelling off of remittances. (See Table 1.)

Egyptians employed abroad remain a major source of foreign exchange. Since remittances flow largely through internal channels, this financial resource goes

Table 1. Percentage of Work Force by Sector

	1974	1979	1983
Agriculture, hunting, forestry, fishing	47.34	41.84	40.97
Mining, quarrying	0.23	0.24	0.28
Manufacturing	15.28	16.02	14.72
Electricity, gas, water industries	0.46	0.69	0.87
Construction	2.63	4.69	5.37
Trade, restaurant, hotel	11.63	9.60	8.84
Transportation, storage, communication	4.47	5.11	4.95
Finance, insurance, real estate	0.97	1.22	1.29
Community, social services	16.48	19.03	21.07
Others	0.53	1.57	1.63

Source: Calculated from Table 3B in *ILO Yearbook of Labour Statistics 1986.* Copyright ©
1986, International Labour Organisation, Geneva.

directly to private citizens and is not available to the government. A "hidden economy" has developed, large in scope and scale, that remains outside government control and co-exists with the formal economy.[15] The government continues to devise means to reduce the scope of this economy by liberalizing exchange rates. The results to date are mixed.

Education and Technology

Investments in education increase the capabilities of the population, and the "technology" of the society. Egypt's population is a relatively well-educated and skilled resource. Emphasis on education by all three governments since the revolution has transformed the country. A major commitment, sustained by a large budgetary outlay, has been made. Though some 60 percent of the semiskilled workers in public industry are still illiterate, as are many of the rural poor who emigrate temporarily to work elsewhere in the Arab world, nevertheless enormous strides have been made. Even illiterate workers have some skills, as in the construction sector.[16]

On the primary school level, enrollments went from 75 to 84 percent of the relevant age group between 1965 and 1984. Secondary school enrollments went from 26 to 58 percent, and university enrollments from 7 to 21 percent.[17] University education is free for those who qualify, and the government has also sent thousands of Egyptians abroad, to universities in both the East and West for specialized training. In comparison with most other lower middle income countries, the gains at the secondary and university levels are really impressive. (These are averages for male and female—in every case the Egyptian males have higher enrollments than do females.) The problems surfacing now are the relevance of curriculum and the maintenance of quality, as demand outstrips supply and class sizes swell. There exist shortages of certain kinds of skills in the public sector: math and science teachers, computer scientists, and specialized medical personnel, all of whom can find better paying jobs overseas or in the emerging private sector.

Egypt in fact bears the cost of educating much of the Arab world. Until recently students from other Arab countries have also been educated tuition-free at the University of Cairo, which has distinguished graduate schools in many fields. Egypt has supplied teachers, school administrators, engineers, physicians, managers and other professionals throughout the Arab world since the 1930s. Some critics question whether Egypt recovers the cost of those it has educated, even through remittances. The whole system is expensive, but it serves political and cultural purposes, reinforcing Egypt's ties with Arab states.

The country's 11 universities have generated cohorts of Ph.D.s. Most of them are employed in national laboratories and research institutes—the National Academy of Science, for instance, has 4,000. Trained individuals are not a scarce resource—the issue is the quality of training and the organizational difficulties of utilizing them effectively. All of this bears on the country's technology, and on the ability to fully utilize its skilled work force.

Already, higher education policy is a source of tension because the government is trying to cut back its annual support. A related question is whether Egypt can maintain its investments in education as the current baby boom matures to parenthood and doubles the number of classrooms and teachers required. There is already grave concern that Egypt is not giving sufficient attention to nurturing and developing its human resources to maintain its international comparative advantage and assure its continued "market share" of this important "product."

Natural Resources

Egypt's human resources appear to be the only ones in abundant and reliable supply. Her natural resources—rich alluvial soil, the waters of the Nile, petroleum and natural gas—are all more finite. Egypt's total area is 386.7

thousand square miles (about the size of Texas and New Mexico), of which 2 percent is cultivated.

Agriculture

Traditionally, agriculture sustained Egypt, and the Nile sustained agriculture. The sector remains central to the economy despite decades of emphasis on industrialization. There has been some decline in arable land and permanent cropland (from 2,653,000 hectares 20 years ago to 2,469,000 in 1982–84) due to urbanization,[18] but agriculture still accounts roughly for 18 percent of the country's gross domestic product, and employment in this sector claimed 41 percent of the work force in 1983. Cotton is the country's second largest export after oil. Livestock, food, and beverages are among its principal imports.

The agricultural sector's performance is fraught with problems, many of which are induced by a government pricing policy that has been explicitly biased against food crops. Nonetheless, agricultural production grew consistently over the past 20 years. Using 1974–76 as a base for an index of 100, performance for the previous decade was 82, and for 1982–84 the index was 114.[19] Productivity per worker also increased, although more modestly and not as fast as increases in most other developing countries. A near tripling of fertilizer per hectare of arable land accompanied a substantial increase in total food production over the past 20 years, but production has dropped in per capita terms. And yields for all major food crops have stagnated or declined since 1970 by comparison with most developing countries.[20] More critical, however, is the decline in calories produced domestically as a percentage of total supply, from 91 percent in 1967–70 to 79 percent in 1977–80.[21]

Productivity in food crops, however, appears high. The average annual grain yield per hectare increased from 3,921 kilograms (1974–76) to 4,254 kilograms (1981–83). This latter looks strong next to a figure of 4,075 for the United States[22] and compares well with other developing countries—until one remembers that almost 100 percent of Egyptian farmlands are under irrigation. If only *irrigated* yields were compared, Egyptian yields would be lower considering the excellent soil, sunshine, and water inputs in that country. The rate of yield growth for major food crops in Egypt declined between 1963–67 and 1978–82 compared with that of 36 other developing nations.[23]

A joint study by Egypt's Agriculture Ministry and AID in the summer of 1982 was reported to show a possible long-range tripling of yields from existing farmland with better management.[24] Decades-old central government planning has mandated which crops would be planted and rotated and has restrained productivity. To compound their hardship, prices paid to the farmers have been fixed irrespective of costs of inputs. As these went up during the 1960s and 1970s, prices for the key crops covered (rice, wheat, cotton, sugar, maize, and meat) remained artificially low. When wages skyrocketed after 1973, the terms of trade actually became negative for the farmer, who in many cases was violating rotations and dealing in the black market. In 1975, controls on food crops were eased somewhat, and the farmgate price of cotton more than doubled. Poverty in rural areas declined appreciably in the 1970s, due not so much to development policies as to remittances, 20 to 40 percent of which are estimated to find their way into the countryside.[25]

Among the economic reforms announced by the government for 1987 were progressive increases in prices for farmers. This move had been one condition for International Monetary Fund credit, and is being pushed also by AID.[26] An additional boost is expected as controls over what farmers may produce are phased out over three years.[27]

Consistent with the government's industrialization strategy, agriculture's share of public investment remains small. It declined from 24 percent in the mid-1960s to 8 percent in 1978, and most has gone into sometimes questionable and always expensive drainage and land reclamation projects, not to improved management, seed, and fertilizer.[28]

Contributing also to declining agricultural production is the encroachment of urbanization on productive farmland. The assault remains unchecked, as even the government continues to build on scarce agricultural land.[29]

Because the population continues to outstrip agricultural production, food imports in 1987 cost the government over $10 million a day.[30] Wheat and flour imports for 1986 have been put at $1 billion.[31] Such voluminous food imports, both purchased and donated, along with subsidies to favor the more politically influential urban dweller have continued to keep prices for staples low.

In terms of agricultural output, cotton production must be considered separately from food production, because different policies and different market conditions have variously affected performance. Cotton, Egypt's chief export crop, appears to fare respectably. This crop, in particular, has benefited from pesticide subsidies.[32] Preliminary estimates for 1986/87 showed it to be a great year, with Egypt producing only slightly less than Turkey, the biggest producer in the Middle East. Plans called for increased cotton acreage and improved yields.[33] Some industry observers suggested, however, that targets may be somewhat overambitious. They expected exports to decline in 1986–87 to 660,000 bales from 700,000 bales in 1984/85. Sales should have been worth $400 million.[34] But the future is clouded by a depression of the world market price for cotton.

Cultivation in Egypt is highly mechanized by most developing countries' standards. Nonetheless, observers have argued that a relatively slow rate of mechanization has contributed to the stagnation of labor productivity.[35] But the data bear reviewing: in 1964–66 there were 5.5 tractors per 1,000 hectares of arable land; by 1981–83 the number of tractors had grown to 16.2.[36] Heavily subsidized gasoline prices may encourage tractor use. In one remittance-rich village, the number of tractors increased from one to 200 over the last 20 years.

Yet even with 100 mechanical water pumps, the cultivated area of the village increased by only a little over 10 percent.[37]

The Egyptian leadership's "consistent neglect of agriculture" has led to what one analyst identifies as "development without qualitative structural change."[38] The combination of controlled prices, a misdirected investment policy, and other institutional factors has debilitated the agricultural sector. Remittances have reduced rural poverty, and clearly reinforced social equity, but they have not been invested substantially in agriculture. Major changes in agricultural investment directions and the introduction of technologies that will improve the productivity of very small farms—neither of which is yet apparent—will be required to revitalize this sector.[39]

In addition to declining productivity, agriculture is plagued by a series of environmental problems—many of them caused, ironically, by "development." These are discussed later in the chapter.

Energy

Energy production and consumption in Egypt has experienced phenomenal growth over the last two decades. Oil, gas, and hydroelectricity are the important sources, with potential, still, for bioenergy, solar energy and conservation efforts.

Oil, and gas which was developed in the 1960s, took off after the embargo in 1973. Led by a significant increase in petroleum production, Egypt multiplied its total energy output four times in less than a decade.[40] As an international petroleum producer, Egypt ranks fifteenth, with nearly 900,000 barrels a year. The country now produces more crude oil than Algeria or Qatar and more natural gas than Iraq. As the fifth largest non-OPEC free market producer of crude oil (after the United States, Canada, Mexico, and the United Kingdom), Egypt is becoming a player of note in the world oil markets.[41] Indeed, petroleum has become Egypt's most valuable official earner of foreign exchange, amounting to $1.1 billion in 1986. Oil production has placed Egypt's trade balances in a solidly favorable position and has literally fueled industrial development.

Crude oil accounts for most of the country's growth in production, but natural gas is of increasing importance to select industries and many households.[42] Further development of natural gas is a major objective of the country's current energy plan and a "gas clause" is included in every foreign contract for exploration and development.

The petroleum sector in Egypt—both extraction and refining—is effective, well managed, and performs strongly. Attractive crude blends and aggressive promotion have developed markets, principally among Western nations, though exports to Japan are increasing. Refinery capacity has been devoted mostly to energy: more than half the product is residual fuel oil, but a small fraction goes to lubricants and asphalt.

Hydropower (mostly from Aswan) is the second major source of energy, accounting for 46 percent of electricity production, but this source is expected to be less important in coming years.[43] Solar energy has high potential for Egypt. Analysts believe that solar energy may be useful for the development of water resources in remote areas of Egypt. A major experiment is under way in Alexandria, where the largest unlined solar pond is being built.[44] But this source of energy has received minimal attention from the authorities, and there is no incentive for private development.

Domestic consumption of energy has dramatically increased over the past 10 years, when petroleum use alone rose annually at an average rate of 10 percent.[45] It paralleled a rapid growth in the economy, confirming the relationship between energy consumption and gross national product in an expanding economy that is experiencing industrialization and urbanization. The Egyptian government, concerned that existing electric power capacity is barely enough to keep ahead of demand, plans the addition of several gas- and oil-fired plants in the next couple of years. Longer term proposals include plans for coal-fired plants at Zaafarana and Ayun Musa, and up to eight 1,000-megawatt nuclear generating stations by 2005. Plans to build the first of these, at Alexandria, were put on hold after the Chernobyl disaster, and have been further dampened by AID and World Bank concerns both about the gross underpricing of electricity and the possibility that the demand has been exaggerated. AID has announced that its future involvement in Egypt's energy programs will be limited to efficiency improvements.[46]

Increased consumption reflects population growth to some extent, but much more important have been the government's domestic subsidized price policies, which have literally induced an upward spiralling of consumption, encouraging waste and inefficiencies in industrial processes and in residential and transportation use and adding to pollution problems. Fuel oil, for example, is sold to the Electrical Authority at $5.40/ton, and to other public sector users at $11–23/ton, compared with $115/ton on the open market.[47] Energy subsidies cost the government about $4 billion per year.[48] Local consumption at rates around one-fifth the world price eat into the amount available for export and reserves for the future, give false signals to other sectors of the economy, and contribute to air pollution in the cities. According to one energy analyst, "Energy is not only cheap in Egypt, but it is getting cheaper."[49] Indeed, continued growth of domestic consumption remains a significant obstacle to the country's energy performance.

A second constraint on the future is geological: of the four provinces with considerable oil or gas beneath them—the Nile Delta, the Gulf of Suez, the Northern Sinai, and the Western Desert—only the last, and the largest (in geographical span), remains largely unexplored. At current rates, production of known resources can easily be sustained for another 15 years or so. Beyond that time, given existing knowledge about reserves, decline sets in, and production costs will increase substantially. Geological conditions and the size of unknown reserves will determine Egypt's energy future. Reliance on international oil companies for both capital and technology increases Egypt's dependence on international economic conditions—and on the world price of oil. With declining prices, incentives for exploration are reduced; drilling declines. Egypt does not really know what the Western Desert holds—or does not hold.

The conventional view is that raising domestic prices to their international equivalents will reduce consumption and force a great degree of efficiency in industry and manufacturing. Yet it is worth remembering that technologies in place in select large energy-consuming industries (such as the Helwan steel plant or the Kima fertilizer plant) cannot readily adjust to price changes. Engineers have pointed out that the outdated designs and technological constraints are more responsible than price distortions for Egypt's "energy waste" in the steel plant or the fertilizer plant.

In energy as in agriculture, Egypt appears through its selection of development projects, its subsidies, and its support for the poorer segments of society to be living off its resources in a way that cannot be sustained over the long term.

Environmental Quality

Egypt's environmental concerns fall into three categories, according to their source. Degradation of the land and of water quality are primarily the result of development efforts to expand and improve agriculture. The urban problems of air and water pollution, and the health implications attending both, are manifestations of a generation of rapid urbanization and industrialization. The phenomenal growth of the 1970s and early 1980s in particular have an environmental price that has not yet been paid. A third set of environmental impacts have their cause in practices that are international.

These problems place further constraints on economic growth, or make it more difficult and costly, at the same time that population increases multiply demands for food, water, sanitation, energy, and jobs. The decades ahead will not easily enjoy the kind of phenomenal growth that over the last two decades put Egypt in the World Bank's "middle income" countries. Patterns of environmental degradation, none of which has yet peaked or declined, are not widely recognized in Egypt or the United States as the major components of resource security. They are certainly not thought to be threats in any sense to political security. But the Egyptian government's ability to deal with these problems and the extent to which such issues impede the efficiency with which resources can be converted to meet domestic demand will increasingly shape national security. The question is: at what threshold does public concern with the environmental problems themselves, or with their negative effect on growth, lead to a challenge of the legitimacy of the government?

Soil and Water Degradation. From the first years after the 1952 revolution, the government has been aware of the need to expand agricultural production. Wisely or unwisely, the control of the Nile through construction of the Aswan Dam was the primary solution advocated. The results are mixed. Agricultural production increased as water became available year-round for irrigation, but the elimination of the annual flooding over the banks and year-round cultivation have created serious problems. Waterlogging, downstream problems from runoff, and attendant health problems have since been documented by Egyptian and international analysts.[50] These were not unexpected in the 1950s, but in Egypt as elsewhere round the world they were ignored as big dams were seized upon as the key to agricultural development, assured energy supplies, and increased political independence.

Due to perennial irrigation and inadequate drainage, the water table rose in many areas within a few years after completion of the High Dam in 1969. Estimates of resulting waterlogging and salinization vary from 28 percent of Egypt's productive land to 50 percent more or less affected, and almost all irrigated land has been found to be potentially salt-affected.[51] By one estimate, 10 percent of Egyptian agricultural production is lost every year due to the deterioration of soil fertility. Stretches of once-lush green farmland have a sparkling white salt crust and reddish halophyte vegetation.[52] Only in Iraq and Pakistan is a higher percentage of irrigated land affected by salinization.[53] Corrective drainage systems are very expensive and their implementation further constrained by the small size of Egyptian farms, shortages of materials, and difficulties in coordination. Although AID has made a major commitment to help the government install drainage tiles, the program remains behind schedule.

At the same time nutrient-rich silt—some of it from the mountains of Ethiopia—is piling up behind the dam. Before 1969 it was spread by annual flooding over the fields. This loss of natural fertilization is now compensated for by an annual application of 13,000 tons of calcium nitrates,[54] which further contributes to salinization of runoff.

Siltation in Lake Nasser behind the dam has also had effects in the Mediterranean off the Delta coast, where it previously augmented the supply of plankton that fed a productive sardine fishery. That fishery, which produced 18,000 tons in 1962, has virtually disappeared—due also to offshore pollution and overfishing. (At the same time, it should be noted, new fishing communities came into being all along the 1,400-kilometer perimeter of Lake Nasser,[55] and fisheries are not scarce nationwide.) Siltation in Lake Nasser also deprived the delta shorelines of sediment replenishment and contributed to shore erosion.

Perennial irrigation and permanent water supplies, not known in many areas before the High Dam, also provide year-round habitats for water-related diseases. Their control is an environmental as well as a medical problem. Schistosomiasis has greatly increased, migrating south from Cairo, and now 36 percent of the population suffers from the disease. The portion is higher among rural people, for whom it is an occupational hazard. The disease is extremely debilitating, and it costs Egypt on the order of $500 million a year. Water sources can be cleaned up, but are very easily reinfected.[56]

Aquatic weeds, especially the notorious water hyacinth, are no longer swept away by annual flooding. Eighty percent of Egypt's waterways are said to be affected. Strong weed growth in Delta canals is a particular problem. Controls—mechanical cutting, herbicides, and introduction of carp—are only partly effective in keeping the waterways clear.

Soils and water are also polluted by pesticides, especially in connection with growing cotton. Egyptian farmers make intensive use of organophosphorus and organochlorine pesticides, supplied by the government, to protect their crops. The average annual use of pesticides in Egypt is almost 30,000 tons, of which 70 percent is directed at controlling cotton pests. No attempts are yet made to control pesticide use or avoid pesticide penetration into food and the soil. Overuse of pesticides leads insects to develop a resistance to them. Farmers then have to shift pesticides frequently. The number of Egyptian insects resistant to pesticides grew from 14 species in 1948 to 364 in 1976.[57]

Egypt spends over $200 million each year to subsidize pesticides—without rigorous assessment of the benefits returned. In a 1986 World Resources Institute study of pesticide subsidies in nine countries, Egypt's subsidies were extensive and expensive. The government bore 83 percent of the cost of pesticides to farmers through allocation of foreign exchange at preferential rates, exemption from import duties, and consumption taxes.[58]

These figures do not count the health and environmental costs associated with pesticide use. As in other countries, these chemicals are sold to untrained farmers without adequate control or supervision. The subsidy amounts to $4.70 a year for every man, woman, and child in Egypt, whereas the government spends $7.34 per annum on health and $33.06 on education. And as in other countries, the government has no way of knowing whether these subsidies are accomplishing their purposes. The development, environment, and health questions raised have not yet been answered: might this money be better spent on other programs, such as integrated pest management? Or on increased productivity, reclamation, or the draining of water-logged soils?[59]

The problems attendant on irrigation and pesticide use are not without solution. Construction of drainage has been alluded to already, and alternative pest strategies are being employed in other countries. But existing technical knowledge is not always used in Egypt. An AID report said Egyptian policy and international lending agencies are all to blame.[60]

Even if the damage to soil and to human health were much less than reported here, the dimensions of the problems would still be serious. As in many other areas around the world, Egypt's current and future generations are paying for the environmental consequences of past development schemes. In Egypt, the full seriousness is masked by remittances and social equity policies that have lessened the impact, especially on the rural poor who might otherwise have experienced severe hardship.

The Urban Environment. As of 1987, 48 percent of Egypt's people lived in cities. Urbanization was growing at an average of 3.7 percent from 1980 to 1987. Cairo, one of the 10 largest cities in the world and still growing, is a bustling, sophisticated capital where a person can find anything and everything. And as in other metropolises, air and water pollution problems are obvious even to the untrained eye. Enteric diseases and dysenteries are still the major causes of death among young children.[61]

Water pollution problems are exacerbated by strains on aging sanitary facilities. In particular, the sewage systems of Cairo and Alexandria are heavily overloaded. In greater Cairo about 75 percent of the effluent, partly treated or untreated, is released into open drains.[62] In 1982, sewers in the Giza section broke, flooding the city. Most of Cairo's sewers were built in 1914, for a capacity of 48,000 cubic meters/day; by 1974 the system carried 1,250,000 cubic meters/day.[63] The sewage system in Alexandria, Egypt's second largest city, is similarly overtaxed. Lake Maryut is presently used as a holding tank for the wastes from the western and eastern districts of Alexandria. Central Alexandria's raw sewage is released directly into the Mediterranean Sea, and some of it has been washed back on the beaches, causing a public outcry. Alexandria's wastes include organic municipal wastes as well as 579 kilograms per day of heavy metals from industrial waste.[64]

When wastes find their way into waterways, agricultural productivity and livestock health suffer as well. Because much Egyptian water use comes from the Nile, the effects of water pollution are sometimes multiplied for all subsequent users downstream.

AID, with assistance from the U.S. Environmental Protection Agency, has a major program to help Egypt rebuild its sanitation systems. The largest AID infrastructure projects in recent years have been in water and wastewater systems, which are also the highest priority in the government of Egypt's last two Five Year Plans. Since 1978 AID has committed over $1 billion to rehabilitate and expand the water and waste water systems of Cairo and Alexandria; of the Canal cities of Ismailia, Suez, and Port Said; and of three provincial cities, Minia, Fayoum, and Beni Suef. The government of Egypt has also dramatically increased its investments in this area. Recent agreements have made U.S. assistance for the project conditional on institutional and financial reforms that will make the system financially viable. Parts of the project are complete and others continue. (AID has also funded some 2,000 drinking water projects and 311 sewage projects in rural areas.)[65]

Air pollution has not received the same attention as waste water. Though regulatory legislation was introduced in 1971, it has not been enforced. Insufficient paving, heavy automobile traffic, a very dry climate, dust from the Mokattam Hills, and combustion products combine to produce high particulate and chemical concentrations in urban areas.[66] The clouds of pollutants from the Helwan cement plant south of Cairo are legend. An October 1982 report on the plant found that pollution was the result of dust coming from old, inefficient furnaces that lacked appropriate filtering systems. Even those with electric filters broke frequently. Particulates in the air reduce solar radiation and contribute to a high rate of respiratory illnesses. The heavy daily coating of dust kills trees and plants downwind.[67]

International Dimensions. A third class of environmental problems is international in source. The Mediterranean coast is polluted by releases from Egypt's neighbors, by passing tankers that flush their tanks (deballasting) in the Eastern Mediterranean, as well as by Egyptian coastal activities. The Mediterranean coast is polluted by Egyptian refineries and from transferring petroleum and oil from pipelines to tankers at Mars al Hamra and Sidi Kerir. However, most coastal pollution comes from the operational cleaning of tankers' holds in two areas approved by the International Maritime Organization (IMO) in the Eastern Mediterranean. Although banned by the new entered-into-force 1979 amendments to the 1973 IMO Dumping Convention, the practice continues because few ports have yet installed the costly reception facilities necessary for cleaning tanker holds. Coastal pollution threatens tourism, fishing, and the health of swimmers.

The Red Sea coastal tourist facilities, coral reefs, and fisheries are also potentially threatened by oil pollution in the open seas, and by sewage and waste disposal from neighboring countries. Oil pollution comes from tanker deballasting, the Egyptian oil fields at the Gulf of Suez (which, at 35 million metric tons in 1982, accounted for 1.3 percent of the world market), the Saudi Arabian oil processing and loading terminal at Yanbu al-Sinaiyah, and offshore exploration.[68]

Pollution in the Mediterranean is covered by the 1976 Convention for the Protection of the Mediterranean Sea Against Pollution, the 1976 Protocol for the Prevention of Pollution of the Mediterranean Sea by Dumping from Ships and Aircraft, the 1976 Protocol Concerning Cooperation in Combating Pollution of the Mediterranean Sea by Oil and Other Harmful Substances in Cases of Emergency, and the 1980 Protocol for the Protection of the Mediterranean Sea Against Pollution from Land-Based Sources. Egypt has ratified all these treaties. Although not all the necessary central facilities in Mediterranean countries are yet completed, scientists think that the Mediterranean's quality has not declined significantly since 1977.

At the downstream end of the Nile, Egypt is heavily dependent upon Nile waters for irrigation, yet can only receive sufficient volumes if upstream states agree not to withdraw excessive amounts. Dependence on this lifeline complicates Egypt's relations not only with Sudan, but also with Ethiopia (source of the Blue Nile) and with Kenya and other nations surrounding Lake Victoria, from which the White Nile originates. Egypt shares the Nile with eight other countries—all upstream. (See Figure 1.) In the past, Egyptian needs have dominated diversion of the waters—always with British help. Nile water is so important to Egypt that it has always been an essential part of her foreign policy to have a friendly government in Khartoum. The first Egypt-Sudan agreement was signed in 1929 when an Egyptian-British consortium ruled Sudan. With support from the United Kingdom, Egypt completed a highly favorable agreement with Sudan in 1959, after sending troops to the border. Egypt is guaranteed 55.5 billion cubic meters of water annually, and the Sudan is allowed to extract 18.5 billion.[69] A professionally staffed Permanent Joint Technical Commission set up under the 1959 treaty performs limited research, data gathering, planning, and coordinating functions. And it has facilitated cooperative efforts to finance and build the Jonglei Canal in southern Sudan—a project meant to increase water available to northern Sudan and Egypt.[70]

So far the bilateral arrangements seem to work well, though as Sudanese needs increase, competition for Nile water could create tension. There is already evidence of water deficits in the Sudan, although the 1988 floods have created other problems for the time being. So far the other upstream nations have not been taken into account in discussion of distribution of Nile water. At least 86 percent of the Blue Nile waters flow from Ethiopia—a point not lost on Ethiopia, which might one day want to divert some of that water for its own development purposes, though no projects are currently planned.[71]

The White Nile, which supplies the other 14 percent of Nile water, flows from Uganda, Kenya, Tanzania, Rwanda, Burundi, and Zaire. Today Egypt still oversees the outflow of water from Lake Victoria, more than 1,400 miles away from its own southern border. All these countries will one day lay claim to the Nile waters for their own hydropower and irrigation needs. The United Nations Environment Programme took an essential step in 1985 to bring these nations together for the first time to discuss joint needs. But sovereignty remains strong: none was willing to commit to any cooperative agreement that would limit its rights to control the Nile water in its territory.[72]

Institutional Responses to Resource Security Issues

Although official Egyptian recognition of the need for population policy came as early as 1962, and the "plan", or National Population and Family Planning Policy, was developed for 1973–82, the 1978–82 Five Year Plan was the first to propose action programs. Earlier efforts relied on industrialization, reduction of infant mortality, improved social security and communications, and modest provision of family planning services, whereas the 1978–82 Plan boldly set a goal of reducing annual population growth from 2.31 percent in 1977 to 2.02 percent by 1987. Emphasis was now placed on establishing family planning centers throughout the country, especially in Upper Egypt (the south), where family size is highest, and on longer-term efforts to change basic socioeconomic

Figure 1. The Nile River

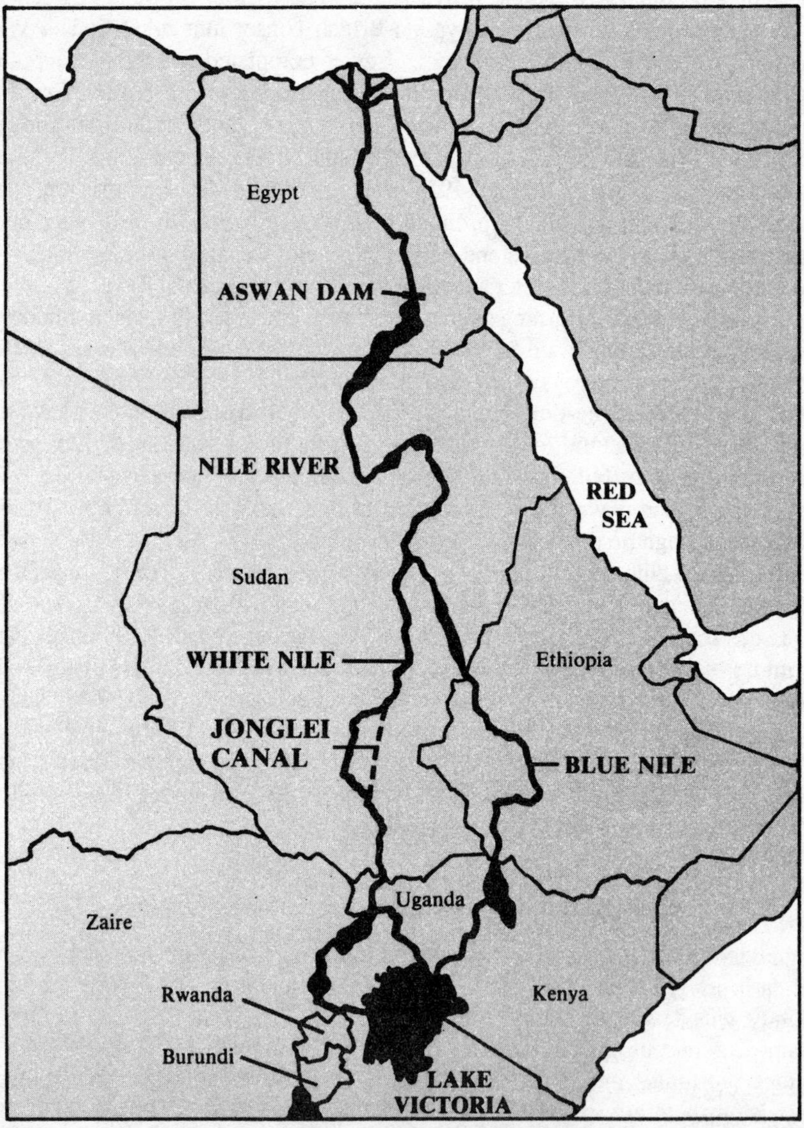

Source: From *World Resources 1987*, by the International Institute for Environment and Development and the World Resources Institute. Copyright © 1987 by the International Institute for Environment and Development and the World Resources Institute. Reprinted by permission of Basic Books, Inc., Publishers.

conditions in education, female employment, agricultural mechanization, etc. The plan also sought to move people to underutilized areas, to distribute the growing urban numbers to cities other than Cairo and Alexandria (largely through investment in housing), and to encourage international migration.[73]

A new strategy was put forth by the Supreme Council for Population and Family Planning (SCPFP). It called for integrating family planning with basic health and welfare services and improved managerial capacity to deliver services at the local level. By October 1980, 70 percent of the rural population had such services. The program was supported by the United Nations Fund for Population Activities (UNFPA) from 1977, with AID joining in 1980. Beginning in fiscal year 1981/82 the Egyptian government also allocated $4.3 million to the program.[74]

In the Socio-Economic Development Five Year Plan 1980–84, the salience of the population problem was again underlined and a strategy developed to tackle it indirectly through increasing job opportunities, and by giving priority to food security, desert development, and housing. Five percent of the public investment budget was allotted to building population centers outside the narrow crowded strip along the Nile. While experts agree that both family planning services and improving the quality of life and expanding economic opportunities are essential to reducing fertility, in Egypt the health-based approach of the SCPFP and the Planning Ministry's concept of redistributing limited resources often seem competitive rather than collaborative.[75] The Five Year Plan 1987–88 to 1991–92 continues this dual approach, but heightens the importance of population, making "population and regional dimensions of development" one of three key "principles" of the Plan period, and once again the government set goals to reduce the natural increase from 2.8 percent in 1986–87 to 2.6 percent by 1991–92, and to 2.1 percent by 2001–02.[76]

The SCPFP, chaired by the Minister of Health, oversees implementation of population policy, but the Ministries of Education, Social Affairs and Security, Agriculture Planning, Labour Force and Training, Culture and Information, and Youth and the census bureau all share some responsibility. Delivery of services is carried out by 3,942 units (in 1982) attached to the Ministry of Health and by 670 clinics of the Egyptian Family Planning Association and other voluntary organizations, largely funded by foreign donor agencies. These organizations use modern advertising and marketing techniques (including television, which is widely watched in urban areas) to promote birth control and sell subsidized contraceptives. Government agencies are often criticized as lagging behind private organizations, though it should be noted that the private agency activity is concentrated in urban areas that traditionally display greater receptivity to change.[77]

The government has clearly succeeded in reducing the crude death rate, and has made some slight progress in fertility decline—from 6.56 births per woman during 1960–65 to 5.23 or even 4.8 during 1980–85, depending on which United

Nations estimates are used.[78] Contraceptives are used by about 30 percent of married women.[79] And the quality of life of Egyptians has markedly increased since the revolution thanks to post-revolutionary governments' commitment to equity, employment, education and health services, and, since 1973, thanks also to the large annual remittances returned by 3 million overseas Egyptian workers. Indeed, Egypt has a Physical Quality of Life Index that places her squarely in the middle of the range of Arab countries, despite a substantially lower per capita income.[80]

But the population growth rate continues to hover somewhere above 2.5 percent per year, and the government's assumptions are that the population, estimated at 50.6 million in 1986/87, will reach nearly 70 million by 2000 (5 million more than the United Nations projects).[81] Egypt simply does not have the luxury or the time to deal with growth at this pace without facing serious stress on the resource base and/or distinct deterioration of the quality of life. The lowering of fertility rates remains too slow to allow the government to keep ahead of the numbers.

Compared with his predecessors, President Mubarak is the most earnest supporter of population programs. He has spoken on occasion of the adverse effects of population expansion, including famine, unemployment, and terrorism. He has proclaimed population control a national priority. Nor does the connection between population growth and economics go unnoticed. President Mubarak put it bluntly: "We increase by about one million and a half each year....It threatens to choke all our efforts in all fields and quashes all hope of growth, production and development."[82] He formed and chairs a new National Family Planning Council, supports the initiative of private organizations, but continues to live with a national program whose effectiveness is hampered by bureaucratic limitations. One senses in Egypt a continuing national concern about family planning that is also not fully organized to be entirely effective. And, on political grounds, the opposition includes family planning efforts high on their list of many issues on which they regularly attack the government.

Regarding environmental problems, in the last seven years Egypt has begun to respond with financial assistance from AID, the U.S. Environmental Protection Agency, and other donors. In 1981 a Ministerial Committee for Environmental Affairs was created by President Sadat. At the Committee's request, in 1982 the People's Assembly adopted Law Number 48 for Protecting the River Nile and Other Bodies of Water Against Pollution. This updated an unenforceable 1962 statute regulating pollution of the Nile. A license from the Ministry of Irrigation, after consulting the Ministry of Health, is required for disposal of wastes into the Nile and its tributaries from houses, shops and tourist centers, industrial and trade establishments, and sanitary drainage plants. A precise specification of wastes, tolerable limits, and recommended technologies remains to be drawn up. Further studies of the discharge of effluents through the sewer system, of marine pollution by oil, and of radiation pollution are still under preparation.

In 1982 Directives were issued by the Minister of Industry and Mineral Wealth (Decree 385) and the Minister of Electricity and Energy (Decree 595) requiring both ministerial review of the availability of pollution control technology before construction and the retrofitting of all factories, power plants, and mines with pollution control equipment. The Prime Minister issued a directive stating that Environmental Impact Statements should be drawn up and reviewed before new industrial plants are built. The Minister of Agriculture and the Governors issued decrees on the protection of wildlife and the creation of national reserves. In 1983 the Ministry of Health issued a Directive (Decree 89) requiring the pharmaceutical industry to install pollution control filters in all factories. Evidence is not available on enforcement of these measures, or on follow-up efforts.

Decree Number 631 of 1982 created a new environmental agency within the Prime Minister's office. With a staff of 10, the agency is responsible for preparing draft environmental legislation, specifying environmental standards, and studying and analyzing environmental proposals submitted by other agencies. Its 1982–83 budget was $8 million.[83]

In January 1983 President Hosni Mubarak announced that water quality and sewage treatment was the number one national priority for the next five years. Egypt has committed itself to constructing sewage treatment facilities for Cairo and Alexandria. For the 1982–83 to 1986–87 Plan, Cairo sewage projects alone were estimated to cost in excess of two billion Egyptian pounds.[84] In addition to the AID contribution, the U.K. Overseas Development Administration has committed 50 million pounds, with another 100 million pounds on the way from private lenders. The Ministry of Industry's Environmental Project, a subsidiary of the AID-funded Industrial Production Project, has committed $24.6 million for pollution control.[85]

In the 1970s, following the rapid industrial and irrigation expansion of the Nasser years, Egyptian scientists became concerned about and documented the environmental effects of certain economic development programs. Their pressure led the government to develop institutions, policies, and laws to deal with the problems. Important changes have taken place in the last three years. Authority rests in the cabinet. Several ministers are knowledgeable about the issues and determined to figure out what needs to be done. A Cabinet commission chaired by the respected Mohamed Kassas led to the creation of the modest Department of Environment.

But looking at the record, and at budget allocations, it is clear that environmental concerns are not yet a priority commensurate with the mounting difficulties.[86] Concern is with conventional pollution issues, and the government wants AID to give more hardware and technical assistance—to help with monitoring and control technologies. Agricultural practices are not really included as a priority concern, nor are the environmental consequences of energy use, and the connections are not being made among drinking water, pollution, irrigation, and health problems. In addition, the responsible agencies are understaffed and underfunded.

Conclusions

The hard irony of Egypt's plight is that the interests that pose a political challenge to the Mubarak regime—that is, dissatisfaction within the military and domestic instability—in dealing with the nation's growing population pressures on limited natural resources. The military's concerns lie in continued large military assistance from the United States, the development of a lucrative arms export business outside the control of the national budget, and forgiveness of military debt by the United States. Various political factions, including the fundamentalists, do not support birth control, and their economic and social agenda demonstrates no support for the policy, price, and technological changes the government will have to make to achieve sustainable development.

The government needs to deal with the severe environmental degradation and population growth threatening resource security, and to devote more resources to address other problems. And popular concern about resource security considerations—cushioned thus far by policies of social equity, a vigorous informal sector of the economy, and remittances worth several times the value of export earnings—has not yet developed a countervailing support for the necessary measures.

Resource degradation, population pressures, and pollution are accelerating and converging in Egypt. The question is, of course, whether the nation can count in the future on the outlets that have up till now reduced the resulting strains. Can the Mubarak and subsequent governments provide jobs for more than 400,000 entering the work force each year, and provide housing and health care for another 20 million who will be added to the population by the end of the century? Can the government meet the expectations of a greatly expanded population for continued subsidies—which are already estimated at $7 billion a year? Can the Arab oil-producing states absorb twice again as many Egyptian workers, especially if they may not be as well educated as in the past? Will adequate supplies of oil be discovered in the Western deserts? Can the private sector, including the informal sector, expand and assume a greater economic role?

Some of the answers to these problems are internal, and some answers lie outside Egypt. What happens with respect to overseas employment, oil prices and foreign assistance will affect Egypt's ability to respond to resource security demands. Increased reliance on foreign sources of supply, although improving the immediate political security pressures on the government, makes the government vulnerable to longer-term uncertainties of market and political influences. This vulnerability may at times even threaten the government's own conception of sovereignty.

Other answers lie at home. More-efficient pricing policies by the Egyptian government might stimulate domestic agricultural and energy production, although at the risk of triggering urban political resentment and further challenges to political security.

In short, threats to resource security may be resolved through a number of policy responses, at some political cost. But focusing exclusively on the political security exposes Egypt to much more severe long term resource security crises.

The future of Egypt's overall national security rests upon the careful balancing of these different challenges. It depends also on giving more attention to the sustainability of its underlying resource base.

U.S. Policy Toward Egypt

The United States should recognize its political interests for what they are—important to all U.S. relations with the Middle East—and think of the Economic Support Funds and development assistance given to Egypt not as a typical collection of AID projects, but as a political insurance payment. Egypt has thousands of underemployed educators, scientists, and engineers and does not require U.S. technical assistance except in a few rare areas of expertise. Washington should therefore give Egypt the money outright, as it does to Israel, and dismantle Cairo's large AID mission.[87] This would reduce U.S. visibility and blunt the anti-American accusations raised against the Mubarak regime.

Then the United States should, as far as possible, leverage its generous contributions to the Egyptian treasury and urge Egypt on to a more sustainable road to development. Recognizing the importance of resource security to military and political security, the United States should use its access to top Egyptian leaders to affect macro-economic and development decisions—to step up the restoration and conservation of soil, to improve the productivity of small farms, to rationally control the use of pesticides, to tackle urban pollution, to lower the subsidies of energy and water. Egypt is beginning to make some progress along all these lines. It deserves support, encouragement, even pressure to do more. Such policy efforts must, of course, be coordinated with those of the International Monetary Fund and the World Bank. But there, too, the United States—being more conscious than those institutions of the importance of resource security—should use its influence to heighten the importance of the policies that affect resource management.

The United States cannot, of course, tell the Mubarak or any other Egyptian government what to do. But it should continue in all its relations with Egypt to emphasize mutual interests in respect for the resource base and the population/resources balances. A high profile posture is invariably dangerous and can potentially backfire, as we have seen elsewhere in the Middle East and in other parts of the world. Supporting Egyptian development means, in the last analysis, adopting policies and postures that would reinforce (or buttress) rather than threaten (or undermine) the country's overall security—in all its interconnected dimensions. The goal of U.S. policy should be to use persuasion and leverage, to be supportive with a low profile, to help shape Egyptian development policies in ways that ensure all three components of national security.

References

1. This section is based on Alaf Lutfi Al-Sayyid Marsot, *A Short History of Modern Egypt* (Cambridge: Cambridge University Press, 1985).

2. Walter J. Burns, *Economic Aid and American Policy Toward Egypt, 1955–1981* (Albany, New York: State University of New York Press, 1985), 23, Figure 19.

3. See Ahmed Hashem, "U.S.-Egyptian Military Relations," unpublished manuscript (Cambridge, Massachusetts: Massachusetts Institute of Technology, 1987), for a more detailed analysis.

4. Fouad Ajami, "Stress in the Arab Triangle," *Foreign Policy*, No. 29 (1977), 99–108.

5. U.S. Agency for International Development, *Congressional Presentation, Fiscal Year 1988*, Annex No. 2, Asia and the Near East, 84; and Joseph C. Story, *U.S.-Arab Relations: The Economic Dimensions*, National Council on U.S.-Arab Relations, Occasional Paper Series, No. 6 (Washington, D.C., 1985), 10–11.

6. Report of the Task Force on Foreign Assistance to the Committee on Foreign Affairs, U.S. House of Representatives, February 1989 (Hamilton-Gilman Task Force), 7, Table 4.

7. *Egypt's Second Five-Year Plan for Socio-Economic Development (1987/88–1991/92) with Plan for Year One (1987/88)*, Vol. 1 (Cairo: Ministry of Planning, 1987), 48. Since 1980/81, investment loans from the United States were converted to nonpayable grants. Initially this commitment was at the level of $750 million annually. Since 1983 the figure was $15 million per year.

8. Personal Communication, Adolph Y. Wilburn, Washington, D.C., June 1987.

9. Arid Lands Information Center, "Draft Environmental Report on Arab Republic of Egypt" (Tucson, Arizona: University of Arizona, May 1980). This survey was produced for the U.S. Agency for International Development. No final report was completed. Though it depends on data from the 1970s, it is still a useful overall assessment of Egypt's environmental problems.

10. The World Bank, *World Development Report 1988* (New York: Oxford University Press, 1988), 222, 274, 276; and Population Reference Bureau, *1987 World Population Data Sheet*, (Washington, D.C., 1987).

11. World Resources Institute and International Institute for Environment and Development, *World Resources 1986* (New York: Basic Books, 1986), 248.

12. World Resources Institute and International Institute for Environment and Development, *World Resources 1986*, 230.

13. International Labour Organization, *ILO Yearbook of Labour Statistics 1986* (Geneva: International Labour Organization, 1986).

14. International Labour Organization, *ILO Yearbook of Labour Statistics, 1986*.

15. Nazli Choucri, "The Hidden Economy: A New View of Remittances in the Arab World," *World Development*, Vol. 14 (1986), 697–712.

16. Fred Moavenzadeh and Tarek Selim, *The Construction Industry in Egypt* (Cambridge, Massachusetts: Massachusetts Institute of Technology, Technology and Development Program, June 1984).

17. World Bank, *World Development Report 1987* (New York: Oxford University Press, 1987), 262.

18. John Waterbury, *The Egypt of Nasser and Sadat: The Political Economy of Two Regimes* (Princeton, New Jersey: Princeton University Press, 1983).

19. World Resources Institute and International Institute for Environment and Development, *World Resources 1986*, 262.

20. Richard H. Adams, Jr., "Development and Structural Change in Rural Egypt, 1952–1982," *World Development*, Vol. 13, No. 6, 1985, 713.

21. World Resources Institute and International Institute for Environment and Development, *World Resources 1986*, 266.

22. World Resources Institute and International Institute for Environment and Development, *World Resources 1986*, 47.

23. Adams, "Development and Structural Change in Rural Egypt, 1952–82," 713.

24. Reported in Liz Thurgood, "Egypt's Agricultural Showpiece Faces a Crucial Year," *Middle East Economic Digest*, April 15, 1983, 15.

25. Adams, "Development and Structural Change in Rural Egypt, 1952–82," 708.

26. U.S. Agency for International Development, *Congressional Presentation, Fiscal Year 1988*, Annex No. 2, Asia and the Near East, 86–88.

27. *Middle East Economic Digest*, December 13, 1986.

28. Adams, "Development and Structural Change in Rural Egypt, 1952–82," 713–14.

29. M.A. Kishk, "Land Degradation in the Nile Valley," *AMBIO*, Vol. 15, No. 4, 226–230.

30. United Nations Trade Statistics 1987 (unpublished).

31. Economist Intelligence Unit, *Country Report: Egypt*, No. 3, September 26, 1986, 17.

32. Robert Repetto, *Paying the Price: Pesticide Subsidies in Developing Countries* (Washington, D.C.: World Resources Institute, 1987), 22–23. This

succinct publication draws on a more detailed paper by Ahmed Galal, "Implicit Subsidization in the Market for Pesticides: The Case of Egypt," prepared for the World Resources Institute, March 1985.

33. Economist Intelligence Unit, *Country Reports: Egypt*, No. 2, June 13, 1986, 17; and *Summary: Egypt*, No. 3, September 26, 1986, 17.

34. *Middle East Economic Digest*, May 31, 1986.

35. World Resources Institute and International Institute for Environment and Development, *World Resources 1986*, 266.

36. World Resources Institute and International Institute for Environment and Development, *World Resources, 1986*, 264.

37. Judith Miller, "A Village in Egypt Sits for a Post-Modern Portrait," *New York Times*, November 21, 1985.

38. Adams, "Development and Structural Change in Rural Egypt, 1952–82," 716.

39. Adams, "Development and Structural Change in Rural Egypt, 1952–82," 715–18.

40. The data for this section are from the United States Department of Energy, *International Energy Annual, 1985*; United Nations, *Energy Statistics Yearbook*, various years; British Petroleum, *Statistical Review of World Energy*, June, 1986; Economist Intelligence Unit *Country Report: Egypt*, No. 2, 1986.

41. Nazli Choucri and Christopher Heye, "Introduction" in Nazli Choucri, ed., *Energy and Development in Egypt* (in preparation).

42. For an earlier assessment of natural gas opportunities in Egypt, see EGPC-IEOC, International Seminar on Natural Gas and Economic Development, select papers, Cairo, February 26–27, 1982. For a review of geological prospects for natural gas, see M. G. Barakat, "General Review of the Petroliferous Provinces of Egypt with Special Emphasis on their Geological Settings and Oil Potentialities" (Cambridge, Massachusetts: Massachusetts Institute of Technology, Technology and Development Program, June 1982).

43. World Resources Institute and International Institute for Environment and Development, *World Resources, 1987* (New York: Basic Books, 1987), 302.

44. Donald R. F. Harleman and E. Eric Adams, "Demonstration of Solar Pond Technology in Egypt: Proposal for Continuation July 86–June 87" (Cambridge, Massachusetts: Massachusetts Institute of Technology, Technology and Development Program, May 1986). See also Atrel Salhorta, E. Eric Adams, Donald R. F. Harleman, "Solar Pond Feasibility Study for Egypt—Preliminary Report" (Cambridge, Massachusetts: Massachusetts Institute of Technology Adaptation Program, January 1983).

45. Since 1981–82, the average annual growth of electricity consumption was around 10.1 percent per year according to *Egypt's Second Five Year Plan*, Vol. 2, 67. Growth in residential and commercial use declined from 21.5 percent in 1982–83 to 7.4 percent in 1985–86.

46. Peter Kemp, "Tariff Wrangle Threatens Egypt's Energy Plans," *Middle East Economic Digest*, February 28, 1987, 24, 29; and *Middle East Economic Digest*, August 29, 1987, 6, and July 11, 1987, 13.

47. *Middle East Economic Digest*, March 28, 1987, 8.

48. Gerald F. Seib, "Foreign Insight," *Wall Street Journal*, January 30, 1986.

49. Gouda Abdel-Khalek, "Income and Price Elasticities of Energy Consumption in Egypt" (Cambridge, Massachusetts: Massachusetts Institute of Technology, Technology and Development Program, November 1984), 21.

50. Arid Lands Information Center, 1980, "Draft Environmental Report on Arab Republic of Egypt."

51. Kishk, "Land Degradation in the Nile Valley," 228. The 28 percent figure is from Arid Lands Information Center, 1980, "Draft Environmental Report on Arab Republic of Egypt," 44, citing El Gabaly, 1978.

52. Kishk, "Land Degradation in the Nile Valley," 228.

53. World Resources Institute and International Institute for Environment and Development, *World Resources 1986*, 280.

54. Arid Lands Information Center, 1980, "Draft Environmental Report on Arab Republic of Egypt," 41.

55. Arid Lands Information Center, 1980, "Draft Environmental Report on Arab Republic of Egypt," 46, citing Benedick, 1978.

56. Arid Lands Information Center, 1980, "Draft Environmental Report on Arab Republic of Egypt," 47.

57. A.H. El-Sebae, "Biochemical Challenges in Future Toxicological Research," *Journal of Environmental Science and Health*, Vol. 15, No. 6, 1980, 691.

58. Repetto, *Paying the Price*, 5–6.

59. Repetto, *Paying the Price*, 3–4, 6, 11, 22–23; L. Brader, "Integrated Pest Control in the Developing World," *Annual Review of Entomology*, XXIV, 1979, especially 235–38.

60. Arid Lands Information Center, 1980, "Draft Environmental Report on Arab Republic of Egypt," 49.

61. The World Bank, *World Development Report 1989* (New York: Oxford University Press, 1989), 229; Arid Lands Information Center, 1980, "Draft Environmental Report on Arab Republic of Egypt," 63.

62. Egypt, *National Report of the Republic of Egypt*, submitted to the United Nations Conference on the Human Environment, Cairo, 1971, summarized in "Summaries of National Reports on Environmental Problems," *The Human Environment*, Vol. II (Washington, D.C.: Woodrow Wilson International Center for Scholars, 1972).

63. Khalid Ikram, *Egypt: Economic Management in a Period of Transition* (Baltimore, Maryland: Johns Hopkins University Press, 1980), 157.

64. United Nations Industrial Development Organization (UNIDO), "Pollutants from Land-Based Sources in the Mediterranean," prepared under the joint UNIDO/UNEP Environmental Program, July 12, 1988, 31.

65. U.S. Agency for International Development, *Congressional Presentation, Fiscal Year 1988*, Annex No. 2, Asia and the Near East, 89–90.

66. Arid Lands Information Center, 1980, "Draft Environmental Report on Arab Republic of Egypt," 60.

67. M. Talaat Abou Saada, "Environmental Protection in Egypt with Particular Emphasis on Wastewater Management," January 1987, mimeo, 1.

68. United Nations Environment Programme (UNEP), "Management and Conservation of Renewable Marine Resources in the Red Sea and Gulf of Aden Region," UNEP Regional Seas Reports and Studies, No. 64, 1985, 19–20.

69. Irene L. Murphy and J. Eleanora Sabadell, "International River Basins," *Resources Policy*, Vol. 2, No. 2, June 1986, 133–144; Bonaya Adhi Godana, *Africa's Shared Water Resources* (London: Frances Pinter, 1985).

70. World Resources Institute and International Institute for Environment and Development, *World Resources 1987*, 184–85. Work on the canal has been completely halted by the Sudan civil war.

71. Leonard Berry, "Land, People and Resources in Sudan," unpublished study for World Resources Institute, 1987, 24.

72. World Resources Institute and International Institute for Environment and Development, *World Resources 1987*, 185–86.

73. *The Five Year Plan 1978–82*, Vol. 2 (Cairo: Ministry of Planning, August 1977), 22, 32, 45. Ten to 15 percent of the labor force is estimated to be working abroad (Hansen, *Egyptian Labor Market*, 12). Their numbers are estimated to have increased from 34,000 in 1973 to about 3 million in 1983 (Economist Intelligence Unit, *Country Profile: Egypt 1986/87*, 9).

74. A. D. Kelly, A. M. Khalifa, and M. N. El-Khorazaty, *Population and Development in Rural Egypt* (Durham, North Carolina: Duke University Press, 1982), 179.

75. Hussein Abdel-Aziz Sayed, "The Population Family Planning Program in Egypt, Structure and Performance," *Population Studies*, Vol. 11, No. 70 (1984).

76. *Egypt's Second Five Year Plan (1987/88–1991/92)*, Vol. 1, 1–2, 186.

77. Sayed, "The Population Family Planning Program in Egypt," 21–38.

78. World Resources Institute and International Institute for Environment and Development, *World Resources 1986*, 238 (using data from the U.N. Department of International Economic and Social Affairs, *World Population Prospects: Estimates and Projections as Assessed in 1982* (New York: United Nations, 1985), and United Nations, *World Contraceptive Use Chart, 1987*, U.N. Secretariat, Population Division of the Department of Economic and Social Affairs, 1987.

79. Dickey, "Egypt's Soaring Population Outstrips Efforts to Control," citing figures compiled by the Family Planning Council and USAID.

80. Morris David Morris, *Measuring the Condition of the World's Poor: The Physical Quality of Life Index* (New York: Pergamon Press for the Overseas Development Council, 1979), Appendix B, Table 1.

81. *Egypt's Second Five Year Plan (1987/88–1991/92)*, Vol. 1, 37.

82. "Egyptian Population Growth Strains Resources and Society," *New York Times*, July 8, 1989.

83. *World Environment Handbook* (New York: World Environment Center, 1985), 175.

84. Economist Intelligence Unit, *Egypt Country Profile, 1986/87* (London: The Economist Publications, 1986), 28.

85. See Peter M. Haas, "Dishonorable Discharges: International Collaboration for Mediterranean Pollution Control," Ph.D. thesis, Massachusetts Institute of Technology, Department of Political Science, 1986, for details.

86. President Mubarak's national priorities are thought to be the maintenance of internal security, domestic political stability (including restraint of the political opposition), protection of important new institutions (the Parliament and Shura, the new supreme court), and energy production.

87. This recommendation remains controversial, given the fact that USAID activities in Egypt have been central to public policy measures in the environmental area and have sensitized the Egyptian government to respond appropriately.

V

Land, Resources, and People in Kenya

*Richard B. Ford and Janet Welsh Brown**

Kenya is surrounded by countries whose names make headlines only as examples of trouble and tragedy—Ethiopia, Somalia, Sudan, Uganda, Tanzania. In the last two decades, Eastern Africa has experienced political upheavals, famine, and crushing poverty—drought and starvation in Ethiopia, political chaos and economic destruction under Idi Amin in Uganda, relentless ethnic civil war in Sudan, and civil strife in Somalia.

It is precisely because Kenya does not receive such coverage that it deserves U.S. attention. In the midst of crises and chronic troubles, Kenya has enjoyed relative peace and prosperity. It has survived drought without famine, maintained an elected parliament, avoided military conflict, experienced economic growth, and broadly expanded education, health, and other social services.

But continuing peace and prosperity for Kenya are not assured. Rapid population growth, combined with slowing growth of Kenya's agricultural sector, portends a crisis in food production. If current trends continue, by early next century Kenya could have twice as many people to feed, with land that may have lost in some areas up to half its productive potential from soil erosion alone. Because Kenya is heavily dependent on agriculture to sustain its economy, such a crisis could well lead to political and economic disruption. If Kenya's fundamental problems of productivity and population are *not* dealt with, Kenyan crises could be on our front pages.

It is in the U.S. interest to support significant human and material resource management initiatives in Kenya that will stabilize the natural resource base and the population, and increase Kenya's sustainable production. U.S. assistance is

The authors wish to acknowledge the assistance of Clark University colleagues Hussein Adam, Beverly Grier, Ruth Katz and Barbara Thomas-Slayter who worked on the case study on which this chapter is based.

particularly important given that Kenya's ecological and demographic stability hold two keys to its political viability.

Kenya is in a critical location in one of Africa's most sensitive political zones. It sits astride the equator in a pivotal coastal strip along the Indian Ocean—a vital supply line for oil shipments from the Middle East to Europe and North America. It is home to East Africa's busiest port, Mombasa, which is the best docking, repair, and fueling depot between Egypt and Durban, a distance of about 5,000 miles. The U.S. fleet calls at Mombasa for rest and relaxation as well as for demonstrations of good will between the two nations, providing the United States a naval presence close to the strategically important Persian Gulf.

Mombasa is also the access point for trade with Kenya and the landlocked nations of Uganda, Rwanda, and Burundi. United States trade with tropical Africa remains small, but it has been growing in recent years. As trade with South Africa declines, the United States has an increased interest in strengthening such relationships in other parts of Africa in order to develop its relationships elsewhere on the continent.

Ethiopia and Sudan, on Kenya's northern border, are torn by continuing civil war. Uganda, on the west, is only beginning to recover from economic ruin following 15 years of political chaos and economic destruction. To the south, Tanzania's production in food and export commodities has been unable to keep pace with rising national expectations and expenditures. Somalia's withering national infrastructure has precipitated a decline in currency exchange from six Somali shillings to the dollar in 1982 to 400 shillings to the dollar in mid-1989, and the nation is paralyzed by political conflict.

By comparison, Kenya has generally maintained political and economic stability. There has evolved a political culture that is genuinely multiracial, that defends the right to vote, that maintains a parliamentary government, and that affords a mostly free press. Both East and West have access to Kenya. And its independent and pragmatic approach to foreign policy has made it a moderating political force in the region and has allowed it to play an important role in softening North-South tensions in East Africa—especially important because the area is on the edge of the troubled Middle East/Gulf region.

Economically, Kenya has also done well. In recent years, it has become a financial and communications center for the East African region, a bold experiment in blending public and private sector initiatives, and an example for other states to emulate. The economic record over 20 years, and in the last year in particular, suggests achievement well beyond the rest of sub-Saharan Africa. The good rains in 1985–86 and in 1987–88 have enabled Kenya to recover from the severe drought of 1984 in record time and in orderly fashion. As of June 1986, gross domestic product was growing at an impressive annual rate of 5.7 percent.[1] Agricultural production, at least for the current year, has been good; the industrial sector is growing moderately; export income is high. Three of Kenya's best years ever for tourism were 1986, 1987, and 1988. In addition, the price of petroleum, which Kenya must import for its transportation and industrial sectors, has been generally low in recent years.

Kenya's present economic prosperity, however, is built on important factors beyond Kenya's control. There is, therefore, a built-in vulnerability that government planners and donor agencies must consider when organizing new initiatives. It is hard for Americans, who have enjoyed an expanding frontier and great degrees of national self-sufficiency throughout most of their history, to fully comprehend a situation like Kenya's where the country is heavily dependent for its national wellbeing on factors outside its control—the weather, world prices for its basic commodities, the price of oil, and international terrorism and other factors affecting tourism. Kenya cannot set the world price of tea or coffee. It cannot control the conditions in Europe and the United States that shape the fashions or fears governing the flow of tourists to its beaches and game parks. It cannot count on the crucial inches of rain at the right time. It cannot predict world oil prices 10, five, or even three years ahead. Kenya's inability to control these factors suggests the critical importance of managing wisely the primary resources over which it does have control—its land and its people.

Development projections for Kenya's next few decades yield ominous signals, especially in food production, soil loss, deforestation, and population growth. Per capita food production has declined 38 percent since 1952, and there is no reason to expect a reversal in the short term if current circumstances continue. Land in areas with high productive potential appears to be almost fully utilized, causing greatly increased settlement of arid and semiarid areas that offer unreliable productivity, less dependable water supplies, sparse woodlands, and soils more susceptible to erosion. Soil erosion from deforestation, agricultural use, and new settlements—in spite of several successful programs—is running at rates that portend food production crises in the next 10 to 15 years.

On top of this, Kenya's population growth rate is one of the highest in the world, around 4.1 percent per year. At this rate, total population will double every 18 years. An already stressed ecological capacity will have roughly twice as many mouths to feed by the first decade of the 21st century. One estimate predicts declines in potential food output by as much as 50 percent in some areas if soil loss does not receive immediate attention.[2] Similarly, Kenya's demand for fuelwood is projected to double by the end of the century, and the nation's forests are projected to be able to supply only about one-third of that demand on a sustained basis.[3] The land will also have to continue to supply most Kenyans with their livelihood, since manufacturing and other urban jobs, although growing, form only a small portion of employment and are not increasing fast enough to absorb the number of those entering the job market over the next two decades.[4]

At the same time, Kenya's political stability depends on conditions that make it vulnerable to disruptions. Competition among ethnic groups and inequities in access to power and economic resources create potential for internal discontent. These inequities fall hardest on the rural poor, the majority of whom are women who manage small farms. Their access to political power and government assistance is limited. Political instability is not an immediate cause for concern, but a severe and prolonged drought, an international economic down-turn, persistent declines in resource productivity, and continued population pressure could exacerbate tensions and create hardship conditions threatening Kenya's viability as a friendly political ally.

The Physical Setting

Several significant physical features dominate Kenya's landscape and shape its economic and political life. Perhaps most dramatic is the Rift Valley. Stretching from the southern to the northern border and including several important lakes, the Rift is one of the world's great natural wonders. Fifteen million years ago, the African continent collided with Eurasia, creating internal pressures beneath the surface of modern Kenya and Ethiopia. At that time, the Kenyan landscape was mostly gently sloping and lush forest that extended from the western part of the nation all the way to the Indian Ocean.

Two potential eruptions simmered beneath the surface. One lay under the present Kenya highlands in the southwestern portion of the country; the second bubbled beneath Ethiopia's future highlands. Eventually the simmering erupted, forcing hot lava to the surface and pushing the forestland up by at least 1,000 meters. The lands adjacent to these eruptions could not withstand the pressure and cracked, leaving the great depression that has become the Rift Valley. The depression is at least 1,000 meters deep and roughly 100 kilometers wide.

The newly formed hills and highlands intercepted moist air coming in from the Indian Ocean and, while causing plentiful rainfall in the upland regions, made the Rift Valley mostly dry. In the middle of the Rift depression, vegetation withered and, especially to the north, dried up almost entirely, leaving a deep desert. Areas adjacent to the Rift have retained some rainfall and support varying degrees of vegetation. The great diversity of this vegetation in and near the Rift may have accelerated the evolutionary stages to produce early hominids, while the dryness of the Rift allowed their remains to be preserved.[5] Today the low and dry areas of the Rift support game and limited livestock grazing, but have little significant agriculture other than in irrigated areas adjacent to the valley's lakes—which are home for much aquatic life and birds, especially the famous pink flamingos.

Kenya's second geologic wonder is the highlands and their associated mountains. This region encompasses most of the southwestern third of the country and is split by the Rift Valley. Mount Kenya, reaching up more than 5,000 meters (16,500 feet), straddles the equator but is snowcapped year round. Growing out of a volcanic chain that also produced Kilimanjaro in Tanzania,

Mount Kenya is spiritual home for the Kikuyu people and provides habitat for hundreds of unique species of flora and fauna.

At elevations of 3,000 to 4,000 meters, the ecology changes from alpine to highland. Rainfall is good, with averages varying from 500 to 1,000 millimeters (mm) per year (20 to 40 inches) and with much of the highlands receiving 750 mm 80 to 90 percent of the time. Productivity of the highlands varies from good to very good, partly because of the rainfall and partly because of the area's rich volcanic soils. These fertile lands have attracted human occupation for centuries. Today the Kenyan highlands are among the most densely populated parts of sub-Saharan Africa, along with similar highland zones in Rwanda, Burundi, Tanzania, and Ethiopia. The highlands also include the nation's capital and largest city, Nairobi.

The southwestern-most corner contains Kenya's third major physical feature, Lake Victoria and the surrounding lake basin area, which is shared with Uganda and Tanzania. Lake Victoria is the world's second largest freshwater lake; only Lake Superior is bigger. The water flows north through Uganda and becomes the White Nile. By virtue of treaties and agreements dating back to colonial times, Egypt has rights to most of the water in the lake and keeps a monitoring team on duty in Uganda to assure the waters are fully delivered into the Nile. The lake supports a substantial freshwater fishery. Catches in Kenya average 30,000 tons per year and provide large amounts of protein for Kenyans, especially those who live in the basin.

The lake basin also is fertile and well watered, and produces many crops. Much of it has high or medium potential for agriculture, forestry, and intensive pasture use. In recent years, the U.S. Agency for International Development (AID) program has focused on western Kenya as one of its priority areas, based on the region's good land potential and considerable population base.

Kenya's fourth dramatic feature is the coast. Stretching more than 400 kilometers along the warm waters of the Indian Ocean, the coast receives approximately 1,000 mm of rainfall each year. In most coastal areas, the underlying limestone causes surface water to drain away quickly; there are no major lakes near the coast. Nevertheless, small farms in this area produce coconuts, sisal, cashews, and many local food crops.

The coast attracts tourists from other parts of Africa, Europe, and North America. Coral reefs, sport fishing, glittering beaches, nearby game parks such as Tsavo, charming ancient towns such as Lamu, and historic 600 to 700-year-old ruins are among the attractions. The thriving port of Mombasa normally handles about 1,300 ships each year and is a lifeline for Kenya and its landlocked neighbors.

The rest of Kenya, about two-thirds of the country, consists of low plateaus and plains. This region, to the north and east of the highlands and west of the coast, is dry and sparsely populated.[6]

Figure 1. Ecological Zones

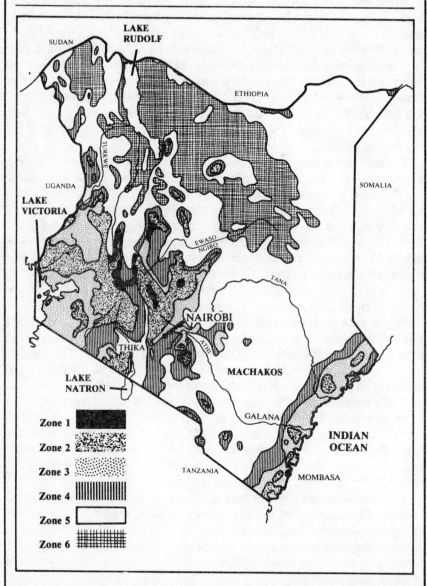

Source: D.J. Pratt, M.D. Gwynne, (eds.), *Rangelands Management and Ecology in East Africa,* (Hodder and Stoughton, London, 1967): 6, 7

Key to Figure 1: Ecological Zones

Zone and Area, (% of total)	Characteristics and Land Use
1. Afro-alpine **800 sq. km. (0.1%)**	Very high altitude above forest lines. Mostly barren with use limited to water catchment and tourism.
2. High potential **53,000 sq. km. (9.3%)**	High moisture, mostly high altitude. Used for forest, coffee, tea, pyrethrum, intensive livestock, maize, and cotton (at low altitude).
3. Medium potential **53,000 sq. km. (9.3%)**	Generally lower moisture and altitude than Zone II. Used for mixed farming: hybrid maize, wheat, pulses, cotton, groundnuts, oilseeds, cashew, coconuts, and livestock.
4. Semiarid **48,200 sq. km. (8.5%)**	Marginal agricultural potential mostly limited to sisal and quick-maturing grains. Productive grainlands. High density of wildlife.
5. Arid **300,000 sq. km. (52.9%)**	Moderate rangeland potential. Wildlife important in some areas.
6. Very arid **112,000 sq. km. (19.8%)**	Low potential rangeland limited to nomadic pastoralists.

The most salient facts about Kenya's geography are these: 18 percent of the land has excellent or good productive potential, but 80 percent cannot be relied on for adequate harvests, and that means the population and most economic activity are concentrated on one-fifth of the land. Only 3 percent of the land is in forests.

Kenya's six ecological zones are indicated in Figure 1. The high and medium potential lands in Zones II and III are the basis for most of the country's economic life.

Zones IV, V and VI account for about 80 percent of Kenya's land and are dry to very dry. Rainfall is 612 mm (25 inches) or less. About 9 percent of this land has sufficient rainfall to support limited agriculture, but only in years of good rain. In northeastern Kenya, rainfall declines and even occasional agriculture is difficult. These areas support nomadic pastoralism, in which trekking herds are moved from place to place, depending on the quality of rainfall and grasses. In most years, even during drought, sufficient local variations in rainfall provide adequate grass somewhere within the region. Crisis occurs when, as in 1984, the rains fail.

Even Kenya's highly productive land has some special vulnerabilities. The character of the rainfall in tropical Africa—long dry seasons, high rainfall variability, torrential and intense tropical downpours, and regular periods of prolonged drought—makes climate patterns in Kenya far different from temperate Europe, North America, or much of Asia and Latin America. These weather patterns mean that drought will be more frequent than in temperate zones, that soil erosion may be more severe, that bare ground is a greater liability, and that livestock management poses different challenges than in temperate climates. These factors call for different responses in mulching, cultivation, weeding, fallowing, pest control, soil management, and intercropping patterns.

In addition, large areas of Kenya's soil are fragile and easily eroded when exposed to wind and water. As long as vegetation remains mostly in place, the soil will survive. However, if excessive grazing or clearing takes place, soils become highly vulnerable. Given these conditions, agricultural intensification and population growth, if not properly managed, can cause far greater soil erosion problems in Kenya than in other parts of the world.

Another important characteristic of Kenya's agricultural land is its variability. The turbulent geologic history of the region has created a rough and varied terrain. Even in zones of high and medium productivity, agricultural lands differ widely in elevation, slope, soil types, vegetation, and the amount, duration, and predictability of rainfall. Kenya's traditional agricultural responses have been locally adapted to particular environmental settings, with strategies calling for mixes of crops and combinations of crops and livestock as a hedge against variable climate. Thus in many areas, small-scale farmers who can tailor their agricultural strategies to the local microclimate have the most productive success. These characteristics underscore the need for considerable variety in land use and resource management practices. In this, Kenya is representative of the agricultural challenges and conservation needs typical of other countries in this region.

The Cultural Setting

Kenya's ecological diversity is mirrored by ethnic variation. Much of Kenya's cultural life thrives on this diversity, but the cultural pluralism sometimes also leads to competition and conflict. Three African groups form almost 99 percent of Kenya's population. Two more recently arrived groups—Europeans and Asians—account for 1 percent.

Kenyans who speak one of the Bantu languages, found mostly in the East and Southeast, are linked culturally and linguistically with the peoples of central and southern Africa. They form 65 percent of the country's population, and practice agriculture, including some livestock management.[7] Bantu speakers are by far the dominant political and economic force in Kenya. The largest group, the Kikuyu, accounted for 21 percent of the nation's population in 1979. Mzee Jomo Kenyatta, the first president of Kenya and one of Africa's great nationalist heroes, was Kikuyu.

Nilotes and Nilo-Hamites, who form about 30 percent of Kenya's population, migrated from the Nile Valley and first penetrated Kenya territory in substantial numbers about 600 to 900 years ago, after the Bantu speakers had established themselves. Most are pastoralists although some, such as the Luo, have settled down over the centuries and today are mostly agricultural. Nilotes have stayed generally in western Kenya.[8] The largest Nilotic group today (13 percent of the population) are the Luo, an energetic and productive people who are clustered mostly along the shores of Lake Victoria and in the greater lake basin. They have adapted quickly and thoroughly to western values and education, and are heavily represented in the professions and academia.

Kenya's third and smallest African community, about 4 percent of the population, is the Cushitic-speaking group who live in the drylands of the north. Related to Somali and Oromo peoples to the north and east of Kenya, these groups are mostly pastoralists. Their comprehensive knowledge of dryland management, livestock, wildlife, rainfall, soil, and vegetation has created a fiercely independent and self-reliant people who feel little need for centralized political institutions.

These nomads continue to move freely between Somalia, southern Ethiopia, southern Sudan, and Kenya, ignoring national boundaries. Notwithstanding such independence, some have entered the cash economy, even moving into regional towns such as Isiolo or to Nairobi, where they work as *askaris* (guards), drivers, police, soldiers, or in other wage activities. But many of the Cushitic speakers continue their pastoral traditions.

After independence, the number of European settlers sharply declined, and most of their prime agricultural holdings were transferred back to African ownership. Today, only about 4,500 Europeans hold Kenyan citizenship, but they continue to have substantial influence in finance, agriculture, tourism, and commerce. In addition, some 35,000 European expatriates live in Kenya, including the large United Nations, business, and technical communities of people who either work on Kenyan projects or for the United Nations Environment Programme, or who live in Nairobi and environs because of the splendid year-round climate and the high-quality transportation, communication, and logistical infrastructure that prevails in the urban areas. Asians, who were originally brought to Kenya by the British to construct the railroads, were prevented in colonial times from owning agricultural lands; to this day, they are concentrated in commerce, where their small numbers (75,000) belie their economic importance.

The Political Setting

Kenya's constitutional-parliamentary form of government, bolstered by a modern bureaucracy and a national party, the Kenya African National Union (KANU), has demonstrated an amazing durability. Kenya has had only two presidents in 23 years. A 1982 coup attempt by the Air Force badly shook the political system but did not destroy it. While the nation has held up well in the face of internal and external challenges, its political problems should not be overlooked: for example, ethnic rivalries for political power and economic resources, a broadening gap between rich and poor, and a growing civil service that creates rivalries between central and local government priorities.

Uprisings, political change, and conflicts in neighboring countries have periodically encouraged sympathetic disruptions in Kenya itself. The government's pragmatic approach to problems with Uganda, Tanzania, Somalia, and Ethiopia and its ability to respond constructively in these situations is a factor making it a valuable keeper of the peace in East Africa.

Historically, different ethnic groups have found ways to cooperate, even to intermarry, but ethnic competition remains a continuing factor in Kenyan politics. National policy officially deemphasizes ethnic ties, and formal ethnic associations are illegal. Even so, ethnic identity continues to be one of the strongest forces for mobilizing local groups. The most intense rivalry, between the Luo and Kikuyu, is the most obvious characteristic of political life, despite determined efforts by President Daniel Arap Moi to place power outside the established Kikuyu elite since the 1982 attempted coup.

This phenomenon of ethnic complexities that produces internal tensions and deemphasizes national boundaries imposed by colonial imperatives is common to all of East Africa. What is much less well understood—and important when devising development strategies—are ways in which traditional jurisdictions, leadership, and social institutions have been overlaid with a powerful national government and a modern bureaucracy. That the success of that process accounts for Kenya's progress and stability should not obscure the difficulties the centralized institutions will have in leading a development process that demands increased productivity and labor-intensive schemes from local and regional microsystems whose very diversity calls for other than a macro approach.

Traditional jurisdictions and leadership were destroyed or radically changed in the colonial era, and the centralized institutions strengthened since independence. Examples of moves taken to centralize power include a 1969 policy that placed authority for revenue issues solely with the central government, the establishment in 1982 of KANU (the multiethnic dominant political party) as the nation's only legal political entity, and actions since the coup to reduce the autonomy of local associations that might cause political rivalry, including a variety of church groups and organizations assisted by foreign governments such as Libya.

Recent attempts at decentralization have caused competition between central and local decision-making. On resource management questions, for example, central decision-makers tend to show concern for overall economic viability, balance of payments, and increased exports, while local decision-makers are more concerned with maintaining the well-being of their own productive resources. Conflicts develop when local groups seek funds for small dams, water supplies, health programs, schools, soil control, or reforestation, while central authorities seek assistance for larger scale projects and are more concerned with increasing production of export commodities or strengthening the infrastructure to support tourism. Moreover, the overburdened central ministries frequently find it difficult to collect good local data needed to make sound decisions about Division, Location, or Sub-Location policies. Local leaders may have good local information, but have little input or authority in the central development decisions.

Given this tension, assistance for local projects typically tends to go to those local politicians and elites who have managed to develop some special access to the central government. Until recently, this situation benefited primarily the Kikuyu, adding an ethnic element to this local-national tension. As the ethnic group best organized and with good access to the center, local Kikuyu leaders had been able to capitalize on mechanisms such as *harambee*, self-help projects to benefit local communities. However, President Moi's efforts to broaden ethnic participation to the high ranks of government has progressed and has already led to changes.

Kenya has made a significant effort over the last 10 years to decentralize development planning by increasing the role of the 41 District Development Committees, which develop local projects such as new schools or hospitals, organize new infrastructure projects such as roads and water supplies, and review programs proposed by individual ministries. But much of the financial authority for such initiatives continues to lie with the central government, as does the authority to approve requests for foreign exchange, and political power remains mostly centralized. This inherent dysfunctional relationship—not unknown in other developing countries—makes it difficult to accomplish what planners recognize needs to be done.

As elsewhere around the world, Kenya's government has been primarily a government of the elite, and access to productive resources has been far from equal. The losers in this system are rural Kenyans. According to 1974 figures, 98 percent of Kenya's poor (as opposed to 90 percent of the population) live in rural areas. At least one-third of rural Kenyans live below the poverty line, compared with only 5 percent of people in the urban areas. More than 70 percent of the rural poor are smallholders, defined as farmers with less than 20 hectares of land, and the remainder are pastoralists, landless farmers, squatters, or migrants to semiarid areas. About 11 percent of rural Kenyans own no land.[9]

Although Kenya experienced significant economic growth in the 1960s and early 1970s, the benefits of this growth accrued primarily to those who were already better off. The 60 percent of the smallholders who were the most well off received most of the benefits from the expansion; the 40 percent of smallholders who were the poorest achieved little or no gain in real income.[10] And as might be expected, the distribution of benefits reflects ethnic patterns. Dominant groups are likely to have greater access to Kenya's resources, including development funds and investments. Kikuyu, for example, have received 45 percent of the total land allocated to private holders since independence though they comprise only 20 percent of the population. And government services, in a pattern that is familiar even in industrialized countries like the United States, may be most available to those least in need of them. According to a recent AID country strategy study, the most prosperous farmers, including those most likely to contribute to exports, account for 59 percent of field extension officer visits; poor smallholders receive 4 percent.

The Economic Setting

Kenya's comparative political stability since independence has been enhanced by the country's relative economic success. Just as the patterns of ecological and ethnic diversity feed and complicate the politics of Kenya, so also are they reflected in the economics.

In the first decade after independence, gross domestic product (GDP) grew at an annual average rate of more than 6 percent and in recent years it has continued to grow at a rate of 2 to 4 percent. In 1986, GDP grew at a rate of 5.7 percent.[11] Kenya's gross national product (GNP) growth has exceeded that of any of the other East African nations, and its 1987 per capita GNP was significantly larger than that of neighboring nations in the region.[12]

In most years, Kenya has been self-sufficient in basic foodstuffs. Small manufacturing enterprises and light industry have been encouraged in its vigorous private sector. At the same time, Kenya preserves national parks, wildlife, and, to the extent possible, a number of endangered species. Kenya maintains a positive foreign-exchange balance, manages a mostly stable currency for which the black market and official rates of exchange are relatively close, and meets International Monetary Fund guidelines for domestic budget deficits.

Managerially, Kenya has progressed in recent years. The expanding civil service and ministerial infrastructure deals well both with day-to-day affairs and emergency situations. Good management paid off in the drought of 1984–85, for example. Although initially unprepared to deal with the food shortage, the government was able to regroup, establish emergency committees, cooperate with the private sector, coordinate donor assistance, and deal in a systematic way with emergency needs for food, transportation, and health. Although Kenya's losses in food production and livestock were considerable, the drought brought no famine or loss of human life.

Agriculture has been and is expected to remain the mainstay of Kenya's economy. Including farming, forestry, and grazing, agriculture accounts for about 35 percent of the value of gross domestic product.[13] It contributes more than half of Kenya's annual export value and is by far the largest source of jobs and subsistence for Kenya's population. About 85 percent of the rural population—and most Kenyans are rural—is engaged in agricultural and pastoral activities.[14]

Both domestic food production and export crops are critical in Kenya's economy. Maize and beans are the principal food crops, plus bananas in some areas. Wheat is the second most important cereal crop. Of the export crops, coffee and tea are the most important.[15]

But both food and export crop production are highly vulnerable to factors outside Kenya's control. Drought, which occurs on the average every 8 to 10 years, can have devastating impact. In recent years, the government has had to import food and seek aid to feed its people during drought years.

Coffee and tea usually are grown on lands with the most reliable rainfall, which are less susceptible to drought, but these products—coffee in particular—are more vulnerable to world price fluctuations. For example, in 1986 coffee was highly profitable for Kenya, due to drought in Brazil. Coffee exports set a new record, yielding one-third of the total export revenue for Kenya and representing an increase of 66 percent over 1985. But by 1987 prices had returned to normal, and by 1989 were at a 10-year low.[16] Moreover, income from coffee exports has been increasingly less able to pay for imports. For example, a ton of Kenyan coffee paid for 24 tons of imported cement in 1958; by 1976 it paid for only 11 tons.

The superior quality of Kenyan tea consistently brings above-average prices on the world market, and tea is not as susceptible as coffee to world price variations. Other food exports, including pineapples, mangoes, avocados, beans, and tomatoes, have risen from 260,000 tons in 1980 to 370,000 tons in 1984, but are still a relatively small part of Kenya's agricultural exports.[17]

Tourism is Kenya's second largest earner of foreign exchange, and may finish in first place in 1989. In 1986, over 600,000 tourists visited Kenya, generating upwards of 250 million Kenya pounds, or close to U.S.$300 million. Earnings from this sector more than doubled from 1981 to 1985. The number of tourists is expected to rise by at least 10 percent a year, and one source predicts tourist revenue could approach $1 billion in the next decade.[18]

But tourism is a fickle business and dependent on factors largely beyond Kenya's control. The health of the European and North American economies, the

Table 1. Percentage of Fuel Consumption by Sector and Source of
          Energy, 1980

Sector	Wood (63%)	Charcoal (8%)	Agricultural Residue (3%)	Petroleum (24%)	Electricity (2%)	Total (100%)
Urban homes	1	50	—	5	36	6
Rural homes	72	37	100	5	—	53
Agriculture	—	—	—	9	10	2
Industry	26	12	—	24	31	24
Commercial	1	1	—	1	22	1
Transportation	—	—	—	56	1	14
TOTAL	100	100	100	100	100	100

Source: O'Keefe and Raskin, *Ambio*, Vol. XIV, No. 4-5, 1985, 221.

international political situation, and the price of aviation fuel have more influence on tourism than, for example, the quality of Kenya's hotels. A combination of lower air fares, favorable reaction to the film "Out of Africa," and political turmoil in the Middle East and Mediterranean are probably responsible for the recent strength of Kenya's tourist industry. Internal political events can also influence tourism: after the 1982 coup attempt, visits to Kenya dropped by 5 percent.

As in other countries, Kenyans debate the pros and cons of increased tourism. The lure for scarce foreign exchange and jobs are weighed against charges that the scarce resources and profits benefit foreign-owned airlines, absentee hotel owners, and limited regions, while the ecological base bears the wear and tear, and people outside the tourist centers do not share the benefits.

Kenya's expanding manufacturing sector increased more than 40 percent from 1983 to 1985, but it is more capital- than labor-intensive and accounts for only 2 percent of employment. In 1984, Del Monte exported $44 million worth of canned pineapple, almost 10 percent of total food and beverage exports that year. Automobile and truck assembly is growing. Auto and truck factories in Mombasa and Thika put together vehicles for numerous overseas companies, and Nairobi manufactures a Kenya family sedan, the "Uhuru," and truck. Small businesses are expanding their manufacture of textiles, leather, paper, cement, tires, batteries, and glass.[19]

Employment in manufacturing increased about 6.6 percent per year from 1972 to 1980, but this provided only about 44,000 new jobs, all in urban areas, in a total population of 20 million.[20] And even the manufacturing sector is subject to non-Kenyan decisions. The many foreign-dominated companies in Kenya, such as Firestone, General Motors, Leyland, or Del Monte, have high mobility and may leave the country if they consider conditions unfavorable.

Energy production adequate to meet Kenya's growing demand is a central concern of the nation's planners. In a real sense, the whole economy is hostage to world oil prices or dependent on declining forests. Kenya has three main energy sources. (See Table 1.) Wood and agricultural residues are the largest and account for almost all energy consumed in rural areas. The modern sector is fueled primarily by imported petroleum, while a small amount of electricity (from hydro and geothermal sources) contributes to urban and industrial use.

Until a few years ago, most Kenyan analyses of energy needs and economic development were, like those of other countries and the donor agencies, focused exclusively on energy for the "modern" commercialized sector, but in this decade the role of biomass fuels has been widely recognized. Three-quarters of all energy consumed in Kenya is derived from wood or agricultural residues. For rural homes, 99 percent of the energy need is met with wood or wood products. Urban homes also get a significant portion of their energy from charcoal. There will be few alternatives to fuelwood for most Kenyans for many years to come. Yet only 3 percent of Kenya is forested. Deforestation is projected to continue throughout the remainder of the century.[21]

Kenya's modern sector relies heavily on petroleum. Major users are cars and trucks, the industrial sector, civil aviation, and marine transportation. Although oil exploration has been under way for some years, no domestic oil resources have yet been discovered in Kenya.[22]

As in other countries dependent on imported oil, world price swings have grave effects on development. In 1981, when oil prices were high, petroleum imports used up more than a third of the income from all of Kenya's exports. Even as prices have declined, petroleum imports have remained a substantial factor in the economy. In 1985, lower prices permitted a 10-percent increase in imports, and required 47 percent of Kenya's export income to pay for it.[23] Inevitable world oil price increases in the 1990s will once again cause a situation where most of the national export income is needed to import energy.

Kenya's refinery in Mombasa, opened in 1963, can process over 4 million tons of petroleum per year. Kenya has helped finance its petroleum imports in part through the domestic sale of petroleum products, such as fuel sales to foreign airlines, and by exporting petroleum products to other East African countries. However, both domestic sales and exports of petroleum products dropped in the 1970s and early 1980s with the oil price rise. Oil products exports, for example, declined from about 50 percent of the refinery's output in 1981 to about 34 percent in 1984. Volume has risen again recently with the fall in petroleum prices, but it can be expected to contract with anticipated world price increases in the 1990s.

Only 2 percent of Kenya's total energy consumption is supplied by hydropower and geothermal generated electricity, most of it generated domestically, plus a small amount from Uganda. Electricity is nevertheless important for urban and industrial purposes, and Kenya is seeking to expand these sources of energy. Current installed capacity for hydropower is about 350 megawatts (MW), mostly on the Tana River system of dams. Hydropower produces three-quarters of total electricity. One new dam, which will produce 130 MW, is under construction on the Tana; another 110-MW dam (with potential also for irrigating about 12,000 hectares) is getting under way in Turkwell Gorge in the northwestern part of the nation. Although there are severe problems with siltation in the Tana River reservoirs, on the whole Kenya's hydro generation has been well operated.[24]

There is also geothermal power potential in the Rift Valley, where the unique geology makes steam available in large and reliable quantities. Thirty megawatts are produced at the Olkaria facility near Mount Longonot, with an additional capacity of 15 MW near completion and 60 MW planned.[25]

City dwellers and large commercial and industrial users receive by far the largest share of the supply. In 1984, for example, domestic and small commercial users consumed only 500 kilowatt hours of hydropower-generated electricity, while large interests used 1,200 kilowatt hours. For the majority of Kenyans in the rural areas, electricity is not a realistic expectation.

In 1989, though coffee is weak, Kenya is feeling buoyant—the economic outlook is positive. Tourism and tea are up, oil prices are down, the rains have been good. The slump that created hardship in the late 1970s and contributed to frustration behind the 1982 coup attempt for the time being are in abeyance. But a look at the number of external factors on which that well-being rests and at population factors necessarily tempers optimism.

In one sense, Kenya's high birth rate is quite "rational": it is bolstered not only by traditional values but also by economic conditions and needs in the rural areas where most Kenyans live.[26] But the actual numbers for Kenyan population growth are dramatic. In 1902, the population was estimated to be 4 million. It took 60 years to double, reaching roughly 8 million in 1960. The second doubling took only 20 years, to 16 million by 1980. If present trends continue, Kenya's population will grow from 20 million in 1987 to 34 million in 2000, 40 million sometime between 2005 and 2007, and as many as 80 million by 2020.[27]

Two factors are causing the rapid rise. First, the number of live births per female (the fertility rate) is increasing. In 1962, the total number of live births per woman aged 15–49 was 6.8; this number rose steadily to 8.0 live births per woman in the early 1980s. It had dropped to 7.7 in 1987 and is expected to decline to 6.5 by 2000.[28]

Demographers attribute increases in fertility to improved health and economic conditions, which result in fewer problems during pregnancy and birth, as well as in overall better health for both mother and child. There also seem to be correlations with education level: women with two to three years of education, but less than seven years, have higher fertility rates than those with more or fewer years of schooling. This phenomenon suggests that a few years of education increases a mother's basic familiarity with nutrition, sanitation, water management, and personal cleanliness, but not with an overall understanding of population pressures. At least seven years of schooling seem to be necessary to create an awareness of the adverse impacts of large families, both in a micro and macro sense.

The second factor causing population growth is declining mortality. The crude death rate has dropped from 24 per thousand in 1960 to 12 per thousand in 1980.[29]

Little suggests that there has been or soon will be a substantial downturn in population growth rates. Short of a major health crisis or epidemic,[30] a natural disaster of enormous proportions, or a massive political upheaval, the growth rates will probably continue at high levels for the next decade or more. In 1989, 53 percent of the population was estimated to be under 14 years of age and just getting ready to enter their childbearing years.[31] (See Figure 2 for a picture of population structure.) Given the current age structure, even if fertility rates were cut in half, to four births per woman, it would still take at least two decades or more to show significant stabilization in total population.

Kenya's government is well aware of the population pressure and has taken a number of policy and program steps to address it, as discussed later in this chapter. Official government policy is to support family planning programs and to reduce the rate of population growth, but the intended effect is not yet apparent. Strong incentives, especially in the rural areas, to have large families still exist, and there is not yet clear evidence that simply moving to a city reduces fertility rates, although there are indications that middle- and upper-income urban residents are having fewer children. Nor has Kenya yet developed a social security and retirement system to look after the elderly; children are the only old-age support most Kenyans can look forward to. One careful analysis of the factors at work in the last generation also documents the effect of agrarian policy, including the tenure system, and the organization, financing, and quality of government services, especially in education and health, and family law.[32]

Finally, the cultural values of Kenya continue to place priority on having children. Influence, prestige, and respect all accrue to the couple with many children. Most national leaders have many children. Thus, values and institutions will have to change before there is a meaningful increase in the use of family planning and a significant decrease in the rate of population growth.

This does not mean that programs in population planning should be stopped —far from it. Over the long term, population planning will be an important part

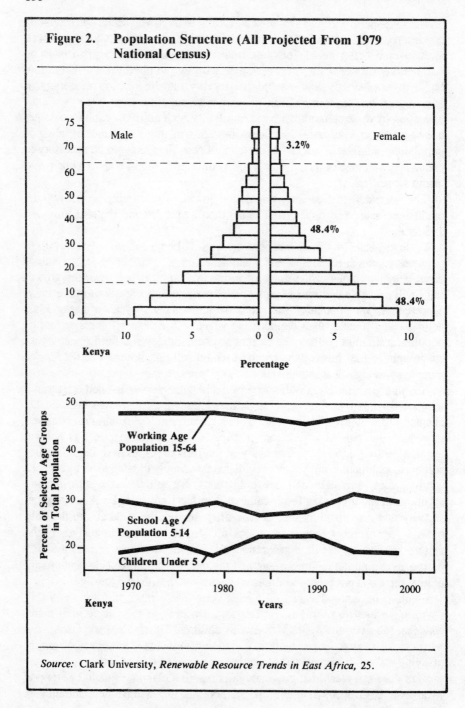

Figure 2. Population Structure (All Projected From 1979 National Census)

Source: Clark University, *Renewable Resource Trends in East Africa,* 25.

of the solution to Kenya's high population growth rate. But it does indicate that the present programs in family planning and birth control techniques will probably not reduce population growth in the next decade or two.

Urban areas are growing roughly twice as fast as the country as a whole. In 1969, there were 48 towns and cities with populations of 2,000 or more; by 1979 this number had increased to 90. Urban population in Kenya is projected to rise from its 1985 level of 19.7 percent of the total population, to 23.6 percent of the total by 1990. Job opportunities in the cities cannot nearly match the demand of migrants from the countryside. Manufacturing jobs, although increasing, covered only 2 percent of Kenya's employment. Wage employment accounted for only about 14 percent of total employment in 1980 and is growing more slowly than the population.[33] Urban unemployment is not officially recorded in Kenya. Estimates, especially in Nairobi, range from 10 to 20 percent. Overall labor productivity in manufacturing was judged by the World Bank to be four points lower in 1986 than in 1980.[34]

Some rural inhabitants migrate not to the cities but to less productive semiarid areas. Population densities are lower in such areas, but the resource base is ill suited to absorb large numbers of new people. Farming on the semiarid lands may be unpredictable, cause ecological damage to the soils, and lead to conflict with pastoralists who inhabit these areas.[35]

With a rapidly growing population that exceeds new urban opportunities for employment, and 70 percent of the people engaged in agriculture, there is clearly growing pressure on Kenya's limited arable land. It is no surprise that increased agricultural productivity and adequate supplies of fuelwood and water are highly desired development goals that may be increasingly difficult to achieve.

Emerging Resource Shortages

The requirement of having to feed twice as many people 18 or 20 years from now underlines the importance of emerging resource shortages in Kenya: declining agricultural yields, fuelwood scarcity, and water problems.

Food Production: Declining Agricultural Trends

Per capita production in agriculture is declining significantly in Kenya, and apparent downward trends in absolute productivity must be carefully watched. Kenyan planners hope to continue and even to increase total per capita output of cash crops for export. The question is how can food production—which even now lags behind population growth—also be increased at the same time?

Between 1955 and 1970, the value of agricultural production increased at an average annual rate of about 4 percent—an acceptable rate that kept just barely ahead of population growth. But from 1970 to 1979, agricultural growth slipped to 2.2 percent. The 1980s have been highly uneven, given fluctuations in climate

Table 2. Overall Per Capita Agricultural Production, 1976-85

(1976-78 = 100)

Year	Total Agriculture	Food
1976	95	99
1977	106	103
1978	98	98
1979	90	89
1980	91	86
1981	94	89
1982	92	94
1983	91	89
1984	89	75
1985	87	83

Source: U.S. Department of Agriculture, *World Indices of Agricultural and Food Production,*
1976-85.

and related problems. The overall growth rates averaged 3.2 percent from 1972
to 1983, thus falling well below the levels of the 1960s.[36]

Per capita production has also declined. (See Table 2.) Production in the base
period (1976–78) has not been achieved in any subsequent year. The decline has
been particularly severe in domestic food crops—17 percent since the base
years—indicating that Kenya is losing ground in its effort to continue feeding its
growing population. From 1980 through 1985, Kenya's production of basic
cereals did not meet consumption needs. (See Table 3.) Figures show greater
than 10-percent per capita declines in the availability of milk, wheat, pulses, and
cassava in the periods 1965 through 1970 and 1976 through 1980, but with
encouraging rises in the mid-1980s. (See Table 4.)

In addition, there is growing unease that long-term trends in maize and beans
may show declines in yield per hectare—despite the fact that the 1985/86 harvest
showed an increase. Precise assessments of productivity will be difficult until
data on smallholder and locally produced food have been collected over a longer
period.

Explanations of reduced agricultural growth in recent years are readily
understandable, but worrisome. Rapid growth rates in the 1960s were made
possible with only modest efforts from the government to manage resources or to
boost productivity. The weather was generally favorable during the 1960s and

Table 3. Production and Consumption in Basic Cereals

Year	Production ('000 metric tons)	Consumption (kilos)	Per Capita Use (percent)	Shortfall
1980/81	2330	2694	164	14%
1981/82	2769	2738	160	(-1%)
1982/83	2796	2740	154	(-2%)
1983/84	2508	2840	153	12%
1984/85	1957	2806	145	30%

Source: U.S. Department of Agriculture, *World Food Needs and Availabilities 1985: Update.*

early 1970s, with no severe drought. A new high-yield maize seed was introduced in Kenya in 1964, and by 1967 half the nation's smallholders were using it, greatly boosting production. But the increased yields have now been realized, and no comparable technological breakthrough lurks on the horizon. Land redistributed when white settlers departed was farmed more intensively by African smallholders than it had been previously. Productivity was stimulated by the demand for cash crops. In addition, the postindependence government abolished colonial land-use restrictions that had prohibited Africans from farming in certain areas or from growing particular crops. Hence, growth rates of 4 percent per year in 1960s were routine.[37] It was a period in which a kind of slack was taken up, under circumstances that cannot be recreated. The next steps to boost production will be more difficult.

Today, much of the available high and medium potential lands are in production, and evidence suggests that they are being farmed close to their productive potential, given present technologies, inputs, and soil conservation practices. In some high potential areas, there is less than one hectare of agricultural land per person. (See Table 5.)

There is evidence of out-migration from these areas, both to urban areas and to marginal lands from some of the areas of medium and high agricultural potential. About 85 percent of Kenya's population lives in three areas of dense concentration—the Lake Victoria Basin, around Nairobi, and along the coast. In these regions, rural densities of 200 per square kilometer are common and in some places reach as high as 600 per square kilometer. These are also areas that have the highest percentage of land registered into private ownership—i.e., there is little or no new land available. Population growth rates in some of these older agricultural areas are below the national average of 4.1 percent, whereas the rate is as high as 7.2 percent in some districts with marginal land. And farming in

Table 4.   Per Capita Availability of Selected Food Items (Kilograms
           per year, period average)

	1965-70	1971-75	1976-80	1981-85
Milk*	74.8	56.0	62.5	70.4
Beef	—	12.5	13.5	9.0
Mutton	—	2.5	3.6	4.0
Pork	—	0.5	0.3	0.2
Eggs	1.4	1.4	1.6	2.0
Poultry	—	—	1.9	2.2
Fish	3.1	2.5	2.8	3.4
Maize	95.1	97.4	100.1	120.0
Wheat*	17.0	15.7	13.6	19.2
Rice	1.3	1.9	2.0	3.0
Pulses*	25.9	22.6	17.2	20.4
Sugar	12.2	15.9	19.1	18.0
Fats/Oils	4.2	6.4	7.3	8.2
Potatoes	19.2	27.0	24.8	28.0
Cassava*	59.8	53.3	49.9	54.3
Sorghum/Millet*	8.0	6.7	5.6	7.5

* indicates decline of more than 10 percent between 1965 and 1970 and
between 1976 and 1980.

Source: National Development Plan, 1989-1993, 22.

more marginal areas is more susceptible to drought and can cause serious soil erosion.[38]

In the 1960s and 1970s, Kenya's increased agricultural production was based to a significant degree on an increase in cash crops. Like many countries in Africa, Kenya's growth rate for food production fell in the period 1970–82 compared with the 1960s, but only in Kenya and Malawi did food production slow while nonfood production accelerated.[39] In the 1970s, land planted in tea doubled and cotton increased by 63 percent, and hectares in coffee grew by 50 percent. (See Table 6.) During the same period, the hectarage in pulses remained about even and land in maize grew only 8 percent. In addition, farmers tend to plant tea and coffee, as compared with food crops, on their higher potential fields where soil erosion is less likely to occur. They tend also to plant the cash crops in higher rainfall areas that are less prone to drought, and use mulching and fertilizer in greater quantities and in more systematic ways because commercial crops provide higher cash return. And, as in many other countries, government

Table 5. Percentage of Per Capita Agricultural Land in Selected Districts

District	Growth from 1962-1979 (in percent)	Agricultural land per capita (1979) (in hectares)
Kericho	38.4	.56
Kiambu	40.7	.25
Machakos	45.9	1.23
Meru	43.7	.71 (high potential)
Nakuru	54.6	6.78 (medium to low potential)

Source: Republic of Kenya, *Farm Management Handbook* (Nairobi: Ministry of Agriculture, n.d.)

policy has favored cash crops. Because of the importance of export crops, the independent Kenyan government's research and extension services have been focused, as in colonial times, more on cash crops than food products. The marketing infrastructure for cash crops is also better developed than that for food crops.

In the future Kenya will want to maintain or even increase growth in cash crop production to earn the hard currency it needs to pay for increasing amounts of petroleum, industrial supplies, and other imports. But it will also need to make major improvements in food production for consumption at home. For that, new policies and technologies will be required.

Kenya may eventually increase the amount of arable land through irrigation, but no substantial increases from this source are likely in the near future. Estimates of potentially irrigable land in Kenya range from 200,000 to 500,000 hectares, primarily in the Tana River and Lake Victoria catchment areas. But so far, irrigation has been only moderately successful in Kenya.[40]

In 1979, for example, a cluster of five donor agencies, mostly European, introduced an ambitious irrigation plan, dependent on foreign loans, for a site at Bura in the Tana River basin in eastern Kenya. The first segment called for irrigation of 6,700 hectares, at a projected cost of $91 million, eventually to be expanded to 70,000 hectares. Smallholder settlement plots were to be allocated to landless Kenyans, with most of the land to be devoted to cotton production.[41]

Actual costs, however, far exceeded projections, as happened in other sub-Saharan countries. By 1983, about $200 million had been spent and an additional $70 million still was needed just to bring the first 6,700 hectares into production. The irrigated areas fell far short of the projected 13-percent return on

Table 6. Total Area of Major Crops and Production on All Farms and Smallholder Contribution

Crops	Area ('000 ha)				Production ('000 tons)				Percentage of Smallholders Growing Crop	Smallholder Contribution to Marketed Production (%)
	1969-71	1978	1979	1980[f]	1969-71	1978	1979	1980[f]		
Maize	1,383	1,490	1,400	1,500	2,060	2,169	1,800	1,900	86.0	43
Wheat	133	119	117	122	223	175	207	210	0.1	n.a.
Rice Paddy	6	7	7	7	27	42	43	40	0.3	100
Pulses (total)	565	600[e]	550[e]	550	267	274	234	240	69 (beans)	100
Sugarcane	26	31	34	40	1,645	2,819[e]	4,034[e]	4,474	n.a.	45
Pyrethrum	—	—	—	—	16	27	28	38	9	95
Cotton (lint)	74	126	90	140	57	84	75	91	9	100
Coffee (green beans)	85	122	119	125	38	93	99	90	27	60
Tea (made tea)	30	55	59	62	—	—	—	—	12	36
TOTAL CROPS	2,070	2,170[e]	2,270	2,270	—	—	—	—	—	—

f = forecast
e = estimate
n.a. = not available

Source: Area and Production Data: FAO Production Year Book (1980); Data on Smallholders: Statistical Abstract (1981)/Economic Survey (1982) and Integrated Rural Survey 1974-75.

the sale of cotton. The huge cost overruns and the disappointing performance of the project will be a debt burden on the Kenyan government and many smallholders for many years. The Bura project demonstrates the difficulties in planning, implementing, and managing large-scale irrigation efforts in areas far removed from supplies, markets, social amenities, and suggests that it will be some time before irrigation becomes a major part of Kenya's agricultural production.

The Threat of Soil Loss, The Promise of Soil Conservation

One veteran Kenyan expert calls the accelerating loss of topsoil Kenya's "most serious resource crisis." As in other places around the world, its causes are destruction of vegetation in catchment areas, overgrazing, and expansion of human settlements on steep slopes and marginal land. Poor land use management techniques and government policies contribute to the loss of topsoil, which Simeon Ominde calls "the life support" of Kenya's population. Restoration and conservation of the soil is therefore central to increasing agricultural productivity.[42]

No comprehensive, nationwide studies exist on soil erosion, but a number of point-specific analyses suggest that soil loss from Kenya's agricultural land is already severe and is getting worse in spite of some impressive soil control programs such as those sponsored by the Ministry of Agriculture and by Sweden. Most of the erosion, according to two studies, is on land growing domestic food crops rather than cash crops.[43] A 1982 study in Kiambu and a 1983 survey of Murang'a, both high potential areas in the rich highlands, monitored sites producing food crops—primarily maize and beans—and others planted in cash crops—mostly coffee. Most of the plots planted in food crops experienced soil losses in excess of a generally accepted threshold level of 10 metric tons per hectare per year. One site was losing soil at the rate of 57 tons a hectare annually. These sample data, when projected to the districts as a whole, indicate that many fields in Kenya's lands with the highest potential, such as Kiambu and Murang'a, are under intense pressure and are losing soil at precarious rates.

For most of the monitored sites, low-cost, labor-intensive, simple technological innovations—such as changing cultivation techniques, installing cut-off drains, putting grass lines along ridge edges, and constructing bench terraces—could reduce erosion rates considerably. Agriculture, in cooperation with the Swedish International Development Authority, terraced 365,000 farms in 10 years and amply demonstrated that soil conservation also conserves water, reduces nutrient losses, and boasts yields, even without purchased inputs.[44] In a progressive village in Machakos, such labor-intensive improvements have preserved soil moisture so that even during the 1984 drought, maize, bananas, and beans planted on the improved terraces were green, while crops on nearby unimproved slopes died.[45]

In Kiambu, a farmer growing tomatoes on a steep slope lost about 50 tons of soil per hectare a year. When a simple monitoring device showed him the rate of loss, he changed his cultivation techniques, carefully maintaining his tomatoes in ridged rows that followed the contours of the slope. A different application of labor reduced annual soil loss to less than 10 tons a hectare, and production will probably continue at comparatively high levels for a long time to come.[46]

Although a number of regional efforts are underway, no countrywide program to halt soil loss exists, but there is compelling evidence for such an effort. A 1981 modelling study by M. M. Shah and G. Fischer predicts that Kenya will suffer major food production problems if it fails to implement soil conservation measures.[47] The authors argue that failure to control soil loss will result in 50-percent declines or more in the production potential of Kenya's arable land in the next 10 to 20 years. On the other hand, the model anticipates that introduction of *both* soil conservation and agricultural inputs could increase the amount and quality of Kenya's arable land, and significantly increase its productivity.

The study looked at the effectiveness of low, intermediate, and high levels of agricultural inputs (capital, labor, tools, fertilizer, pest controls, mechanization, etc.) in increasing arable land and at production with and without conservation measures. Conservation measures include primarily soil control efforts to reclaim, restore, and enhance the land. Even at the low input level (low capital, high labor, hand tools, no fertilizer), conservation measures lead to substantial production increases. In combination with higher levels of inputs, the increases are even more striking. On the other hand, if inputs are used *without* conservation measures, the model predicts that the projected potential will decrease by up to 74 percent.

The study is optimistic that low inputs and soil conservation measures could double Kenya's arable land (6.36 million hectares compared with 3.17 million hectares), and that land with less potential could be upgraded, possibly tripling the amount of land with very good potential, from 257,000 hectares to 1,037,000 hectares.

Soil conservation also increases productivity per hectare, although not as much as if inputs are also increased. Together, the combination of conservation measures and increased levels of inputs has the potential to achieve dramatic increases in food production that would allow the Kenyans expected by century's end to be fed. Even more striking is the analysis by Shah and Fischer showing how much production potential is reduced by *not* using conservation measures. (See Table 7.)

The model's predictions must be used with caution, but even if the anticipated gains are wildly optimistic, there would still remain the possibility of solid gains at low cost. With looming food shortages as the population spirals upward, Kenya cannot afford to neglect measures that could make such a critical difference in food supplies.

**Table 7.   Percent Reduction in Production Potential If Soil Erosion
Controls Are Not Applied**

	Low Input	Intermediate Input	High Input
Maize	74	61	52
Beans	68	56	49
Cassava	64	52	41
Bunded Rice	8	6	8
White Potato	73	55	51

Source: Shah and Fischer, 1981, "Assessment of Food Production Potential: Resources,
Technology and Environment — A Case Study in Kenya."

Deforestation and Shortages in Fuelwood

Kenya's energy requirements are closely related to the questions of agricultural productivity and soil loss. As noted earlier, only 3 percent of Kenya is forest, yet trees and other biomass are the source of 74 percent of the annual energy used nationwide, and of 99 percent of rural energy use. Cooking accounts for 60 percent of all wood energy use—the rest is used in agricultural and industrial processing: drying and curing of tea, tobacco, and sugar; tanning; and making charcoal and bricks.[48]

Despite widespread acknowledgment of deforestation and government planting programs, trees are being cut much faster than they are being replanted. The main cause is population pressure on the land: most clearing is done to plant food crops— maize, millet, sorghum, and beans. Cutting trees for charcoal and fuel for agricultural processing and household fuel are contributing factors. The problem is severe both in the prime agricultural areas where vast areas have been cleared for smallholders, and in the semiarid savanna and rangelands where about 70 percent of the total standing wood stocks are to be found.[49]

Energy is essential to every aspect of Kenya's development program, and the government has ambitious plans to more than double the production by 2005 (from 5.6 million tons of oil equivalent in 1985 to 12 million) with fuelwood increasing its dominance slightly to 77.6 percent of the whole, and petroleum declining slightly, to be compensated for by hydro, geothermal, and conservation.[50] These goals will be very difficult and expensive to meet, and all of them have serious environmental impacts.

There are insufficient wood stocks to meet the projected demand on a "business-as-usual" basis—as Figure 3 dramatically shows. Even by 1990,

Figure 3.   National Wood Report Demand and Supply Base Case

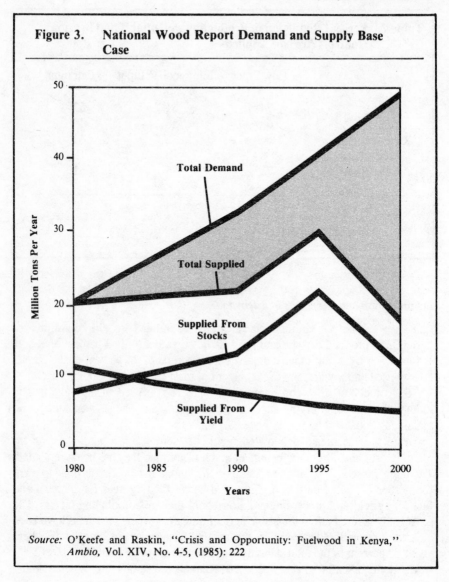

Source: O'Keefe and Raskin, "Crisis and Opportunity: Fuelwood in Kenya," *Ambio,* Vol. XIV, No. 4-5, (1985): 222

available wood will fall one-third short of meeting requirements, so it is not an exaggeration to say that Kenya faces now and in the immediate future a real fuelwood *crisis.* Such a large shortfall will have serious social, economic, and ecological effects. Collection of fuel will become even more onerous and the cost of fuel will rise further. Reduced cooking time or fewer cooked meals will alter diets; use of animal wastes for wood substitutes could rob the soil of nutrients. And the removal of trees and woody plants will hasten the soil loss and reduce water carrying capacity of the soil—leading to the downward spiral of productivity described in the previous section. This is not an acceptable scenario, and only major efforts in tree planting can head it off.

The Kenya government is aware of these trends and is developing programs to accelerate tree planting, but much more will be required. Data and experience indicate that most of the tree planting will take place on privately owned farms—even on the smallest of them—and in woodlots, windrows, and hedges, using agroforestry techniques. Of vital importance is a stepped-up training program in agroforestry that is controlled by and directed toward women, who do as much as 70 percent of the managing of trees and farmlands, but who have no legal rights to make decisions about them. Natural forests also need to be replanted and managed to be more productive. Urban areas that have been denuded of trees will need suburban plantations to help meet energy needs in the cities, and industrial plantations can meet some of the needs for agricultural and industrial processing.[51]

Equally important is the further development and distribution of improved cookstoves. Kenya has some very good experience in this respect. Despite technical problems with the ceramic liners, lack of credit, and distribution problems, a private stove-making industry is thriving in Kenya that is now offering technical assistance to other East African countries.[52] This outside aid is given through the auspices of KENGO, an umbrella organization of 200 energy nongovernmental organizations (NGOs). And there is also room to greatly improve the efficiency of kilns, ovens for drying tobacco and baking, briquetting techniques, and all the other direct heat and steam-making processes that use traditional fuels.

Improvements in efficiency can reduce pressure on remaining forests and buy time for planting and reforestation efforts. Many programs for doing these things are under way—with support from AID and European bilateral programs—and numerous examples can be cited of successful community-based efforts, many involving women and schoolchildren. Awareness of the problems has been greatly heightened in recent years and articulated at the presidential level, but the total effort is not yet up to what is required to keep up with population growth and protect the productivity of the land. A still greater sense of urgency and effort is called for.

Water Resources

Rapid population growth is also straining Kenya's ability to supply clean water to its people. In large urban areas, particularly in Mombasa, Kisumu, and Nairobi, the government is mostly keeping up with demand, and the goals of "water for all" in urban areas may be met by 2000. Achieving the goal, however, will cost a great deal of money, especially in Nairobi. Whereas Mombasa's piped water system is paid for indirectly with tourist investments in the large hotels, Nairobi's is not. The rapid expansion of residential and commercial construction in Nairobi creates a constant need for new sources of water. Such growth overextends the entire system. In 1984, for example, the drought reduced water levels in reservoirs to the point that severe water rationing was required toward the end of the year. New water systems installed since 1984 and planned in the future may provide adequate water supply, but these gains may be offset by leakages in Nairobi's aging pipes.

The water supply problem is much greater in rural areas. As part of the United Nations Decade of Driking Water and Sanitation, Kenya hoped to provide clean water for the entire nation by the year 2000, but it is now virtually certain that this goal will not be met in the rural areas. Even so, the Ministry of Water Development has been active. Since 1978, over 1,100 boreholes have been drilled at an average cost to donor agencies and the government of approximately $120,000 each, or a total cost of about $132 million. Believing that such costs are a major drain on the treasury, with little hope of repayment, the ministry is now encouraging a variety of alternative means to provide low-cost rural water, including roof catchments, hand-dug shallow wells, and increased tree planting to retard water runoff.[53]

Not only do water shortages loom as a potential problem, but water development can also cause new resource pressures. Rural water supplies, mostly for cattle, frequently lead to new or expanded settlements, especially in semiarid areas. The drift of population to the drylands requires special attention. Sustainable dryland development requires careful resource management, including management of soil, vegetation, tree planting, and water use. Developed with caution, the dry areas can be productive and supportive for many generations. Careless use can spell irreversible disaster.

Availability of water for agriculture will also be an increasing problem in rural areas, particularly in times of drought. The removal of trees and brush in woodlands adjacent to cropland can cause severe soil erosion, lowering soil moisture and the ability of the soil to retain water, and ultimately reducing water availability for crops. Soil erosion from croplands themselves has the same effect. Controlling deforestation and simple soil and water conservation measures can make the difference in whether or not a farmer's crops have enough water to survive drought. In addition, soil erosion in some areas is causing tremendous siltation and reducing the storage capacity of water supply reservoirs, reducing expected lives of reservoirs from 30 to as little as 15 years, for example, in the Tana Basin.

Smallholders and Natural Resources Management

The problems of declining food productivity, the impending crisis of rural energy, and potential water shortages are all interconnected. A deterioration—or

Table 8. Agricultural Output by Size of Holding

	Number (thousands)	Area ('000 ha)	Output per hectare (KShs)
Under 0.5	206.4	53.7	4,335
0.5-0.9	265.8	180.7	2,213
1.0-1.9	400.4	560.6	1,104
2.0-2.9	224.1	533.4	904
3.0-3.9	131.9	445.8	713
4.0-4.9	107.0	467.6	800
5.0-7.9	96.4	610.2	519
8.0 and over	51.5	664.4	224
TOTAL	1,483.4	3,516.4	841

Source: Central Bureau of Statistics *Integrated Rural Survey, 1974-75 (IRS I), Basic Report,* including unpublished data (Nairobi: Republic of Kenya, 1977).

improvement—in one affects all. These problems have their most adverse impact at the village-level, especially on women, who represent about 70 percent of small farmers and are also the wood gatherers and water carriers. These three problems are contributing to increasing resource degradation and have the potential to push village level resources beyond the threshold of sustainability.

With Kenya's dependence on its land resources to provide food, jobs, energy, and crops for export, current resource trends are disturbing. Anticipated shortages in food, energy, and water supplies will seriously strain Kenya's economic and political stability and will make it more vulnerable to external disruptions such as drought, regional political upheavals, or predictable increases in the cost of imported oil. Fortunately, the situation is not irreversible. Kenya has already undertaken major efforts, although additional steps are needed to assure national progress and security over the next 10 to 15 years.

Kenya is fortunate in that it has many small plot owners— women and men who farm fields of two or three hectares or smaller—located in the high and medium potential lands of the southern third of the nation. These smaller farms have significantly higher output per acre than larger farms. (See Table 8.) They produce 60 percent of the country's total production on about one-third of the arable land. And the good news is that, with the correct policy incentives and assistance, they could be much *more* productive.

A major program to increase productivity on these farms could reduce poverty at the same time, for most of Kenya's poor are rural, and these women and men include the 30 percent of the rural population who live below or close to the poverty line. They can afford few if any inputs. Many of them are farmers who have had little access to central government services and who have benefited but slightly from Kenya's past economic success.

Smallholders are more productive farmers primarily because they have access to plenty of labor, mostly women and children in the family. They are knowledgeable about local climate and soils and frugal in their use of scarce inputs. But their output could benefit greatly from improved resource management and modest inputs, and that makes them the best bet for increasing national food production in the short run—to meet rising demand while larger infrastructure projects provide for future improvements. Assistance to these farmers will have the added advantage of restoring degraded lands.[54]

The World Bank has determined that working with smallholders is a priority and has developed a program to provide inputs, mostly fertilizer and improved seed. Planners at the World Bank believe these inputs could increase output by as much as 100 percent. What is needed is a parallel program to improve management, since soil conservation will greatly enhance the effect of inputs. Better resource management means organizing rural resources such as water, soil, vegetation, woodlands, labor, and locally available capital in ways that will maximize production without degrading the resource base. Both crops and trees are included, and indeed must be worked on jointly. Activities include on-farm tree planting, terrace building, gabion (small check dams) construction, grass planting, traditional intercropping, water conservation—all of them labor-intensive strategies. And it should be accompanied by the introduction of more-efficient stoves and kilns, ovens, milling and other machinery that uses wood and agricultural residues for fuel, and by national policies that provide incentives to pursue such a strategy.

Fortunately Kenya has already had some good experiences with these approaches, and should therefore be able to adapt and disseminate the information and technologies involved. In selected villages of Machakos, an arid and semiarid region of high population density east of Nairobi, Kamba women, relying on generations-old self-help institutions known as *mwethya* groups, have worked collectively on each other's farms to construct soil and water management devices. In the village of Katheka, for instance, where gully erosion and water runoff had become severe, the *mwethya* groups gather on Wednesday and Saturday mornings, rotating from farm to farm and working sociably together to maximize their labor and share the latest local news. In the last seven or eight years, they have constructed more than 600 small check dams, 600 cutoff drains, and several kilometers of bench terraces, and they have planted many trees. During the drought of 1984–85, Katheka fared better than neighboring semiarid areas. Their experience suggests that modest government resources, for example, to line and protect well, plus good local management, can raise productivity.[55]

In other areas of Kenya, women have organized tree planting through local KANU chapters, churches, and women's organizations. In Murang'a, north of Nairobi, women's groups have devised credit schemes and cooperatives to improve the quality of cattle and milk production through pooled savings and improved production and use of fodder. In a parallel nationally supported research project, the Integrated Program for Arid Lands has devised means for the pastoralists in the arid northern areas to improve marginal grazing lands, giving them greater resilience to deal with the all-too-frequent drought.

Local participation in the organization of these efforts is clearly one of the keys to their success. Perhaps relative local autonomy is another. To multiply such successes, much more effort will have to be put into identifying the elements of success, the policy and institutional barriers, and dissemination of the strategy. The organizational and training tasks are staggering, but the payoff could be large increases in national food production. Strengthening local capabilities is fundamental to reaching the goals. This strategy could provide the hedge against hunger in the next 10–15 years and greatly increase rural employment while the longer term projects spelled out in the Five Year Plan—strengthening agricultural research and educational institutions, building feeder roads to serve the rural areas, reforestation, water development, credit schemes, and land adjudication and registration—hold hope for the future. But programs directed to improve the productivity of low-input smallholders will provide the necessary economic and ecological base on which to build them.

Population

Despite many efforts, even the best conceived schemes for increasing productivity cannot lead to a better life for Kenyans if the population keeps doubling every 18 to 20 years. Longevity—barring some calamity—is likely to increase further, to 65 years by the year 2000, and the childbearing age cohort is large. So it is entirely probable, despite all kinds of efforts, that the population will indeed double in less than 20 years. With good resources management and equity, Kenya could theoretically absorb that many without turmoil—providing that the necessary steps are taken now to assure a quick leveling off of population after that 20 years.

In 1963 the newly independent Kenya government recognized the potential problem of rapid population growth (the rate was then around 3 percent per annum) with the early appointment of an advisory commission that produced a report, *Family Planning in Kenya 1967*. Many of its recommendations were pursued, including the establishment of the National Family Planning Council (1967) and a clinically based national family planning program—the first in sub-Saharan Africa—that provided supplies and services (pills and intrauterine devices) to eligible women. The program, appropriately placed in the Ministry of Health, grew with substantial help from the World Bank, the United Nations

Fund for Population Activities (UNFPA), and AID. By 1978, family planning services were available throughout the country in 505 maternal and child health clinics; 416 were run by the central government, the rest by local agencies or churches and the Family Planning Association of Kenya.[56]

The programs have not, however, had significant effect on population growth rates. A survey in 1977–78 estimated that only 4–5 percent of married women of reproductive age were using modern methods, with another 2–3 percent using "inefficient methods." A 1984 AID survey (after the Reagan administration reversed U.S. policy on contraceptive assistance) found 17 percent to be using contraception. But most of the increase had been in traditional methods—abstinence and rhythm. And all the time the mortality rates were going down and the fertility rate up.[57]

While there has been an apparent increased endorsement of family planning goals by national leaders, there is no sense of urgency in the sole paragraph devoted to the subject in the previous (1984 to 1988) Five Year Plan, which promises to continue "informing and educating actual and potential parents" and to provide family-planning services "mainly in the rural areas."[58]

Lack of example at the top does little to stimulate demand for services, which in any case is low. There are exceptions: in Kibera, the large Nairobi high-density housing area, services cannot meet demand.[59] But in general, despite a commendable record in education and reasonable economic growth, there remain formidable cultural and economic restraints on demand—especially in agrarian policy, the organization and delivery of government services (particularly health and education), and in family law (especially marriage and divorce, inheritance and access to land). As in other countries, Kenya's experience demonstrates that family planning education and services will have only minimal effect, unless they are part of a larger development strategy that takes into account persistent values and social arrangements, and recognizes that seemingly irrelevant elements like agricultural policy, land registration, and the centralization of bureaucracy have implications for fertility rates and the demand—or lack of it—for family planning services.[60]

With respect to population policy, as in other aspects of development strategy, Kenya deserves no special opprobrium. Except for some "shallowness of commitment," the government has done what all the experts advised—its own Population Council, the World Bank, the UNFPA, AID, and the private voluntary organizations. The outcome was in some senses inevitable. The question is, what to do now? And the answer is surely more complicated and more difficult than "more and better family planning education and services."[61]

The underlying causes of high fertility—a strong and continuing desire for large families by both women and men—is based on profound contradictions. The Kenyan woman must provide basic subsistence for her family, but she is not usually the head of that household. She defers to her husband, having and raising "his" children and providing him with her labor on "his land." This "structural and status dependency of women coexists with the virtual requirement of economic self-sufficiency." In managing this "ambiguous and paradoxical" arrangement, fertility is an instrument, and a large family the "byproduct."[62] Traditional family obligations have been further reinforced by the way in which title to private lands was given after independence (i.e., to men), and by 25 years of agricultural and social policies.

Obviously the family is changing in Kenya, as more and more women work away from home, as the pressures of urban life or smaller plots for each succeeding generation of rural farmers increases economic motivation for smaller families, as more and more women find themselves single heads of households. These pressures and increased education and opportunity for women will bring modest increases in demand for family planning, but major reductions in fertility are likely to come only with fundamental changes that will be very difficult to introduce—access for women to land titles, agricultural support assistance that recognizes the role of women as 70 percent of farm labor, and assurance of security in old age.

Some changes in the availability and targeting of family planning services can also make a significant difference. Current trends toward more pluralistic approaches and the greater use of nongovernmental agencies promise more effective use of family planning services. And Frank and McNicoll argue that a strong case can be made for concentrating resources on the most receptive groups. These are first of all women who have had five or six children. A "stop-at-six" rule in Kenya would bring about an astonishing one-fourth drop in overall fertility.[63] Second, contraceptive demand to augment breastfeeding and traditional postpartum abstinence might contribute to restoring the longer birth intervals common in the 1950s and 1960s. Third, smaller, high-demand groups—adolescents and educated women, especially urban—should be assured reliable service. Last, the national leadership must do more than just preach "Not-as-I-do-but-as-I-say."

Dilemmas—for Kenya and the United States

The case of Kenya illustrates the dilemma facing many developing countries. The political leadership, government technicians, and *wananchi* (the citizenry) know the problems: rising population and less available land, declining productivity of the soil, and loss of trees, on which subsistence production is based. And all participants, for a variety of systemic reasons, have difficulty altering the existing behaviors because of reluctance to take risks or to increase vulnerability. It is easier to say what needs to be done than to marshall the people and organizations actually to do it. There are values and habits to be recast and vested interests to be considered.

For instance, one of the persistent recommendations is to decentralize government services so as better to incorporate regional and local variations, and to get feedback and better design incentives.[64] And indeed, Kenya is "way ahead of other African countries," having produced district-level development plans in all 41 districts. But the lack of trained staff at the district level renders decentralization a slow process. Central ministries remain reluctant to give up power, uncertain about the possible unraveling of national unity as well as their particular jurisdictions. Thus Nairobi continues to maintain tight control on the budget and foreign exchange, and on many aspects of pricing, marketing and distribution.

Formally, the government has recognized and made a commitment to small farmers to increase food production for domestic consumption. In reality, coffee, tea, commercial horticulture and tourism still have priority. Foreign-exchange earnings are so important that coffee and tea tend to be favored for research and extension funds, tourist hotels receive electricity and water, and concerns for protecting the sustainability of the resource base become a second priority. Even so, work is now under way to strengthen environmental legislation, to increase capacities to carry out environmental impact assessments, and to open new environmental studies programs in schools and the national universities. Pressures from the International Monetary Fund (IMF) and other international advisors to increase foreign exchange earnings are in part responsible, but the government encouragement of exports is driven also by its own desire to buy imported machinery, consumer goods, and military hardware.

The gap between rich and poor is growing and new owners of wealth, such as coffee growers with more than 200 to 300 acres, who may earn as much as $100,000 per year when prices are good, are themselves a political force to be dealt with. They are part of a small number of families of expanding wealth. The cities look prosperous, as do the high potential agricultural areas, but there is little cash in the rest of the countryside where 30 percent live below the poverty line. The poor tend to gravitate to the semiarid belt on marginal lands, where it is difficult to make a living, birth rates are high, and pressure on fragile lands relentless.

There is an honest commitment to strengthening non-governmental organizations—churches or women's associations that are often the organizational center of community projects such as school construction, water projects, basket weaving—so they can play a larger role in rural development. Some excellent examples exist, such as the Machakos women's efforts discussed earlier. But the Kenya government, like others, sometimes feels threatened by genuine local initiatives and has at times been at odds with church groups over, for example, how to manage primary elections.

KANU has been organizing actively and aggressively on the local level, developing projects and building its organizations. It exerts considerable influence on daily affairs in rural areas, and sometimes seems better organized than the government and better integrated than the churches. But critics say their activities are self-serving, that they are more interested in strengthening KANU than in rural development, and that payment of annual dues (10 shillings per person or Kshs 15,000—almost U.S.$1,000—in an area like Katheka) removes funds from rural areas for district and national activities.

There is concern, too, about the development projects under way—that the big efforts like AID's integrated rental development project in Kitui or major irrigation investments in Bura will falter when the donor agencies leave and the government is unable to pay for salaries, Landrover spare parts, and petrol. It is said that these projects are not truly integrated, but represent rather the gluing together of a health project, plus a water system, plus an energy program, etc. Whereas donor assistance can support a communications and transportation infrastructure that can make the large projects work, local government offices cannot. Some are also worried that money will be wasted on inappropriate items like a $1.5 million development information system in one district that is rarely used because the technical staff are not adequately trained to do so, that the government offers verbal support for family planning but has been unable to curb rising fertility rates, or that solutions to water supply problems are still thought of in terms of big projects. Concerns have been expressed, for example, that AID/Kenya and the World Bank and IMF advisors are still placing priority on short-term economic return at the expense of sustaining long-term productivity and are reluctant to take corrective action on a number of long-term environmental concerns.

The effort required for Kenyan leaders and donor agencies to reorient their rural development strategies to a greatly increased rural focus—its targets, techniques, institutions, and emphasis—might be daunting under even the best of circumstances. Given major problems of external debt and scarce foreign exchange, these are not the best of times or circumstances. The problem of how to train thousands of local people and officials, of how to communicate with them and reach them with supplies, seeds and services, of how to get produce to markets, of how to strengthen thousands of rural institutions—of how to *do* all that is the challenge on which Kenyans deserve backing and support.

It is not the kind of task central governments have experience in doing anywhere in Africa or, for that matter, in the world. Nor do foreign advisors from AID, the Bank, IMF, and elsewhere have much experience in organizing and training for grassroots development. Community development cannot simply be relegated to the underfunded NGO sector. Economists are only beginning to understand the kind of macro policies that impede or facilitate this kind of decentralized, small-scale development.

Notwithstanding the problems inherent in this difficult transition period, there are specific steps the United States can take to encourage local-level agriculture, forestry, energy supplies, and family planning. But helping the government to make the major necessary strategic changes—in agricultural policy, decentralization, and family law—is much harder for outsiders to do. And while further support for NGOs is indicated, it is important not to appear to be circumventing official efforts. Nor is it smart to burden NGOs with responsibilities for issues or programs they are not appropriate to handle. It would be tragic to repeat the experience of AID, which chose VADA, a national non-governmental development organization, to be the wholesaler of large sums of AID money for other NGOs. This modest, successful organization was not geared up for such a task, and internal strife over how to use the funds destroyed the organization.

Despite these caveats, the United States, especially through the AID program, can constructively encourage more effective use of natural resources in the rural areas to stimulate increased and sustained food as well as cash crop production on small farms. The work currently supported in Katheka is a model of the way in which development support can attack poverty and environmental degradation and, at the same time, stimulate production at the village level. Conservation of soils and water, planting trees on farms and in larger reforestation projects, better management of remaining forests, controlling water runoff, mobilizing rural institutions, and measures to increase the efficient burning of traditional fuels for cooking, agricultural processing, and small-scale manufacturing—all are essential if Kenya is to keep up with its population growth.

The Katheka experiments demonstrate that villagers fully understand the connections between sound resource management and sustained food production. What they need to improve production is sound local leadership and village institutions to organize the work; technology that village units can manage and maintain; and access to external assistance (technical and financial) that the village can control. In addition, Katheka illustrates that the U.S. assistance programs can successfully support the Kenyan institutions in doing this kind of development.

Cooperative research in agriculture and forestry can also be very supportive to these efforts if the work is truly focused on low-input agriculture, integrates approaches to forestry and agriculture, and involves on-farm experimentation that takes advantage of local knowledge.

On the subject of population growth, Kenya's leadership has grown sensitive to outsiders' criticism, but that should induce diplomatic persuasiveness, not timidness, on the U.S. side. The United States should support continued analysis of fertility trends and policy needs, integrating demographic analysis prominently into all resource management calculations. AID should help target the groups most likely to use contraceptives; there is still unmet demand in the urban areas. U.S. backing for a vigorous "stop-at-six" campaign—for which there is considerable support in Kenya—could be the medium for a broad education campaign. There are many ways in which the United States can provide assistance and training necessary for such programs, while still putting polite pressure on leadership to set an example.

Donor coordination continues to be problem in Kenya, as in other countries blessed with multiple contributors. AID/Kenya needs to work closely with other donors, not just to avoid duplication in research and projects, but also to assure that the macro policy advice being pressed by the multilaterals and other donors does not negate the work being tried at the micro level to help small farmers conserve soil and water, grow trees, and increase productivity.

AID in Kenya must be staffed adequately with professionals—some of whom would work at the macro level, others of whom would benefit from expertise in local-level soil and water conservation, agroforestry, traditional fuels technology, maternal and child health—or, equally necessary, provide training in these fields. Staff working at the macro and micro levels must talk to each other, and all of them should be assigned to the country, usually for four or five years. In addition, organizations such as the Peace Corps should be expanded in Kenya. Its volunteers have been effective workers, with highly encouraging activities in pilot programs in natural resources management in rural areas.

Promising methodologies such as Participatory Rural Appraisal, which integrates technical and socio-economic approaches to natural resources management, need to be expanded. Uses of successful village approaches need to be better analyzed, better understood, and more widely disseminated through training, visitations, and other educational programs. Funds for small-scale project activities also need to be allocated so that they get to village institutions where there is substantial payback in relation to funds invested.

Sustained U.S. effort in local-level natural resources management will be worth it. Kenya is a role model for much of the eastern/southern Africa region, and the U.S. stake in the success of this democratic, pluralistic model is significant.

References

1. Republic of Kenya, *Economic Survey 1987* (Nairobi: Central Bureau of Statistics, Ministry of Planning and National Development, 1987), v.

2. Leonard Berry, *East Africa Country Profile: Kenya* (Worcester, Massachusetts: Clark University, Program for International Development, 1980); M.M. Shah and G. Fischer, "Assessment of Food Production Potential: Resources, Technology and Environment—A Case Study of Kenya," working paper (Laxenburg, Austria: International Institute for Applied Systems Analysis, 1981), 14.

3. Phil O'Keefe and Paul Raskin, "Crisis and Opportunity: Fuelwood Need in Kenya," *Ambio*, Vol. XIV, No. 4–5, 1985, 214–219.

4. Republic of Kenya, *Economic Survey 1987*, 8–17.

5. Richard E. Leakey and Roger Lewin, *People of the Lake* (New York: Avon, 1983), 17–21.

6. For greater detail on natural resources, population and land use, see Clark University, *Renewable Resource Trends in East Africa* (Worcester, Massachusetts: Clark University, Program for International Development, 1984).

7. Bantu speakers include the Kikuyu, Luhya, Kamba, Meru, Ebmu, and, in an indirect way, the coastal Swahilis. Coastal Swahilis are descended from commercial peoples who represent a mixture of coastal Bantu-speakers and Omani Arabs. The Omanis settled along the coast about 1,000 years ago and intermarried with Bantu speakers who had arrived shortly before. The mixture produced the Kiswahili language and culture, which blends Arabic and African languages and cultures.

8. Nilotes (and/or Nilo-Hamites) include the Luo, Kalenjin, Turkana, Kipsigi, Nandi, Maasai, and Samburu.

9. World Bank, *Kenya: Growth and Structural Change*, A World Bank Country Study (Washington, D.C.: The World Bank, 1983), Vol. 1, 45–48.

10. World Bank, 1983, *Kenya: Growth and Structural Change*, Vol. 1, 46.

11. Republic of Kenya, *Economic Survey 1987*, 8.

12. The World Bank, *World Development Report 1989* (New York: Oxford University Press, 1989), 164, Table 1. Kenya's 1987 per capita GNP was $330, Uganda's $260, and Tanzania's $180.

13. Republic of Kenya, *Economic Survey 1987*, 10–14.

14. World Bank, 1983, *Kenya: Growth and Structural Change*, Vol. 1, 5. Agriculture is the source of two-thirds of Kenya's export—84 percent if refined petroleum is excluded.

15. Republic of Kenya, *Economic Survey 1987*, 104–105.

16. Republic of Kenya, *Economic Survey 1987*, 1.

17. Wilfred Machua, "Horticulture, Growth Continues Despite Challenges," *African Business*, March 1985, 69–71. The whole March 1986 issue is devoted to an appraisal of the Kenyan economy.

18. Wilfred Manchua, "Kenya's Tourism Sector Beckons You," *African Business*, March, 1986, 61–62, and Republic of Kenya, *Economic Survey 1987*, 156–166.

19. Robert Shaw, "Can Industry Become the Fourth Export Pillar?" *African Business*, March 1986, 51–55.

20. Republic of Kenya *Economic Survey 1987*, 139–148. For an analysis of Kenya's industrial development strategy, see World Bank, 1983, *Kenya: Growth and Structural Change*, 79–94.

21. Phil O'Keefe and Paul Raskin, "Crisis and Opportunity: Fuelwood in Kenya," *AMBIO*, Vol. XIV, No. 4–5, 1985, 220–224.

22. Don Shakow, Dan Weiner, and Phil O'Keefe, "Energy and Development: The Case of Kenya," *AMBIO*, Vol. X, No. 5, 1981, 206–210; Barbara Gunnell, "The Hunt for Oil Goes On," *African Business*, March 1986, 50.

23. Republic of Kenya, *Economic Survey 1986* (Nairobi: Central Bureau of Statistics, Ministry of Planning and National Development, 1986), 122–127.

24. Barbara Gunnell, "Hydropower Juggling Aid for Cheap Power," *African Business*, March 1986, 55–58.

25. Barbara Gunnell, "Steam Projects Still Produce," *African Business*, March 1986, 59.

26. See The World Bank, *World Development Report 1984* (New York: Oxford University Press, 1984) for an explanation of economic reasons why the poor have big families, and Odile Frank and Geoffrey McNicoll, "An Interpretation of Fertility and Population Policy in Kenya," *Population and Development Review*, Vol. 13, No. 2 (June 1987), 209–243 for an analysis of the relevant policy and cultural factors at work in Kenya.

27. Clark University, 1984, *Renewable Resource Trends in Eastern Africa*, 19; *1987 World Population Data Sheet* (Washington, D.C.: Population Reference Bureau, 1987).

28. Republic of Kenya, *Economic Survey 1986*, 21–25; The World Bank, *The World Development Report 1988* (New York: Oxford University Press, 1988), 276. The Population Reference Bureau's *1987 World Population Data Sheet* shows the figure still at 8.0, but the *World Development Report 1989* estimates the 1987 rate at 7.7.

29. The World Bank, *World Development Report 1984*, 256.

30. No country as yet calculated the implications for development of the growing AIDS epidemic, but since it hits the active young adult age group, which is both primary breadwinners and childbearing, a group in which society has made a major social investment, the prospects are grave. See Panos Institute Study, *AIDS and the Third World*, Panos Dossier 1 (London: The Panos Institute, in association with the Norwegian Red Cross, revised, 1987).

31. WRI/IIED, *World Resources Report 1988–89* (New York: Basic Books, 1989), 248, Table 15.2.

32. Frank and McNicoll, 1987, "An Interpretation of Fertility and Population Policy in Kenya," especially 221–226.

33. Clark University, 1984, *Renewable Resources in Eastern Africa*, 24–27. WRI/IIED, *World Resources 1988–89*, 266, Table 16.2.

34. World Bank, *World Development Report 1989*, 176, Table 7.

35. See Simeon H. Ominde, "Population and Resource Crisis: A Kenyan Case Study," *GeoJournal*, Vol. 5, No. 6, 1981, especially 546–548, 550, for an analysis of the effect of population pressure on resources.

36. World Bank, 1983, *Kenya: Growth and Structural Change*, Vol. 1, 5, 64.

37. World Bank, 1983, *Kenya: Growth and Structural Change*, Vol. 1, 64.

38. Ominde, 1981, "Population and Resource Crisis: A Kenyan Case Study," 546–549.

39. World Resources Institute and International Institute for Environment and Development, *World Resource 1987* (New York: Basic Books, Inc., 1987), 45.

40. World Bank, 1983, *Kenya: Growth and Structural Change*, Vol. 1, 68.

41. The World Bank, *Kenya: Growth and Structural Change*, Vol. 2, 346–349.

42. Ominde, 1981, "Population and Resource Crisis: A Kenyan Case Study," 550; Shah and Fischer, 1981 "Assessment of Food Production Potential: Resources, Technology and Environment—A Case Study of Kenya;" The World Bank, 1983, *Kenya: Growth and Structural Change* also cites soil loss as a major factor in lowered productivity.

43. Laurence A. Lewis, "Progress Report on Assessing Soil Loss in Kiambu and Murang'a Districts in Kenya" (Worcester, Massachusetts: Clark University, Program for International Development, 1983).

44. World Resources Institute and International Institute for Environment and Development, *World Resources, 1987*, 228.

45. Richard Ford, "Global Resources: Is the Future Possible?" *Environment*, Vol. 26, No. 9 (November 1984), 4–5, 40.

46. Ford, field visit to Kiambu, April 1982.

47. Shah and Fischer, 1981, "Assessment of Food Production Potential: Resources, Technology and Environment—A Case Study of Kenya," especially 8–20.

48. O'Keefe and Raskin, 1985, "Crisis and Opportunity: Fuelwood in Kenya," 220–222, and Peter Mutua Mulli, "Energy Use and the Environment in Kenya," draft paper presented at the World Resources Institute, Washington, D.C., April 28–29, 1988.

49. David W. Brokensha, Bernard W. Riley, and Alfonso Peter Castro, *Fuelwood Use in Rural Kenya: Impacts on Deforestation*, Working Paper #8 (Binghamton, New York, Institute for Development Anthropology), and O'Keefe and Raskin, 1985, "Crisis and Opportunity: Fuelwood in Kenya," 220–221.

50. Mulli, 1988, "Energy Use and the Environment in Kenya," 2.

51. O'Keefe and Raskin, 1985, "Crisis and Opportunity: Fuelwood in Kenya," 222; Brokensha, Riley, and Castro, 1983, *Fuelwood Use in Rural Kenya: Impacts on Deforestation*; P.N. Bradley, N. Chavangi, and A. Van Gelder, "Development Research and Energy Planning in Kenya," *AMBIO*, Vol. XIV, Nos. 4–5 (1985) 228–236.

52. Eric L. Hyman, "The Strategy of Production and Distribution of Improved Charcoal Stoves in Kenya," *World Development*, Vol. 15, No. 3 (1987), 375–86.

53. Onyango Omotto and James Koffi, "A DYI Water Supply is Better than None," *African Business*, March 1986, 43–44.

54. The 1983 World Bank study *Kenya: Growth and Structural Change* points out that concentration on small holdings, including further redistributions of land, would increase both employment opportunities and output. See Vol. II, 341–362.

55. For a description of this project, see Barbara P. Thomas-Slayter and Richard B. Ford, *Resources Management, Population, and Local Institutions in Katheka: Examples of the Effect of Natural Resources Management in Machakos* (Worcester, Massachusetts: Clark University, 1987).

56. Frank L. Mott and Susan H. Mott, "Kenya's Record Population Growth: A Dilemma of Development," *Population Bulletin*, Vol. 35, No. 3 (October 1980), 31–34. For a discussion of policy, see also Frank and McNicoll, 1987, "An Interpretation of Fertility and Population Policy in Kenya." The latter is an excellent analysis of the interconnection of economics, tradition, and law.

57. Frank and McNicoll, 1987, "An Interpretation of Fertility and Population Policy in Kenya," 221; World Bank, *World Development Report 1989*, 216, Table 27.

58. *Kenya Development Plan 1983*, 145, cited in Frank and McNicoll, 1987, "An Interpretation of Fertility and Population Policy in Kenya," 240.

59. Isabel Mbugua, "Seeds of Self-Sufficiency in Kibera," *People*, Vol. 13, No. 2 (1987), 17–19.

60. Frank and McNicoll, 1987, "An Interpretation of Fertility and Population Policy in Kenya," 222.

61. Frank and McNicoll, 1987, "An Interpretation of Fertility and Population Policy in Kenya," 227.

62. Frank and McNicoll, 1987, "An Interpretation of Fertility and Population Policy in Kenya," 217–228.

63. Frank and McNicoll, 1987, "An Interpretation of Fertility and Population Policy in Kenya," 235–236.

64. Goran Hyden, *No Shortcuts to Progress: African Development Management in Perspective* (Berkeley: University of California Press, 1983), and Frank and McNicoll, 1987, "An Interpretation of Fertility and Population Policy in Kenya," 225.

VI

U.S. Policy in the Crucial Decade Ahead

Janet Welsh Brown

In the 1970s, critics of the U.S. environmental movement—critics in the United States as well as in the developing world—often called environmentalism "a luxury of the rich." Most poor countries thought they would have to choose between development and conservation of resources, between jobs and the environment.

We now understand better. In less than 20 years, environmental protection has gone from being a luxury of the rich to being a requirement for the poor. Leaders of even the poorest countries—those with the most fragile lands, or the most problematical rainfall, or the most crowded urban barrios—understand full well that future development depends on the sustainability of the resource base. For their part, most environmentalists have reached a better understanding of the necessity for poor countries to develop their resources and provide a better life for their people.

In professional jargon, U.S. relations with developing countries are commonly characterized in terms of "we" and "they," "haves" and "have nots." *We* seem to have all the information, the cash, and the know-how, and *they* have all the problems. Such simplistic analysis will neither protect U.S. interests nor provide for developing-country growth. For the fact is that both the industrialized and the developing world share some ominous problems:

- In agriculture: we are converting more and more prime farmland to other uses. In common with developing countries, Americans face problems such as soil loss, water-logging and salinization, rising costs of inputs, and pollution from runoff. In a world with enough food to feed everyone, more people go to bed hungry and malnourished than ever before.
- In the woodlands: we are parties to rapid deforestation, reduction of fuel and lumber supplies, loss of soil fertility, destruction of habitat. Of the

old-growth forests that flourished in the Pacific Northwest, only 13 percent remain today. By 1980, between 25 and 40 percent of all original tropical forests had been lost, with untold damage to fragile ecosystems and loss of species, the richest concentration of which is found in tropical forests.

- In energy: supplies of both nonrenewable and some renewable fuels are diminishing while the environmental and health costs of their production and use rise. At the same time, we face a quintupling of world energy demand, mostly to meet the needs of developing countries, and unbearable pollution of the atmosphere.
- In population: the earth will need to feed, educate, and support another billion people before the end of the century, putting additional intense pressure on both urban and rural resources. Even for countries that have developed policies to solve their *population* problems, there is still a *resource* problem of how to care for, educate, and employ people already born.

In the 1990s, industrialized and developing countries will have to face these problems together. On one earth, there is an inextricable connection between us and them, between the haves and the have-nots, between the problems of poverty and the pressures on the environment. The times call for burden-sharing with the developing countries. The answers lie in the search for sustainable development, which *Our Common Future*, the report of the World Commission on Environment and Development, defines as the integration of environmental policies and development strategies so as to "meet the needs and aspirations of the present without compromising the ability to meet those of the future."[1]

Our Common Future outlines the strategies required—in agriculture, energy, population, industry, and urban development—to achieve sustainable development in both the industrialized and developing world. Current public opinion polls of American citizens demonstrate consistently high levels of concern over global warming and loss of tropical forests and biological diversity, and an explicit willingness to pay what it costs to stem these ominous trends. Translating this concern and good will into action requires coming to new understandings between the industrialized and developing countries and striking a global bargain between North and South for environmental protection and economic progress. Although the industrialized countries are responsible for most of the global consumption and pollution, the developing countries are rapidly increasing their share. A concerted attack on the problems will thus require close coordination with the developing countries and a sharply increased flow to the South of new financing and new technology for environmental conservation and sustainable development.[2]

Elevating Developing Nations in U.S. Foreign Policy

If poverty and environmental degradation in developing countries are to receive the Washington policy attention they deserve, the profile of African, Asian, and Latin countries must be raised and sharpened. In 1988, spurred by the expectation of a new President in the White House in 1989, development policy analysts advanced a number of proposals that would elevate the importance of Third World countries in the making of foreign policy. One idea was for the Presidential appointment of a prestigious commission to evaluate all U.S. ties with developing countries—trade, debt, development, security, and military ties—and recommend policy directions to the President.[3]

Such a commission might well serve both a policy and public education function. Its work and pronouncements, effectively staged, could heighten public awareness of the importance of the relationships between developing countries and the United States. But Washington bookshelves are already laden with insightful volumes of good recommendations, and institutional changes will also be required if developing countries are to get systematic high-level consideration within the U.S. government. National security has its own Council, as does the Economic Advisers of the President. Third World concerns need a cabinet-level coordinating council, chaired by a Presidential appointee, that would assure adherence to policy priorities and provide government-wide coordination. Such a commission would regularly bring together the people responsible for policy in the trade agencies, the treasury, the Agency for International Development (AID), state and military affairs, the Environmental Protection Agency, drug enforcement, and the Department of Agriculture to provide clear policy direction focused on debt and environmental degradation. This "International Cooperation Council" could also coordinate U.S. trade, development cooperation, security policy, and debt management in Asia, Africa, and Latin America. Guided by the objectives of sustainable development, such organized, high-level attention to developing countries would be a constant reminder that ecologically and economically sustained growth in these nations is in the U.S. interest.[4]

The World Economic Context—Trade and Debt in Developing Countries

Despite remarkable growth in the economic power and influence of some developing nations in recent decades, the factors that shape the world economy are still beyond the control of the vast majority of developing countries so seriously affected by them. World finance, debt, and growth are still controlled by the 10 most powerful industrialized countries. The value of the dollar still determines the cost of key imports, including oil. A one-point increase in the U.S. interest rate still adds billions to the debt-service costs that debtor nations must pay each year, often more than they receive in development assistance. While world trade actually increased by 4 percent in 1986 (and rose again in

1987 and 1988 by 6 percent and 9 percent), prices of commodities other than oil dropped sharply and then rose again over this short period. Historically since the 1950s, non-oil commodity prices have declined relative to the cost of the manufactured goods developing countries typically import. Moreover, the world price of individual commodities may fluctuate wildly from year to year. While diversified and resilient economies can absorb these shocks, countries dependent on the export of one or two commodities and hamstrung by their debt-servicing agreements will find it ever harder to earn foreign exchange.[5] Trade barriers intensify the problem.

Indeed, capital is now flowing from the poor to the rich countries, rather than the other way around. Even Africa, the poorest continent, has a net flow of cash to the North. In 1988, total developing-country principal and interest payments exceeded new lending and development assistance by an astounding $27 billion. This imbalance was compounded by capital flight from developing to industrialized countries and by the failure of private investment and commercial bank lending to resume after the debt crisis of 1982. Thus, while industrial powers debate the nature and size of development assistance, there is a troubling awareness in developing-country capitals that the trade, debt, and financial decisions made by these same powers far outweigh the significance of foreign assistance in determining their development progress.

This awareness is reflected in many voices. The Bangladeshi Ambassador to the United States jokes wryly that his country would happily give up U.S. development assistance if the United States would eliminate its barriers against jute imports. At a 1987 meeting of nongovernmental representatives from developing and industrialized countries—all of them committed to improving the conditions of poor people in developing countries—the message from the developing world was that nongovernmental organizations (NGOs) in industrialized countries can most constructively promote development by encouraging a more supportive policy environment in their own countries, that macro policies governing the terms of trade have a bigger impact, for good or bad, on development than does international development assistance.[6]

The world trade and debt crises are more closely connected to the problem of sustainable development and deteriorating environment than is at first apparent because these crises appear to be hastening the depletion of resources on which long-term growth depends. On the one hand, proposed new capital-intensive development projects will get much more careful scrutiny, and—because of the crises—some will probably not be undertaken, which may ease the pressure on some natural resources. Such misguided programs as the Indonesian transmigration scheme have already been scaled back because of the debt crisis, and environmentally-damaging budgetary subsidies have been cut in some countries. But at the same time, developing-country colleagues warn that financial stringency is slowly undermining hard-fought recent gains in resource conservation and environmental protection.[7]

While available information is still largely anecdotal, the following points are frequently made:[8]

- Conservation usually takes a back seat in times of economic stress. As economic conditions have worsened in developing countries, and as debt pressures mount, there has been a tendency to ignore environmental planning and conservation measures in both industrial and rural development projects.
- The austerity measures that have been required under International Monetary Fund (IMF) adjustment programs and World Bank structural adjustment agreements include government cutbacks in investments and operating expenditures. These are likely to fall disproportionately on weak, fledgling environmental and conservation agencies and programs. This is undermining the earlier efforts that have been made to bring ecological considerations into development planning and projects. In many countries the only money available for new conservation areas comes from international donors.
- Austerity measures and general recessionary conditions also have led to sharp declines in per capita incomes and increases in unemployment. This puts more pressure on the natural resource base as more people fall back on subsistence farming and rely on scarce forest and water resources.
- Pressures to expand primary commodity exports can lead to increased deforestation and to expansion of cash cropping on available good lands. It is extremely difficult for a Central American government or the Philippines to reduce cattle or cotton or log exports in the face of enormous debt pressure. In the process, the rural poor are further marginalized and forced on to poorer, erosion-prone lands.
- Tariff rates that rise with each successive stage of processing discourage processing by countries that supply raw materials and greatly limit the earnings that could be made there on commodity exports. For instance, U.S. tariffs on fabric are higher than those on yarn, which are in turn higher than those on raw cotton. Such tariffs require higher volumes of commodity exports to make up the difference, which may in turn flood the world commodity markets and lower world prices, forcing countries to put still more strain on an already pressured resource base and accelerating a downward spiral of poverty and environmental degradation.
- In countries that must postpone dealing with air and water pollution problems, which have now reached crisis proportions in all the larger cities of the developing world, future public health and clean-up costs will be staggering, as we have discovered in the United States.

In sum, the resource base, already battered, is being required to pay for debt and trade imbalance in ways that won't achieve financial, environmental, or development goals. To assume that this situation can continue is foolishly shortsighted and promises greater impoverishment of future generations. A conscious attack launched through the trade, debt, and monetary policies of the United States and other industrialized countries must be part of the U.S. strategy of recognizing the importance of developing countries.

To be of long-term value, U.S. approaches to these trade and debt crises must meet four criteria: they must be financially sound, they must protect the economically weak, they must not destroy the resource base, and they must contribute to sustainable growth in the developing countries. Although detailed recommendations on trade and debt are beyond the scope of this book, some recommendations designed to meet these criteria should be mentioned:

- All international lending—for projects, policy, and restructuring—should meet exacting standards of sustainability. The World Bank, under President Barber Conable's direction, has recommitted itself to firm environmental standards to govern its lending. The United States, prompted by its own environmental NGOs, has been a major supporter of these efforts, and should continue to monitor and strengthen the Bank's processes. In concert with other donor members, the United States must press for similar changes in the regional banks.
- Commercial banks must also clearly understand that environmentally *un*sustainable projects are *financially* risky. Government-sponsored guarantee and insurance programs, such as the Overseas Private Investment Corporation, should make awards only after convincing evidence that the activities involved contribute to sustainable development is presented. It should be made clear that federal guarantees do not cover loans made for environmentally unsound projects.
- Along with nutrition, health and education budgets, certain natural resources programs (e.g., forest and watershed management, protection of coastal fisheries, and soil conservation) should be exempt from national budget cuts demanded by the multilaterals in the name of structural adjustment.
- International agricultural surpluses exported under Public Law 480 and similar commodity programs should never, except in such emergencies as famine, be distributed in ways that undermine developing-country production of food crops. Supplies should be used in food-for-work and many other food aid programs that offer incentives and financial resources to conserve fragile resources, replant deforested areas, improve the productivity of small farms, and encourage sustainable agriculture.
- As for trade, developing countries should not be forced to exploit natural resources more heavily to increase exports. Given the desperate employment needs of these countries, their labor-intensive exports should be better received in the United States and other industrialized countries. If

developing countries are not permitted to export labor services in the form of value added to commodity exports or other goods, they are likely to export them as migrants, a phenomenon that has long dogged U.S.-Mexican relations.

Recent negotiations within the General Agreement on Tariffs and Trade (GATT) have produced proposals to reduce the subsidies behind many agricultural exports of the European Economic Community and North America. These ample subsidies give industrial farmers a distinct advantage. They influence demand and destabilize prices of commodities in world trade, and they reduce incentives to grow food and create dependency in some developing countries. It is widely recognized that they should be discontinued but doing so is politically difficult since the phase-out would impose a hardship on European farmers and a political and economic burden on their governments. And the proposed decade-long phase-out is too stretched out to help developing countries much anyway. Further difficult changes still need to be negotiated for the international food markets to operate in an economically rational way that does not handicap developing-country exporters and that promotes food security for all countries.

Finally, the United States should explore the several creative proposals that have been floated by developing-country leaders, environmental NGOs, and progressive business and banking officials to swap debt for other development and environmental ends.[9] Some proponents have called for the creation of a global fund to purchase debt and convert it to development purposes, a fund that developing countries would help manage. A study by the World Resources Institute, commissioned by the United Nations Development Programme, and supported by the aid agencies of the United States, Canada, and others explores the feasibility of various options for substantially increasing international conservation financing, including using current channels more intensively. Foremost among such fortification strategies is fully integrating environmental considerations into development plans, while other avenues involve fostering public/private partnerships wherever sound conservation financing can have a commercial payoff. Nature tourism is a case in point.

Debt-for-nature swaps, if tailored to local needs, have proven a promising source for conservation financing. In Ecuador, for example, a debt-for-nature swap was arranged by the leading conservation group, *Fundacion Natura*. It was essentially an external-to-internal debt conversion, with the government bonds assigned to one private intermediary organization exclusively for the benefit of protected areas and environmental education. In 1987, *Fundacion Natura* obtained an agreement from the government's Monetary Board that would allow up to $10 million in debt to be exchanged at 100 percent face value for monetary stabilization bonds in local currency. The interest on the bonds pays for conservation projects while the principal will become the endowment of *Fundacion Natura.*

The first part of the swap was completed in March 1988, when a donation of some $350,000 from World Wildlife Fund of the United States bought $12 million in commercial debt. At 33 percent net interest, the first year's income alone was 82.8 million *sucres*, or the equivalent of Ecuador's entire budget for national parks. This comparison suggests the relative impact of additional funds from the debt-for-nature swaps. In April 1989, World Wildlife Fund of the United States and the Nature Conservancy purchased the remaining $9 million in debt for this swap. Paying some 12 cents on the dollar, World Wildlife Fund used Morgan Guaranty Trust and Bankers Trust to acquire $5.4 million in debt, while the Nature Conservancy purchased $3.6 million through American Express Bank. As part of the Nature Conservancy's purchase, $400,000 in debt was bought by the Missouri Botanical Garden to be used for a national biological research program carried out through local universities. In just over one year, the price of Ecuadoran debt had fallen from 35 cents to 12 cents, and *Fundacion Natura* calculates that the multiplier effect of the exchange of debt into bonds is 8.33 times the value of each dollar donated.

Part of the income from this debt swap will be spent on developing management plans for national parks in the Amazon region, the Andean highlands, and along the Pacific coast. A much-needed plan for managing and patrolling the Galapagos Islands' off-shore marine areas will be devised, and land will be purchased for small reserves elsewhere. Not only will the biological diversity of Ecuador benefit from these activities, but indigenous groups in protected areas will be able to maintain their traditional way of life. Scientific research, training of park personnel, scientific research, and environmental education programs also come under the plans approved for the swap. *Fundacion Natura* will disperse the funds of those carrying out the programs—the Charles Darwin Foundation, universities, and some smaller non-governmental organizations.[10]

As for the further potential for debt-for-nature swaps, the World Resources Institute study notes the recent willingness of bilateral aid agencies to swap some of their debt for local financing of grassroots resource management programs. The amounts involved will not resolve the debt crisis at large, but may substantially increase the on-the-ground availability of conservation financing. For the poorest nations, the study endorses a proposal that one third of the debt be converted into domestic currency bonds, with the income used to finance high-priority programs in natural resource maintenance and human resource development. The study also advocates reforming natural resource management policies as an integral part of a broad-based debt-restructuring plan for any country. Judicious stewardship of the country's natural resources is a pre-condition for a successful development strategy and should be part of the lending policies of the multilateral development banks and IMF.

Beyond debt-related initiatives, the study outlines three other promising ways to increase conservation financing in the developing world: (1) an International Financial Facility (or regional facilities) to identify and foster promising resource conservation programs, in coordination with governments, NGOs, and aid agencies, and to help arrange their financing; (2) a Pilot Investment Program for Sustainable Resource Use ("Ecovest") based on public-private sector cooperation that creates the right incentives to further sound commercial natural resource management ventures; and (3) a Global Environment Trust Fund financed by levies on "greenhouse gases."[11]

Similar concepts have been worked into debt for development schemes, and some have been proposed to swap debt for tenure. The Philippines might finance land reform, for instance, by converting official and private debt (with official guarantees) to bonds issued by a Philippine authority, which would redeem the foreign debt for pesos and use the pesos to purchase agricultural estates. The large holdings would be broken up and parceled out to small farmers, who would pay in long-term installments. The Philippine agency would service the debt out of these installment payments, and the program would be supported by development assistance to smallholders.[12]

Another proposal is for the creation of an international revolving fund to finance land redistribution. To compensate landowners, countries redistributing large private holdings could borrow (in local currency only) in installments for domestic reinvestment in sustainable development projects.

Even in the early exploration and promotion of these concepts, their advocates must move with the fullest participation of developing countries, lest the specter of U.S. corporations, banks and private voluntary organizations acquiring large pieces of developing-country real estate provoke condemnation of the whole idea as some new form of colonialism. The key national and international agencies that have a potential interest in these swaps—the World Bank, IMF, AID, the Japanese government—have been slow to back the concept. Imagination and leadership on the debt issue is coming instead from some developing-country finance ministers and from the U.S. private sector—from NGOs, banks, and investment houses.

Advocates of these ideas should also recognize that debt/environmental swaps might accomplish a great deal on the environmental side or in the distribution of land and still make only the smallest dent in a developing country's debt. Only if accompanied by other debt-relief measures will such swaps stanch the net resource flow out of developing countries and help development and economic growth resume.

What is called for is no less than a "global bargain" between the North and South that recognizes the mutual environmental and economic advantages of conserving tropical resources and forms a partnership to do so.[13] It will be a bargain in which industrialized countries, in payment for their own pollution of the global atmosphere, relieve the debt and trade pressures that drive poor countries to destroy their resource base. North and South would arrange large-scale forgiveness of publicly held Third World debt in return for a country's investment in universally valued resources within their national control, such as protection of habitats and rare species, or investment in energy sources that do not contribute to atmospheric deterioration. The arrangements will require both environmental diplomacy and international leadership with a new vision.

Resource Management's Contribution to Meeting Debt and Trade Problems

While analyzing the negative impacts that crippling debt and unfavorable trade barriers may have on developing-country resource exploitation, consider also that productivity increases from careful management of the natural resources sector—which looms very large in the economies of most developing countries, especially the poorer ones—can provide part of the answer to the debt and trade crises. More effective use of locally available resources can simultaneously reduce the need for foreign investment, save and earn foreign funds, expand domestic production, and reduce resource deterioration. For instance, increased agricultural productivity can translate into big foreign-exchange savings for countries such as Mexico and Egypt, which have large regular food-import bills.

About 15 percent of all debtor-country imports are for food. In Egypt, as indicated in Chapter IV, the figure is higher. Improvements in domestic agricultural productivity are needed to meet the needs of expanding populations, and, as the examples of India and China make clear, they can markedly improve trade balances. Even where net food exports or food self-sufficiency are not a realistic possibility, reductions in food imports are. Indeed, in such countries as Kenya, the possibility of future economic growth rests squarely on the expectation that women and men farming small plots will increase productivity through soil and water conservation measures.

A second example of making better use of available resources is found in irrigated agriculture. The United Nations Food and Agriculture Organization (FAO) anticipates investments of $100 billion over the rest of the century to expand irrigated areas, but if current irrigated areas attained their production potential through better management, only limited expansion would be needed.[14]

Another 15 percent of developing countries' imports consists of fuel. More than 90 percent of developing countries' external financing for energy has gone to hydroelectric and other conventional power projects. Yet, all available studies indicate that the potential for sharp improvements in energy efficiency in developing countries—from Brazil to Kenya—is enormous and represents the least-cost approach to balancing energy supply and demand. Also, in many countries, biomass energy systems hold out considerable promise in reducing oil imports.[15] If international donors focused on an energy-development strategy that makes better use of traditional fuels, substantial positive impacts could be expected on energy supply and the global environment. At the same time, such a reorientation would contribute significantly to the quality of life of the rural poor, especially of the women and children responsible for collecting fuel.

Surprisingly, developing-country imports of forest products exceed $10 billion annually and are increasing steadily. Many countries, including Mexico and Nigeria, that should be able to meet their own needs are instead major importers. In other countries, industrial forestry has been so neglected that exports are declining. Improved management of existing forests, reforestation, and the development, where appropriate, of timber farms can boost exports in some cases and reduce or avoid future import costs in many others. The Philippines is a case in point.

U.S. Cooperation in Development

For the 1990s, the U.S. Congress needs to overhaul the Foreign Assistance Act, the main legislation governing U.S. relations with developing countries. The act determines the policy and authorizes the budget for all military, political, and development assistance, whether disbursed by AID, the Agriculture Department, or the multinational assistance agencies. The act needs fundamental revisions that will make it a *sustainable development* act. As in 1973, "new directions" are called for, even by the act's most faithful supporters, the religious and development groups that regularly lobby for development assistance to alleviate poverty.

The current law is some 500 pages long. Its detailed prescriptions, specific earmarks, and multiple reporting requirements are sometimes mutually contradictory. They reflect, if not cause, that process has become more important than results. The goal of helping developing countries meet "basic human needs"—the goal defined in the last major rewrite of the legislation in 1973—has badly eroded. Two programs in particular—food assistance and contributions to multilateral organizations—have declined in real dollars since 1977. During the Reagan years, in particular, the proportion of assistance provided for military purposes increased. Earlier, military assistance took 25 percent to 30 percent of the budget, but the figure increased to over 40 percent in the mid-1980s. The portion of politically determined "Economic Support Funds" (ESF) also increased, while the share going to development programs decreased from about 50 percent in the late 1970s to less than 40 percent in 1989. (See Figure 1.) Decisions about which countries get how much development assistance are increasingly made on political grounds rather than on need. In fiscal year 1989, 72 percent of the $15.1 billion budget went to seven countries. Israel and Egypt headed the list, with Pakistan, Turkey, Philippines, El Salvador, and Greece following on. (See Figure 2.)[16] The philosophy of meeting basic needs has been

Figure 1.   U.S. Foreign Aid, 1946-89, By Major Program

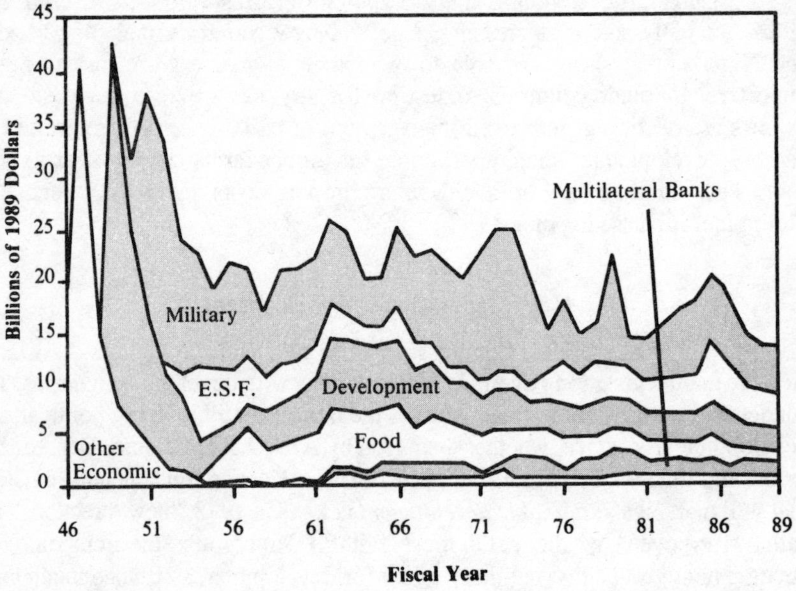

Note: The development category includes U.S. voluntary contributions to international development organizations and programs. Data shown indicates general trends, plotted points do not represent exact amounts.

Source: "Report of the Task Force on Foreign Assistance to the Committee on Foreign Affairs," U.S. House of Representatives (Government Printing Office, Wash., D.C., Feb. 1989): 9

overshadowed by a new goal articulated by AID leadership: "broad-based economic growth, the engine of which is private enterprise."[17]

Congress should scrap the obsolescent and cumbersome Foreign Assistance Act of 1961, and enact a new law, the International Development Cooperation Act. In the process, it should move the Military Assistance Program to the Defense Department budget, where its considerable sums providing training and weapons will have to compete on their merits—by defense criteria. The new act should also shift the administration of the euphemistically called Economic Support Funds, given to beleaguered developing-country allies to serve short-term political interests, to the State Department. The policies governing the

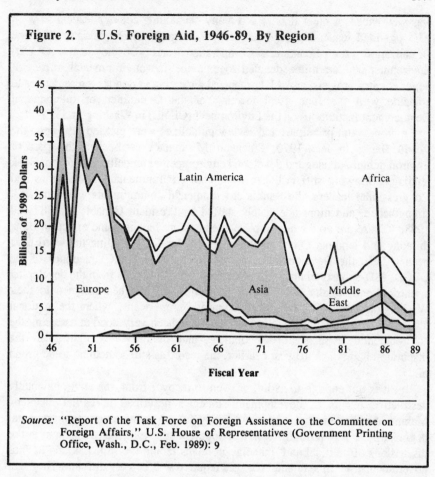

Figure 2.   U.S. Foreign Aid, 1946-89, By Region

Source: "Report of the Task Force on Foreign Assistance to the Committee on Foreign Affairs," U.S. House of Representatives (Government Printing Office, Wash., D.C., Feb. 1989): 9

distribution of these funds would still be coordinated by the President's new International Cooperation Council, but the bilateral program, in the past run by AID, could concentrate on helping countries achieve sustainable development by fighting poverty and environmental degradation.[18]

The United States—through both its bilateral programs and its dominant membership in the multilateral banks and the United Nations development assistance agencies—has historically been a world leader in the struggle against poverty. It has also led the way in its insistence on environmental impact assessments for all its development projects. Enforcement of the environmental concerns, written into the act beginning in 1975 at the urging of U.S. environmental organizations, has been somewhat uneven from one administration to another, indeed from one AID regional bureau to another within the same administration. Nonetheless, in the beginning the United States was well ahead of other donors and many developing-country leaders as well. AID provided leadership for both groups. It was at AID's initiative that the Organization for Economic Co-operation and Development (OECD) Environmental Committee decided to examine the environmental impact of donor country projects, and AID organized a meeting of donor representatives to coincide with the June 1986 meeting of the Committee of International Development Institutions on the Environment (CIDIE) in Washington.[19]

Environmental principles and review guidelines were pressed also upon the World Bank. In late 1970, President McNamara established the post of Environmental Advisor and developed environmental guidelines to govern Bank lending. Following stiff criticism from U.S. environmental organizations and Congressional leaders, the Bank's environmental commitments were renewed, strengthened, and more adequately staffed by President Conable in 1987 and 1988.[20] These are now being implemented and are having some effect on Bank thinking and lending. Other institutional vehicles for spreading the word have been CIDIE, the Development Advisory Committee (DAC) meetings of the OECD, AID-sponsored meetings of environmental officials from the developing countries, and regular meetings of environmental attachés assigned to their Washington embassies by donor countries. Americans, when the national leadership is strong, and even in between, have been very good at assessing the environmental impacts of development, and though one might wish the inspiration had struck 10 years earlier, the record is still something to be proud of.

But it is not enough to avoid, or even to recover from, the environmentally destructive results of development strategies described in earlier chapters. Making headway against ingrained poverty and reversing severe environmental degradation will require different development strategies. As is apparent in the discussions of political and financial problems facing the Mubarak and Salinas governments, the fundamental changes required will be very difficult. They will require a new vision of world partnership inspired by the need to take care of our common future, a new concept of burden-sharing to sustain this earth, its people, and its environment. Tinkering with outmoded assumptions, institutions, and relationships will not be enough to meet the problems of the crucial decade of the 1990s and beyond. Nothing less than *sustainable* national development, development on which future generations can continue to depend, must be the goal on all continents.

Sustainable Development

The term "sustainable development" has been used by different people to mean different things. AID officials tend to use it to identify a project that can be sustained financially after foreign assistance has been terminated. Environmentalists use it in reference to ecosystems' carrying capacity or the management and use of resources in ways that don't deplete "nature's capital." By sustainable development in developing countries, we mean national development strategies that are *environmentally sustainable, economically and financially sustainable, and institutionally sustainable*. No development strategy that draws more heavily on the natural resource base to support one generation at the expense of future generations is sustainable. Agricultural or energy programs cannot be considered sustainable if they use up nature's capital, denude the hillsides, deplete the soil, destroy spawning grounds and fisheries, or otherwise deny the future productive capacity of the biosphere.

Similarly, programs that cannot be funded for the time necessary to bring self-sustaining results or that depend on long-term foreign financing are not likely to be financially sustainable. Economic policies that distort the market or create incentives for destructive practices are not sustainable. Food prices that drive farmers from production, trade barriers that too long protect inefficient manufacturers, technologies heavily dependent on uncontrollable world oil prices—these and other policies and practices cannot be sustained economically. Nor will a national development strategy be institutionally sustainable (except, perhaps, at the cost of politically unacceptable dependence on outside assistance) without well-trained people, analytical capacity, and strong institutions for planning and delivering services.

The notion of sustainability thus links the environmental, economic, and institutional aspects of a country's development operations, though not in strictly parallel ways. A development strategy that is not sustainable in an environmental sense is not economically sustainable either. And a strategy that appears financially and economically sustainable may not necessarily be environmentally sustainable over the generations. To be both environmentally and economically sustainable, a strategy must be built on sound analysis, rely on appropriate institutions for planning and delivering services, and carried out at all levels by adequately trained individuals. To make the best use of limited natural and human resources, national policies must fit environmentally and economically suitable practices together.

The concept of sustainable development is not a static one. It implies limits, but they are not absolute, as *Our Common Future* points out. Indeed, the productive potential of the resource base is relative to the size and growth of the population, the state of technology, and the degrees of social organization brought to bear. Managing natural resources (the air and water and land, as well as the oil and minerals under it) and planning for population increases, selecting and developing the right technologies, and marshalling social skills and shaping institutions—together, these are the factors that lead to sustainable development.[21] *It is clearly more than environmental assessments and a bunch of "environmental projects." Sustainable development is an approach to development that takes the resource base seriously as the foundation of all future growth.*

Improvement in the lot of people in Africa, Asia, and Latin America, particularly those at the bottom of the social and economic scale, is the most practical way to meet the two great, interconnected challenges of our time—the challenges of world poverty and global environmental degradation. It provides the economic and ecological foundation on which sustainable national, and indeed international, development can proceed.

The U.S. development cooperation program in the next decade will not command the popular support it needs in the United States if it does not seek the best returns on its limited development dollars. Fortunately, a consensus is emerging among those concerned with sustainable development on the kinds of activities that will provide such returns.

First and foremost, capacity-building to enable countries to better manage their natural resources is essential. In many countries, this means strengthening environmental ministries and agencies through improvements in their monitoring, analytical, and research capabilities, and enhancing their ability to interact effectively with the planning, finance, and agriculture ministries that have traditionally had more power and prestige. Alternatively, institutional capacity-building can entail integrating environmental and demographic considerations into the work of planning and other ministries. Regional and local institutions responsible for implementation need strengthening as well, as do key private institutions.

Training at all levels is of the highest priority—from economists who shape macro policies to community participants who must keep agricultural records or account for development funds, from truck drivers and repair persons to computer programmers and business managers. AID evaluation files bulge with evidence that "micro-managing" of development projects by passels of foreign consultants is not likely to engender a sense of local "ownership" of the project nor to ensure continuity after foreign funds have expired. A better investment of U.S. tax dollars lies in helping countries to help themselves.

Institutional development, education, and training are areas in which the United States has some comparative advantage and where the investment dollar, by leaving skills behind after the project is completed, goes a long way. Indeed, as capacity-building proceeds, AID should expect to a much greater degree than in the past to fund local costs rather than foreign-exchange costs, paying for the greater use of qualified local and other specialists from developing countries as trainers, consultants, and managers of projects. In these respects, the United States might also help the World Bank to change some of its practices.

Second, the role of policy analysis must be emphasized. Among the key lessons of the 1980s is the importance for development of certain kinds of macroeconomic policies—currency valuation, incentive systems, pricing and marketing mechanisms, to name just a few. Obviously, when government price controls make food prices too low so as to favor city dwellers, farmers become discouraged and production suffers. Artificially high currency valuations encourage proliferation of imports and dependence on foreign technology. In environmental matters as well, some national policies undercut the possibilities for sustainable development. For example, subsidies on pesticides can promote excessive use, thereby threatening human health, polluting water resources, and hastening the growth of pesticide-resistant species. Investment incentives, tax and credit subsidies, farm pricing policies, and logging concessions in public forests often intensify forest exploitation or encourage uneconomic conversion of forestlands to other uses.[22]

Sustainable development requires more than AID's much touted "policy dialogue," a term that masks the promotion of a set of glib, highly selective macro-policy prescriptions—getting the prices right, eliminating all subsidies, and privatizing state-owned enterprises. Sweepingly applied to highly varied developing-country economies with vastly different resources, institutions, and capabilities, this kind of oversimplified AID prescription can only lead to further development failure. Much more careful and comprehensive analyses of policy impacts are called for, country by country.

Changing macroeconomic policies often involves painful adjustments and temporary dislocations that hurt the poor the most. To ease these burdens and encourage developing countries to stay the course on policy reform, the United States and other well-to-do countries must collaborate by training developing-country officials to improve their own on-going macro-analyses. Countries will also require transition funds to tide them over while they make painful adjustments to new policies.

In this reform, as in other measures, the United States must move in consort with other donor nations and agencies, for in most countries"Egypt is one exception"the level of U.S. development assistance is not high enough by itself to leverage major macro-policy changes. The need for better consultation is a common refrain. Particularly important is U.S. consultation and leadership in the International Monetary Fund and World Bank to assure that policy reform efforts support the concept of sustainable development.

And, third, in many countries a greater reliance on non-governmental mechanisms is needed. Many an experienced development-assistance professional in the foreign aid business, and indeed developing-country officials themselves, have expressed frustration and disillusionment with the notion that all development must be engineered and controlled by centralized ministries. National development, of course, remains the responsibility of national governments. Without appropriate national policies and allocation of development funds, sustainable development cannot take place. But the recent encouraging examples of developing-country NGO and private business contributions to development—sometimes in countries heretofore rigidly committed to centralized social philosophy—should be built upon in the coming decade. The United States and other donor countries need to explore imaginatively with developing-country planners the ways in which indigenous non-governmental entities—local community organizations, women's societies, and private entrepreneurs—can contribute to sustainable development.

More specifically, how would a sustainable development strategy work in agriculture and forestry, energy, and population and how could the United States best help? The approaches and proposals put forth below should be incorporated in a new International Development Cooperation Act.

Agriculture and Forestry

Until recently, the "modern" agricultural sector was seen in many countries as the answer to both increased food production and the need for export-earning crops. As a result, the rural policies and programs of developing-country governments overwhelmingly favored better-off farmers working on well-endowed lands that were amenable to big increases in productivity when high-yield varieties and high inputs of fertilizers, insecticides, and mechanization became available. In most countries, this sector received the lion's share of national and international research attention, infrastructure buildup, credit, and subsidies, as well as the greatest bilateral and multilateral assistance from donor institutions. The result was the Green Revolution with its rewarding increases in food production in many countries. AID agricultural assistance continues to favor this sector, but there is wide awareness in developing countries and international agencies that agricultural assistance now needs to focus on the rural poor, who did not benefit from earlier strategies and who may even be worse off than before.

The rural poor are a heterogeneous group, but they share certain characteristics: limited assets, environmental vulnerability, important economic roles for women, and lack of access to services and land. A combination of population pressure, insecure title to land, and lack of credit and technical assistance forces poor farmers and herders onto more and more fragile lands.

Most of sub-Saharan Africa and remote areas of Asia and Latin America fall into this "low-resource" category. Here, per capita production has been declining, and hunger is a critical problem. Furthermore, the consequences in resource degradation are severe—desertification (in arid Africa) and deforestation and soil erosion (in moist, mountainous Central America, for example). Major policy changes—indeed, a new development strategy—will be required to assure food and livelihood for the rural poor and to restore and protect the water, land, and forests on which their survival depends.

In some respects, raising productivity of smallholders and alleviating rural poverty will be harder to achieve than the gains of the Green Revolution were. The main actors will have to be the affected groups—the hundreds of millions of women and men who farm the land, NGOs capable of organizing community activity, and local and regional governments. The strategies required are information- and management-intensive, and will require organization and implementation by people who really know the local agricultural and social system. This approach requires politically difficult decisions, and it will be undertaken in a world economy that is unlikely to grow as fast as it did in the 1960s and 1970s. Fortunately, we now have evidence from societies as different as Kenya and Costa Rica that significant increases in productivity can be made on very small farms, and farmers can draw on experiences like those in Kenya's Katheka District that demonstrate both the technology and organizational technologies required.

In the crucial decade of the 1990s, the United States should target its agriculture and forestry assistance to poor people living on marginal lands because it is there that terrible erosion of the resource base and harrowing poverty come together. Agriculture, forestry, and water development must be tackled *together* in a long-term commitment, a second Green Revolution, to increase the productivity and welfare of subsistence or marginal farmers. All development projects require careful environmental assessment if they are to be sustainable over time, but for farmers who are "resource poor"—the men and women who rely on uncertain rainfall in highlands, drylands, and forests that are hard to farm—restoration of the resource base is essential to increasing productivity and alleviating poverty.

It is clearly in the U.S. interest to provide substantial help in this process. Deforestation and desertification contribute increasingly—as much as 20 percent—to the greenhouse warming effect and to the reduction of biological diversity. In the tropics, forests are being cut at roughly 10 times the rate at which they are being replaced. In Africa, the figure is 29 to 1.[23] The resulting soil and water loss is devastating to productivity, and damage is greatest at the margin, where people are the poorest.

Concern for poor people and for the global environment is widespread in the United States. This popular support is the foundation on which to build a revitalized program of international cooperation that can command long-term public support for the necessary budget outlays in the U.S. Congress.

Promoting sustainable agriculture and food security by strengthening smallholder agriculture and increasing rural employment and income will require intensive application of agroforestry techniques to improve productivity on farms as small as half an acre. But it must also include attention to other means of increasing rural employment and income, such as improved transport, distribution, and marketing; purchase of animals; and support for small-scale, rural-based industries based on efficient and sustainable use of soil, water, and forests. Energy development (discussed below) must be an integrated part of such efforts; so must continued soil and water conservation, watershed rehabilitation and management, and aquaculture.

The United States should take the lead in removing the bias against smallholder agriculture still found in the project- and policy-based lending of the World Bank and the regional development banks. In its bilateral programs, the

United States should target poverty and environmental degradation where they are most severe: in sub-Saharan Africa (where per capita production is likely to grow hardly at all before the end of the century);[24] in South Asia, with its heavy concentration of poor people; and in those Latin American and Caribbean countries (especially our nearest neighbor, Mexico, and troubled Central America) that have severe problems of environmental degradation and deep pockets of poverty despite their middle-income status.

Specifically, in agriculture and forestry, the United States should commit to sustained cooperative efforts in five areas:

1. The United States should draw on its admirable agricultural research and extension tradition to establish cooperative U.S.-developing country programs of research and training devoted to forestry and low-input agriculture. The agenda must include the development of new high-yield, drought- and disease-resistant dryland crop varieties; new crop mixes; new rotation and tillage methods; nitrogen-fixation techniques; new applications of fertilizer and pest-management systems; new systems of water conservation, storage, and processing of foods; incorporation of trees into farming systems; livestock management; and natural forest management.[25] In making good on these ambitious goals, the United States should work closely with international and developing-country research and extension institutions to involve local farmers, fishers, and herders in research and the diffusion of innovation. And because biological systems vary widely even within countries, the site-specific experience of local practitioners, including women, must be incorporated into the research and experimentation. Because many of the barriers to changing rural technology appear to be social and institutional, social science analysis will be an important part of any research agenda.

2. A United States cooperative research agenda must include a major effort to improve the quality of policy analysis and research in developing countries. The United States should help both developing countries and international research institutions understand that perverse agricultural, forestry, and other incentives can affect farmers' land-use practices and technology choices. For example, while research institutions are attempting to develop less erosive cropping systems, crop pricing or input subsidies may undermine farmers' incentives to preserve natural soil fertility. Or pesticide subsidies may undermine the adoption of integrated pest-management strategies.

3. The United States should invest heavily in developing-country institutions of dealing with the remote, the rural, the poor, and the marginal. In some countries, this means developing policy-analysis units in the planning ministry or building and equipping national environmental monitoring systems, biological research laboratories, or agroforestry experimental

field stations. In almost all countries, it will require finding ways to help nations build and strengthen local governments, local transportation, and local community organizations. The United States should apply its extensive experience in training extension workers to help strengthen organizations created to reach marginal farmers, especially women, to promote sustainable technologies.

4. The United States should support government efforts to broaden access to land and equity through land reform and strengthened tenancy rights. According to the United Nations Food and Agriculture Organization (FAO), land redistribution and tenancy reform are "the most fundamental of anti-poverty measures," and they are essential for good resource management practices. It stands to reason that poor people will not plant and tend trees that they do not have the right to enjoy and use, that poor people will not invest meager savings and arduous labor in conserving soil and water on land to which they do not have secure title. And yet in 1979 an estimated 30 million agricultural households were landless, and another 138 million near-landless. In every region of the world are countries whose efforts to prevent deforestation and improve agricultural productivity are blocked because most rural people are virtually landless.[26] In developing countries where landownership is highly concentrated in the hands of a few—a problem endemic in South Asia and Latin America—the best U.S. technical and policy advice on agricultural strategies will not achieve sustainable development unless the United States supports governments' efforts to secure access to land for the poor and landless. Special attention must be given to the roles and rights of women, who are the primary resource managers in many developing countries.

5. United States forestry programs for developing countries must pay greater attention to innovative ways to increase local fuelwood supplies. From 30 to 98 percent of all energy consumed in individual developing countries comes from biomass, mostly trees,[27] but the costs and difficulty of collecting fuelwood have escalated. Much of the reforestation needed to supply energy and to save the land and water will have to be done by small farmers. The United States should help developing countries reform policies that lead to forest destruction and discourage sound forest management, and it should support programs that promote tree planting on farms and throughout rural areas. Specifically, the United States should back decentralized seedling production and distribution programs, help strengthen forestry and agroforestry research and extension, and help integrate tree planting with soil and water conservation programs and with agriculture and energy programs. NGOs and local communities have a major role to play in reforestation efforts and should be a focus of U.S. assistance.

Energy for Development

In the 1990s, U.S. development cooperation should redouble emphasis on energy for development—especially on the energy needs of the poor. Accordingly, attention must shift to traditional fuels—the wood, agricultural residues, and other biomass on which more than half the people (and a much higher proportion of the poor) in the developing countries depend.

The world faces another energy crisis in the 1990s as oil prices rise once again. Experts disagree only on whether the increases will arrive in 1992, 1995, or later in the decade. No other sector is as important as the energy sector for economic development and growth—in both industrialized and developing countries. And every use of energy has environmental implications, whether for greenhouse warming or the denuding of tropical forests. Here, at the juncture of Americans' unlimited appetite for energy and their growing concern for the global environment, lie the compelling reasons for U.S. development assistance programs to give high priority to energy for development.

For developing countries, energy is the key to growth. In most, it is the largest single figure in the national development budget and takes the biggest bite out of foreign exchange. And developing countries' energy needs have just begun to grow. If these countries were to use energy at the rate that industrialized countries do, five times the present global energy use would be required, and the global atmosphere cannot tolerate such an increase.[28]

Low-income urban families, even in middle-income countries, spend up to 30 percent of their budgets on cooking fuel. Some spend more on this each day than on the food they cook. Daily, rural women and children must search ever farther afield through degraded and denuded forest to gather agricultural residues and firewood. In some areas of acute fuelwood shortages, families are eating fewer meals per day and changing their diet to include fewer cooked foods.[29]

At the same time, the production and use of energy has direct and serious environmental costs that developing countries cannot ignore. The burning of fossil fuels and, to a lesser extent, the destruction of forests lead directly to the increase of carbon dioxide in the atmosphere and the associated rise in the earth's temperature through the "greenhouse effect." Air pollution from vehicles, factories and power plants is damaging health, buildings, crops and forests. Huge hydroelectric dams have their own environmental problems, as well as health and social costs. And the demand for fuelwood adds substantially to deforestation and an associated soil loss in tropical areas. Smoke from family cooking fires takes an exhorbitant toll in respiratory diseases and damage to the eyes.

The United States should provide leadership on a world energy strategy in the 1990s. From 1972 to 1980, donor countries contributed $14 billion toward meeting developing-country energy problems, with 90 percent of that going into huge electric power generation station and transmission, mostly from big dams.[30]

Now, rising environmental consciousness, the staggering capital costs of expanding energy production, the threat of rising oil prices, and the need to protect export earnings from the demands of the energy sector call for a radical change in patterns of energy investment—from capital-intensive central power generation to major investments in greater efficiency and development of renewables. It is in the interests of the United States and other industrialized countries—the heavy users of energy and the largest contributors to atmospheric deterioration—to share the burden of developing efficient, nonpolluting energy sources for other parts of the world.

United States leadership should be asserted both in policy matters and through the example of bilateral energy projects. On the policy side, the United States should, through the IMF, World Bank, and bilateral assistance agencies, seek the economic rationalization of energy policies in developing countries. Of special concern are the handsome energy subsidies for both fuel oil and electricity. Policies may also need to be developed to provide incentives for increasing efficiency or cutting fuel costs to the builders and managers of conventional power plants and factories. And aggressive efforts to improve automotive fuel efficiency in industrialized countries could benefit developing-country users, help forestall a rise in the world price of oil, and lessen the global atmospheric impact of exhaust fumes.

Second, AID should help cooperating countries plan "least-cost strategies""for meeting their energy needs—for the urban industrial sector and for decentralized energy production for rural development. Major investments in institution-building and training will be required.

Third, the United States should encourage developing-country governments, international banks, and other investors to support the production or purchase of energy-efficient machines, appliances, and transport. Most developing countries could realize extraordinary savings by making these switches. It has been estimated, for instance, that Brazil could avoid the construction of 22 gigawatts of new electrical capacity costing $44 billion by spending $10 billion over the next 15 years on more-efficient refrigerators, street and commercial lighting and motors.[31]

As a fourth policy concern, the United States should promote in all development efforts the use of the cleanest, least-polluting technology. Because conventional power plants have the potential for contributing to global warming and transboundary pollution, the United States and other industrialized countries have a mutual interest in assuring that developing countries employ the best available technologies, even if it means sharing the extra cost. The United States should, both through its bilateral programs and its leadership in the multilateral agencies, help developing countries improve the efficiency of conventional power plants through retrofitting, improved maintenance, and other approaches. For new plants, state-of-the-art technology for both efficiency and pollution control should be a condition of international assistance.

In its bilateral programs, AID should enlarge its energy efforts, focusing on the point where the energy requirements of poor people and the demands of the environment converge. The principles of conservation and end-use efficiency and the development of renewable energy technologies should guide such programs. One of the lessons learned when oil prices rose precipitously in 1973–74 was that "new" energy capacity can be found in conservation—and more cheaply than building new power plants. Thus, the U.S. economy was able to grow by 30 percent between 1973 and 1986 with no growth in energy use.[32]

Similar savings through more efficient energy generation, transmission, and consumption can be made in developing countries. Primitive technology is not necessarily either cheaper or more efficient. The Tanzanian woman cooking in an earthen pot over an open flame uses eight times as much fuel as her affluent neighbor with a gas stove and aluminum pot. A wick dipped in kerosene gives only one one-hundredth the light of a 100-watt electric bulb for the same amount of energy.

The United States should support greater energy efficiency as a way of buying time to develop renewables. For example, at a small fraction of the billions spent on conventional energy assistance, the United States could support a massive program to develop and market improved cookstoves. In many countries, viable private industries can be developed—they already exist in Thailand, Kenya, and India—using domestic materials. But where the cost of improved stoves is out of reach of the rural or urban poor, distribution should be financed by other means, including international assistance if necessary. The use of more-efficient stoves will reduce the cost of fuel for poor people and slow the rate of forest destruction, giving the world a better chance to catch up on reforestation.

The United States should take major initiatives to help developing countries upgrade the stoves, furnaces, boilers, and kilns that everywhere burn traditional fuels—wood, husks, bagasse—in agricultural and manufacturing processes, using grossly inefficient technology from the 1920s and 1930s. Technical assistance and financial support will be required to upgrade these technologies—to design, manufacture, and maintain more-efficient systems. High on the list should be improved kilns for charcoal manufacture, briquetting techniques that make more efficient use of residues like peanut husks and coffee hulls, and better technology for processing coffee and oil and drying crops. Such efforts can greatly enhance the supply of process heat and steam, and even make the generation of electricity practical for local needs.

By sponsoring demonstration projects, the United States should also support developing-country efforts to tap renewable sources of energy. To the extent possible, such efforts emphasize reliance on local materials, technology, and manufacturing so as to reduce the need for foreign-exchange outlays for energy investments.

Various forms of assistance are appropriate. For example, the United States should expand and accelerate its existing tropical forestry efforts so as to enhance fuelwood supplies through reforestation and agroforestry. Where feasible, it should promote mini-hydroelectric development such as AID supported in Thailand. These small, dispersed dams minimize transmission costs and can be developed and managed with local labor and control. The United States should also promote solar energy (including wind) where practical—for water heating and pumping, for instance—and support the improvement of the local manufacture of solar-thermal and solar-electric technologies. Development assistance can promote the "modern" use of traditional fuels such as wood and particularly agricultural residues and wastes that can be digested to make flammable gas (methane) and liquid fuel (ethanol), but international assistance is required for research and development in order to specify applications and overcome the social, institutional, and organizational constraints.

Population Policy and Family Planning Services

Around the world, one country after another has instituted policies to slow population growth. The most successful of these—in such island countries as Barbados, Cuba, and Sri Lanka and in vast continental China—have featured mutually reinforcing strategies. They offer full access to family planning information and services combined with programs to improve health (particularly of mothers and children), to raise the standards and hopes of the poor, and to educate people (especially women). In their example lie the clues for U.S. policy in the 1990s. As the report of the World Commission on Environment and Development put it, "developing-country population strategies must deal not only with the population variable as such but also with the underlying social and economic conditions of underdevelopment"—education and employment (especially for women), and shelter and sanitation.[33]

The United States urgently needs to resume its traditional international leadership in family planning programs, and AID must try to mesh its population-assistance programs more clearly and deliberately with the other relevant socioeconomic and education programs it supports.[34]

The United States used to be the leading supporter of family planning programs in developing countries and of contraceptive research. For 20 years it was the largest donor to international population programs. But policy changes during the Reagan administration have seriously weakened U.S. support for these vitally important activities. Funding for international family planning has been cut from $290 million in 1985 to $235 million in 1988, a nearly 20-percent reduction. These cuts urgently need to be restored, and budgets increased as necessary.

The Reagan administration took the occasion of the International Conference on Population in Mexico City in 1984 to announce that U.S. funds may not be provided to any foreign organization that has any involvement with abortion, even if its abortion-related activities are supported by private or other non-U.S. funds. This resulted in the withdrawal of U.S. support for programs of the International Planned Parenthood Federation in December 1984, and subsequent cuts and then elimination of the U.S. contribution to the United Nations Population Fund (UNPF). These actions, too, need to be reversed.

But the traditional U.S. leadership role was not just financial. Until current policy eroded this leadership, the nation provided technical leadership in the development of effective birth control systems. Much of the expertise in family planning—biomedical research on contraceptives as well as attitudinal studies—has traditionally been housed in U.S. institutions. In addition, the United States has been the top supplier of inexpensive, high-quality contraceptives.

The national family planning programs that the United States should once again promote and support will have several ingredients. They must be voluntary and should be part of all primary health care programs. National leaders must play a strong, prominent role in promoting the benefits of reduced fertility, and be backed, as in Mexico, by vigorous public education using whatever media is available—newspapers, billboards, radio, and television. There must be a sufficient number of trained workers and an adequate supply of low-cost contraceptives. And they must be coordinated with other programs designed to meet basic human needs and give people confidence that their children will survive. Funding levels, including the U.S. contribution to the UNPF, should be restored to earlier levels, and then increased as necessary to do the task.

Large improvements can be made in agricultural productivity and provision of new energy capacity, as we have seen in the previous sections, but they cannot keep up with demand if population growth is not slowed in the coming crucial decade. The mathematics are inexorable: a generation's delay in reaching fertility replacement levels means 4 billion more people.

Conclusions

Each of the chapters in this book argues to some degree that new and different development strategies are required to achieve sustainable development. This holds true also for the United States and other industrialized countries, of course, as is admirably well spelled out in the report of the World Commission on Environment and Development. But in developing countries, fundamental difficult changes are needs. As Richard Nuccio points out in the chapter on Mexico, "Nothing less than the consensus underlying Mexican stability for the last 60 years is at stake." And as we have seen also in Egypt, the things that most need to be done—to promote smaller families, curtail subsidies, and restrict military expenditures—are the moves least favored by the various opposition groups or the military. In the Philippines, the essential requirements for sustainable development—land reform, sharp curtailment of destructive forestry and fishing practices, and vigorous family planning efforts—would attack the privilege, power and values of the traditional elite that the President (and others before her) depends on for her political base.

And some of the changes required are expensive. The agriculture, forestry and energy strategies emphasized in this book are an exception: indeed, because they are labor-intensive and considerably less capital-intensive than high-input agriculture and central power stations, they may require fewer dollars and greater organizational capability. But some measures will be costly: the United Nations Population Fund estimates, for instance, that it would cost $5 billion a year over the next decade ($2 billion more than the world spends now) to reach a stable 10 billion population by 2100.[35] And significant debt relief, discussed seriously for the first time in 1989 by U.S. policymakers, will likely be paid for in part by the taxpayers. While the kind of trade concessions called for in this chapter may cause near-term hardship and dislocations in specific U.S. industries, more liberal trade policies can create more rather than fewer U.S. jobs over the long term.

Surely, the environmentally destructive accelerating trends detailed in these chapters will not easily be deflected without costs to all concerned. The financial and political obstacles to fundamental changes in Third World development strategies will be difficult to overcome. At first glance, the problems seem bigger than the resources and political will available to deal with them. But there are a number of other trends, not often acknowledged, that give grounds for some optimism.

First is the widespread and growing recognition of the seriousness of problems themselves and of the ways in which they are connected to each other, often across national boundaries. In the United States, the growing awareness of global environmental deterioration, especially of the shared atmosphere, tropical forests, and biological diversity, have once again—after an eight-year hiatus—fueled a new round of environmental activism. Environmental issues are back on the political agenda, and this time the movement is much more international in its concerns. More than a dozen new laws were proposed in the Senate and House in 1989 to curb global warming, make energy use more efficient, and preserve tropical forests. Similar forces are at work in both Western and Eastern Europe. Most noticable were the gains made by the Greens in elections for the European Parliament.

We have already alluded to the recognition given by developing-country leaders to the importance of environment to development. Many have also clearly articulated their parallel concern about population growth. In October 1985, 35 world leaders representing half the world's population, presented the United Nations Secretary General with a "Statement on Population Stabilization," warning that "if this unprecedented population growth continues, future generations of children will not have adequate food, housing, medical care, education, earth resources, and employment opportunities."[36] And in Belgrade at the September 1989 summit of non-aligned nations, the heads of state, noting the widening gap in development levels between the North and the South, declared poverty and the degradation of the environment to be closely related, and asserted that, "Environmental protection in developing countries had to be viewed as an integral part of the development and could not be considered in isolation from it."[37]

Second, the governments of the world are beginning to develop mechanisms for dealing with the international aspects of the problems. The September 1987 *Montreal Protocol on Substances that Deplete the Ozone Layer* is a promising start. Prime Minister Margaret Thatcher's call to the 1989 London conference on ozone registered worldwide concern about the problem, and the latest economic summit (held in Paris in July 1989) had global environment issues on its agenda for the first time. Environmental discussion at the Development Advisory Committee has elevated the importance among OECD countries. And at the first African Ministerial Conference on the Environment (AMCEN) in 1985, participating environmental ministers set up an informational and action-oriented development program. Their "Cairo Programme" incorporates village pilot projects in 50 countries. At their third meeting in 1989, they continued to address practical problems to international environmental policy concerns.

Third, developing countries themselves have all had at least a generation's experience in managing development problems. Of particular importance is the much improved understanding among both developing-country planners and their international advisors of the role of macro-policies—of pricing, tariffs, taxes, exchange rates, subsidies, and incentives and disincentives of all sorts in determining the achievement of development goals. The need for institutional development, and the institutionalization of change is also clearer.

Fourth, most developing countries now have a corps of concerned professionals who know the geology and hydrology of their regions, the biology of their life forms, and the workings of their social and political institutions. Their scientists have studied the effects of siltation and soil fertility. Engineers have tackled water-logged soils and water and sanitation problems and have built every kind of infrastructure. Medical professionals have documented the effects of bilharzia, pesticide poisoning, and malnutrition. In each of the countries discussed in this volume, these professionals, employed usually in their national universities and research institutes, have been the first to articulate and document their concern over the environmental trends. These men and women have often been the cadre who formed the first environmental organizations. In countries as different as Malaysia and Poland, Nicaragua and the Philippines, Friends of the Earth affiliates and other national environmental organizations speak out with increasing effectiveness.

The final promising trend is the burgeoning in developing countries of popular citizens' organizations protesting government neglect of the health consequences of threatening water or air pollution, or the stripping of the resource base. These organizations are often visible first among the urban, more literate, and better informed parts of the populace who understand the importance of and use the media. Students are often the vehicle for organizing demand on governments. But equally significant are the examples of the village women in Kenya, tribal people in the Amazon or at the Narmada dam sites, prawn fishers in Negros, and the Chipko movement in India, where women a decade ago tied themselves to trees to save them from loggers.

This sort of citizen action, the voluntary self-organizing communities of interest that de Tocqueville once thought unique to America, have in fact proved to have indigenous counterparts everywhere in the world. They and their professional colleagues are more effective, of course, when they can operate free of fear of harsh oppressive reprisal. Indeed, there appears to be a direct correlation between the number and effectiveness of such ranks and the openness of the society. The São Paulo state secretary of the environment said at an AID meeting in Washington, D.C., in February 1987 that since the return to democracy in Brazil, vocal citizen pressure had lent greater power to his office. In the Philippines, professionals and NGOs both were intimidated by the Marcos regime. Even the otherwise irrepressible Filipino press was squelched during the 20 years of martial law. But the environmental movement has come alive again, and this time even the Catholic hierarchy has joined the movement with an important statement on the relation between the environment and poverty and development. Just as the citizens' organizations flourish in greater democracy, so also do they contribute to the diversity and pluralism that makes democracy a reality.

When one adds up these four trends that indicate rising consciousness, organization, and determination, the future looks more hopeful. With the right kind of support from the international development community, the necessary changes in development strategy can be made.

Clearly, the United States cannot by itself change the directions of development—the strategies necessary for increased productivity, greater efficiency, and better management. Even if the United States were still the largest donor country, or if it had the greater moral influence that a larger per capita donor does, or a better current record for depoliticized development assistance, it still could not do what's needed alone. Nor would that be appropriate, even if it were possible. The times have changed. The patronizing notion of *assistance* must be replaced by a concept of global *sharing* of responsibility—not just because we really do have equal stake in "our common future," but also because the United States does not have the answers, the skills, and the resources to do the job alone. Developing countries do, and they are the appropriate agents for their own development. They have skills and experience accumulated over 30 years and more of independence and development practice.

Trial and error—lots of the latter, but some successes, too—have more than equipped them to take charge.

The role of the donor countries is to help improve developing-country capabilities to do a better job—to analyze, to plan, to organize, to deliver—and to develop the institutions needed to do the task, from the ministerial to the local government level, and in the non-governmental arena as well.

A second appropriate role for the United States is to exert some farsighted leadership among the other donor countries. In recent years, the United States' fine earlier record of leadership has been diminished. But the United States has particular experience in the technical and training fields, in NGO experience, and even in community organizing—all of which will be needed more than ever in the new development decade. Most of all, it is American environmental consciousness and insights that can now be brought to bear. The United States government, compelled by its own environmental constituency at home, was the first to develop environmental guidelines and goals for its bilateral development programs. More recently, it has been the U.S. Treasury, again propelled by the environmental organizations and like-minded congressional leaders, that has enlivened environmental concerns at the World Bank. And it is a U.S. president of that Bank who has organized and staffed the institution to implement its solid environmental guidelines. The regional banks are coming along more slowly, so U.S. official and private pressure on them needs to be maintained.

The development goals that Japan, now the world's largest single donor, pursues are extremely important. Any perceived Japanese reluctance to participate fully in international development efforts has now, observers agree, been dissipated. As the largest donor, Japan will have a very considerable voice at the World Bank and IMF and in bilateral relations, with Asian countries in particular. How it will use its voice and its money is crucial to the outcome of the problems discussed in this book.

If Japan pursues a program different from that prescribed in these pages for the United States and other OECD countries, its participation could be inimical to the sustainable development goals sought. If it were to import logs in violation of the Philippine ban, or to provide sophisticated expensive diagnostic equipment for central hospitals while other donors finance and encourage community-based preventive health care delivery and family planning services, then success will elude all. So the role that the United States plays in including Japan in a global strategy is very important. Indeed, it should be seen by the Bush administration as a primary diplomatic task. The signs are that Japan is open to genuine dialogue about the nature of global development. The United States should seize the opportunity.

The United States ought also to temper its current indiscriminate enthusiasm for private enterprise as the primary engine for development and be wary of the U.S. Chamber of Commerce's perpetual thrust for a development-for-trade policy. That there is, in places as wildly different as Tanzania and China, a disillusionment with state-run enterprises and a new freedom for the entrepreneur is not to be denied. The greater willingness to have appropriate tasks organized at a regional or local level, to remove market constraints, to recognize the important economic role of the informal sector, and to trust more to private capitalistic efforts is to be welcomed. In the pluralistic experimentation that follows is sure to be found the great variety of answers required for the equal variety of conditions blocking sustainable development.

Pressure from the IMF and the multilateral banks to rationalize currency exchange rates and to release market forces from price constraints or restricting import-export conditions, has, of course, been a very important influence in these trends. But that pressure has often been applied without regard to who pays the costs. In country after country, poor people and the resource base on which they depend have paid the price. "Adjustment" that endangers the future ability to produce is to be avoided.

Because adjustment has brought about some major changes—privatized government-run businesses, forced realistic currency evaluations, and increased farm-gate prices for scarce food commodities—there is a tendency in some U.S. circles to enthusiastically embrace wholesale privatization and to depend on the markets and on world trade to stimulate economic growth. But as the examples in this book indicate, it is hard to make a judgment that Egypt and Mexico with their huge state enterprises and their revolutionary commitment to equity have produced any worse problems of poverty and environmental degradation than the Philippines' venal private capitalism for the rich.

Indeed, it can be argued that the revolutionary-inspired ethic of equality in Mexico and Egypt resulted not only in phenomenal growth, but also in a real sharing of the wealth (and jobs) and in a higher average quality of life than many countries with greater assets and higher average per capita incomes. Comparison of the Philippines with Mexico and Egypt seems to indicate that social progress and peace depend as much on a philosophy of equity as on who owns the banks, cement factories, and oil companies. And, conversely, it is apparent that both privately and publicly held corporations have both been part of systems that, for lack of vision and understanding as well as greed, can destroy the natural systems on which future growth depends.

Big enterprises and big capital investments looking at even bigger world markets—these are activities that tempt the developer's imagination. They also concentrate effort, investment, profit, and the possibility of bigger mistakes and opportunity for bigger corruption. It is not the ownership or the size of the enterprises that make the difference so much as the goals, the development strategy, and the macro policies guiding them. If the strategy is not focused on sustainable goals, there may be no more incentive for the efficient management of resources by private enterprises than in publicly held ones. What the complex task of sustainable development requires is pluralism and diversity and the flexibility to develop new solutions—since those prescribed to date have many drawbacks.

There is a constituency in the United States that will support new strategies for sustainable development, a constituency that will recognize the nation's self-interests as well as its humane interests in spending a fraction of a percent of national income to help end poverty and environmental degradation in developing countries, a constituency that understands that the wise and humane management of human and natural resources in far-flung developing countries is in the U.S interest.

The traditional and dwindling constituency for U.S. foreign assistance has been the humanitarian development-oriented groups (the Lutheran, Quaker, Catholic and other religious groups that lobby heavily for foreign assistance legislation each time around), plus whoever can be drawn into the vote by security concerns, support for Israel, the needs of a variety of export-oriented industries, and concerns within the professional, university, and NGO development communities who make their living in the programs funded by AID. But in each recent budget round, military assistance and politically motivated "economic support assistance" have grown at the expense of development assistance, and the religious groups that are the stalwart supporters on Capitol Hill find less and less reason to support a program that has become dominated by short-term military and political goals rather than development ends. With the proportion of military to development aid at its highest in history, U.S. development programs are in danger of losing their main supporters. The other groups will remain in the fight only so long as it is a vehicle for their particular interests, which may or may not be those of the developing countries. As veteran observer and foreign assistance supporter Congressman Benjamin Gilman lamented, there seems to be less and less support for development assistance on Capitol Hill.[38]

With new legislation, an International Development Cooperation Act that separates development assistance from the military and political, some of the traditional supporters may drop away. Advocates of the political and military goals are likely to follow those monies to another budget committee. Others will remain and support development goals. The Wheat Association and the agriculture states' representatives who understand their constituents' long-range interest in prosperous developing-country markets would continue to support development assistance, especially a large Public Law 480 program utilizing agricultural exports. The pollution-control industry, not yet politically organized on these matters, will eventually discover its interests in developing-country markets, and in development cooperation agreements to end environmental degradation. Governors and state development offices with a longer range understanding of their export markets can also be activated in support of cooperation for sustainable development. The universities and development professionals and their organizations can be expected to remain a part of the constituency because of the emphasis in this development strategy on training and institution-building.

But the important new growing constituency that we expect to be the next core of the U.S. international development constituency will be the great and widely distributed environmentally aware from middle America. They are to be found in all walks of life. Thanks to the activists among their organizations, they are alarmed about threatened tropical forests, encroaching deserts, and the loss of biological diversity. Thanks to the last few long hot summers, with their drought and ruined crops, the scientists' concerns for the warming effect begin to be more widely understood. Polluted beaches in 1988 and multiple oil spills in 1989 further raised the public consciousness of the costs of pollution. Future oil price increases will provide an opportunity for rapid citizen education on the atmospheric damage connected with wasteful energy production and consumption. Indeed, American citizens already seem to be far ahead of their political leaders in understanding the ultimate ecological interdependence that encompasses the current political and economic interdependence.

While national leaders have drifted along, citizen concern for global environmental problems cries out for action. It is time—on the 20th anniversary of the National Environmental Protection Act, which provided the legal charter in the United States for concerted federal action on national environmental problems—to legislate a charter for international cooperation dealing with global issues. Focusing on relations with the developing countries, an International Environmental Cooperation Act would galvanize the federal and multilateral agencies vital to realizing a North-South global bargain to sustain the earth. It would address debt and trade with developing countries, as well as increase the flow to the South of financial and technological help to curb environmental degradation and pursue sustainable development.

To counter environmental deterioration that is now quite literally out of control, time is of the essence. The 1990s are the crucial decade in which we have the opportunity to act on these pressing concerns. If resolute national and international efforts are not vigorously pursued in this decade, irreparable damage will be done to the world's environment, and the problems will prove increasingly intractable, expensive, and crisis-dominated. That will mean human misery on a terrible scale in the developing countries and health risks, and economic deprivation for our own children. There is time, but only a little time, in which to act. In this crucial decade ahead, ending poverty and environmental degradation in developing countries is in the U.S. interest.

References

1. World Commission on Environment and Development, *Our Common Future* (New York: Oxford University Press, 1987), 40.

2. See James Gustave Speth, "Coming to Terms: Toward a North-South Bargain for the Environment," *WRI Issues and Ideas*, June 1989, for a fuller exposition of the global bargain concept.

3. Jerome T. French, retired Foreign Service Officer and consultant to USAID, proposed this idea in a letter to the author, April 1988. The need for coordination of U.S. policy has long been argued by the Overseas Development Council and found expression earlier in the aborted International Development Cooperation Agency. The proposal has been made again in 1988 by parties promoting the reform of the Foreign Assistance Act, such as the Michigan State University Conference, May 16–18, 1988, and the Phoenix Group.

4. For recommendations on policy coordination and reorganization of AID and its missions, see The Phoenix Group, *The Convergence of Interdependence and Self-Interest: Reforms Needed in U.S. Assistance to Developing Countries* (Arlington, Virginia: The International Trade and Development Foundation, February 1988), 26–29.

5. José Goldemberg et al., *Energy for Development* (Washington, D.C.: World Resources Institute, September 1987) 15–17; Richard E. Feinberg, Overseas Development Council, "Third World Debt: Toward a More Balanced Adjustment," Statement before the Subcommittee on International Debt of the Committee on Finance, U.S. Senate, March 9, 1987; and The World Bank, *World Development Report, 1989* (Washington, D.C.: The World Bank, 1989), 8, 9.

6. Peggy Antrobus, quoted in *Curry Foundation Reports*, Vol. 5, No.1, Winter 1988 (Washington, D.C.). See also Feinberg, 1987, "Third World Debt," which arrives at a similar conclusion.

7. We are indebted to colleagues Paulo Nogueira-Neto (Brazil), Marc Dourojeanni (Peru), Osvaldo Sunkel (Chile), and Francesco Szekely (Mexico) for observances on this point.

8. J. Gustave Speth, "The Environmental Dimension to the Debt Crisis: The Problem and Proposals," in Robert A. Pastor, ed., *Latin America's Debt Crisis, Adjusting to the Past or Planning for the Future?* (Boulder, Colorado: Lynne Rienner, 1987), 45–51.

9. See article by Costa Rica's Minister of Energy and Natural Resources, Alvaro Umana, "Costa Rica Swaps Debt for Trees," *Wall Street Journal*, March 6, 1987, 31.

10. For an overview of the Debt for Nature experience to date, see "Debt for Nature in Latin America: A Status Report," Diana Page, World Resources Institute, forthcoming in *International Environmental Affairs, A Journal for Research and Policy*.

11. For more details on these proposals, see *Natural Endowments: Financing Resource Conservation for Development* (Washington: World Resources Institute, September 1989).

12. Memorandum from Robert Repetto, World Resources Institute, to the author, July 11, 1988.

13. See James Gustave Speth, 1989, "Coming to Terms: Toward a North-South Bargain for the Environment." The notion of a global bargain to save the tropical forests was first articulated by WRI President Gus Speth at a press conference in Washington, D.C., May 5, 1984, after the World Resources Institute's Global Possible Conference.

14. *Food 2000: Global Policies for Sustainable Agriculture*, a Report of the Advisory Panel on Food Security, Agriculture, Forestry and the Environment to the World Commission on Environment and Development (London and New Jersey: Zed Books, 1987), especially 60–64.

15. Goldemberg et al., 1987, *Energy for Development*, and Alan S. Miller et al., *Growing Power: Bioenergy for Development and Industry* (Washington, D.C.: World Resources Institute, 1986).

16. For an excellent Summary of the trends in foreign assistance, see *Report of the Task Force on Foreign Assistance to the Committee on Foreign Affairs of the U.S. House of Representatives, February 1989* (Washington, D.C.: U.S. Government Printing Office, 1989), especially 4–23. This was the so-called Hamilton-Gilman Task Force which prepared recommendations for revising the Foreign Assistance Act in 1989.

17. Alan Woods, *Development and the National Interest: U.S. Economic Assistance into the 21st Century* (Washington, D.C.: U.S. Agency for International Development, 1989), and Carol Adelman, Assistant Administrator, AID for Asia and the Near East, speech at the Society for International Development, Washington, D.C., April 12, 1989.

18. Similar recommendations have been made by several studies examining U.S. policy. See, for instance, the recommendations of the Phoenix Group, *The Convergence of Interdependence and Self-Interest*, and a Michigan State proposal, Ralph Smuckler and Robert J. Berg with David F. Gordon, *New Challenges, New Opportunities: U.S. Cooperation for International Growth and Development in the 1990s* (East Lansing, Michigan: Center for Advanced Study of International Development, Michigan State University, 1988).

19. Personal communication from Albert C. Printz, Jr., November 8, 1988. CIDIE was established to monitor and review actions agreed upon in a "Declaration of Environmental Policies and Procedures Relating to Economic Development," signed in New York on February 1, 1980 by the heads of the World Bank, five regional banks, the Commission of the European Communities, the Organization of American States, the United Nations Development Programme, and the United Nations Environment Programme.

20. See The World Bank, *Environment and Development* (Washington, D.C.: The World Bank, 1979), and speech by Barber Conable, at the World Resources Institute, Washington, D.C., May 5, 1987.

21. World Commission on Environment and Development, 1987, *Our Common Future*, 8–9.

22. Robert Repetto, *Paying the Price: Pesticide Subsidies in Developing Countries* (Washington, D.C.: World Resources Institute, 1985), and "Creating Incentives for Sustainable Forest Development," *AMBIO*, Vol. 16, No. 2–3, 1987, 94–99.

23. Food and Agriculture Organization, *Tropical Forest Resources*, Forestry Paper No. 30 (Rome: 1982).

24. Food and Agriculture Organization, *Agriculture: Toward 2000* (Rome: July 1987), Chapter 1.

25. The Consultative Group on International Agricultural Research (CGIAR) has begun to focus on some of these issues, but it needs urgently to suffuse its entire research program with considerations of agricultural sustainability.

26. Food and Agriculture Organization, 1987, *Agriculture: Toward 2000*, 18.

27. *Energy 2000—A Global Strategy for Sustainable Development*, report to the World Commission on Environment and Development, (Atlantic Highlands, New Jersey and London: Zed Books, 1987), 28.

28. José Goldemberg et al., *Energy for a Sustainable World* (Washington, D.C.: World Resources Institute, 1987), v, 1–4.

29. See Lester R. Brown et al., *State of the World, 1988* (New York: W.W. Norton & Co., 1988), 87–90, for a description of the impact of fuelwood shortage.

30. Goldemberg, et al., *Energy for Development*, 18, 86, and *in passim*. This small volume is an excellent discussion of the ways in which energy—through greater efficiency, technology innovations, and improved use of renewable energies—can become an instrument of development instead of a brake, as it so often is today.

31. Howard S. Geller, *The Potential for Electricity Conservation in Brazil* (São Paulo, Brazil: Companhia Energetica de São Paulo, 1985).

32. Goldemberg et al., 1987, *Energy for a Sustainable World*, v.

33. World Commission on Environment and Development, 1987, *Our Common Future*, 106, and Chapter 4, *in passim*.

34. The author is indebted to Sharon Camp of the Population Crisis Committee and Patricia Baldi of the National Audubon Society for assistance in formulating these policy recommendations on population and family planning.

35. Nafis Sadik, *The State of the World Population 1989* (New York: United Nations Population Fund, 1989), 19. Joseph Speidel of the Population Crisis Committee in Washington, estimates $7 billion will be needed annually between now and 2000. Cited in Brown et al., 1988, *State of the World 1988*, 168.

36. *New York Times*, October 20, 1985.

37. Ninth Conference of Heads of State or Government of Non-Aligned Countries, *Environment*, NAC 9/EC/Doc.8/Rev.4, Belgrade, September 7, 1989.

38. Benjamin Gilman, at a Congressional meeting on biodiversity and development policy, Washington, D.C., September 27, 1988.

Contributors

JANET WELSH BROWN

Dr. Brown is a Senior Associate at the World Resources Institute in Washington, D.C., and director of WRI's environment and development policy program. She is co-author and co-editor of *Bordering on Trouble: Resources and Politics in Latin America*. Earlier Dr. Brown was Executive Director of the Environmental Defense Fund, senior program officer on science policy at the American Association for the Advancement of Science, and a professor of political science and international relations.

NAZLI CHOUCRI

Dr. Choucri is Professor of Political Science, and Associate Director of the Technology and Development Program, at the Massachusetts Institute of technology. Dr. Choucri has a longstanding research interest in population and resource issues, focusing on problems of public policy. Among her publications are *Multidisciplinary Perspectives on Population and Conflict* (ed.), 1984, and *International Energy Futures*, 1981.

RICHARD B. FORD

Dr. Ford is a professor of history and international development at Clark University. He has served for several years as Chief Resource Advisor to the National Environment Secretariat, Ministry of Environmental and Natural Resources, Kenya. He specializes in village-level natural resource management systems. He has written numerous articles on East African natural resources issues.

DELFIN J. GANAPIN, JR.

Dr. Ganapin is a member of the Ecology faculty at the University of the Philippines at Los Banos. He is a consultant on highway, energy, agroforestry, and other development projects and has authored numerous papers.

PETER M. HAAS

Dr. Haas is an Assistant Professor of Political Science at the University of Massachusetts at Amherst, specializing in international political economy and international environmental cooperation. His publications relating to these issues include several articles and a forthcoming book titled *Saving the Mediterranean: The Politics of International Environmental Cooperation.*

RICHARD A. NUCCIO
Dr. Nuccio is Director of International Programs at the Roosevelt Center for American Policy Studies. He was a Fulbright scholar at the Centre de Investigacion y Docencia Economica (Center for Economic Teaching and Research) in Mexico City in 1981 and has worked on Mexican and U.S.-Mexican relations for over 10 years. He is the author of *What's Wrong, What's Right in Central America?*

ANGELINA M. ORNELAS
Ms. Ornelas is Press Secretary to Congressman Esteban Torres of California. She studied U.S.-Mexican relations at the University of Mexico City (UNAM). She has published several articles on Mexico's communications industry.

GARETH PORTER
Dr. Porter is Academic Director for Peace and Conflict Resolution at the Washington Semester Program at American University, and teaches also at the University's School of International Service. Dr. Porter is author of numerous books and articles on Southeast Asian politics, particularly those of Vietnam, Cambodia and the Philippines. His most recent book is *Vietnam: The Politics of Bureaucratic Socialism*, forthcoming in 1990.

IVAN RESTREPO
Dr. Restrepo is head of Centro Ecodesarrollo. Located in Mexico City, it was one of the first research centers focussing on environmental issues. Under Ivan Restrepo's leadership, the Center has published extensive studies on Mexican environmtal issues, including the impact of the petroleum sector and of agricultural strategies on the environment.

Appendix

A Public Forum
In the U.S. Interest: Resources, Growth and Security in the Third World

Washington, D.C.
June 22-23, 1987

Chairman

W. HODDING CARTER, III, President, MainStreet, a television production company, Washington, D.C.

Speakers

GOVERNOR BRUCE E. BABBITT, former Governor of Arizona, Phoenix, Arizona

WILLIAM H DRAPER, III, Administrator, United Nations Development Programme, New York City

REPRESENTATIVE CLAUDINE SCHNEIDER, Republican of Rhode Island

Participants

RUTH ADAMS, Director, Program on Peace and International Cooperation, John D. and Catherine T. MacArthur Foundation, Chicago, Illinois

ROBERT O. BLAKE, Senior Fellow, International Institute for Environment and Development, Washington, D.C.

LAWRENCE BRAINARD, Senior Vice President for International Economic and Political Analysis, Bankers Trust Company, New York City

HENRY R. BRECK, private investor, New York City

ROBIN BROAD, Resident Associate, Carnegie Endowment for International Peace, Washington, D.C.

JANET WELSH BROWN, Senior Associate, World Resources Institute, Washington, D.C.

WILLIAM E. COLBY, consultant, Washington, D.C.

FRANCIS MADING DENG, Senior Research Associate, Woodrow Wilson Center, Smithsonian Institution, Washington, D.C.

RICHARD E. FEINBERG, Vice President, Overseas Development Council, Washington, D.C.

EARL W. FOELL, Editor-in-Chief, *Christian Science Monitor,* Boston, Massachusetts

GEORGIE ANNE GEYER, syndicated columnist, Washington, D.C.

JOHN MAXWELL HAMILTON, Director, Society of Professional Journalists project to improve news coverage of the developing world, Washington, D.C.

JAMES A. JOSEPH, President and Chief Executive Officer, Council on Foundations, Washington, D.C.

JESSICA T. MATHEWS, Vice President and Director of Research, World Resources Institute, Washington, D.C.

CHARLES WILLIAM MAYNES, Editor, *Foreign Policy,* Washington, D.C.

JOHN D. NEGROPONTE, Assistant Secretary of State for Oceans and International Environmental and Scientific Affairs, Washington, D.C.

DENIS M. NEILL, President, Neill and Company, Washington, D.C.

MATTHEW NIMETZ, partner, Paul, Weiss, Rifkind, Wharton & Garrison, New York

VICTOR PALMIERI, Chairman, The Palmieri Company, New York

ELLIOT L. RICHARDSON, Senior resident partner, Milbank, Tweed, Hadley & McCloy, Washington, D.C.

HOBART ROWEN, syndicated columnist and Economics Editor, *The Washington Post,* Washington, D.C.

LORET MILLER RUPPE, Director, Peace Corps, Washington, D.C.

MOHAMED SAHNOUN, Ambassador of Algeria to the United States, Washington, D.C.

JAMES GUSTAVE SPETH, President, World Resources Institute

FRANCISCO SZEKELY, Professor of Environmental Policy, Assistant Director for International Environmental Studies, Energy and Environmental Policy Center, John F. Kennedy School of Government, Harvard University, Cambridge, Massachusetts

PETER THACHER, Distinguished Fellow, World Resources Institute, Washington, D.C.

GERALD E. THOMAS, former U.S. Ambassador to Kenya and Guyana, Guildford, Connecticut

IRENE TINKER, Founder and Director, Equity Policy Center, Washington, D.C.

DANIEL YERGIN, President, Cambridge Energy Research Associates, Cambridge, Massachusetts

Invited Experts

SHELDON ANNIS, Visiting Fellow, Overseas Development Council, Washington, D.C.

LEONARD BERRY, Professor, Center for Technology, Environment, and Development, Clark University, Worcester, Massachusetts

NAZLI CHOUCRI, Professor of Political Science, Massachusetts Institute of Technology, Cambridge, Massachusetts

MOHAMED T. EL-ASHRY, Vice President for Policy Affairs, World Resources Institute, Washington, D.C.

RICHARD FORD, Professor and Director, Center for Technology, Environment, and Development, Clark University, Worcester, Massachusetts

RICHARD NUCCIO, Director, Latin American and Caribbean Program, The Roosevelt Center, Washington, D.C.

ANGELINA M. ORNELAS, Research Assistant, The Roosevelt Center, Washington, D.C.

D. GARETH PORTER, School of International Service, American University, Washington, D.C.

ROBERT REPETTO, Senior Economist, World Resources Institute, Washington, D.C.

WRI Colloquium
U.S. Policy in the 1990s: International Cooperation for Environmentally Sustainable Development

Washington, D.C.
March 7–8, 1988

List of Participants

Susan R. Abbasi	Head, Oceans & Natural Resources Section, Congressional Research Service, Library of Congress, Washington, D.C.
Mansur Ahmed	Humphrey Fellow, American University, Washington, D.C.; Assistant Secretary, External Resources Division, Ministry of Finance, Bangladesh
Patricia Baldi	Director, Population Program, National Audubon Society, Washington, D.C.
James Barnes	Senior Staff Attorney, Environmental Policy Institute, Washington, D.C.
Doug Bennet	President, National Public Radio, Washington, D.C.
Peter A. Berle	President, National Audubon Society, New York City
Robin Broad	Resident Associate, Carnegie Endowment for International Peace, Washington, D.C.
Robert S. Browne	Staff Director, Subcommittee on International Development Institutions & Finance, Committee on Banking, Finance & Urban Affairs, U.S. House of Representatives, Washington, D.C.
James H. Caldwell, Jr.	President. ARCO Solar, Inc., Camarillo, California

Tom W. Carroll	Director, Center for Advanced Study of International Development, Michigan State University, East Lansing, Michigan
Jon Clark	Program Director, Environmental & Energy Study Institute, Washington, D.C.
Rene Costales	Secretary, Environmental Committee, Project Analysis Department, Inter-American Development Bank, Washington, D.C.
William Cousins	Consultant, Washington, D.C.
Russell deLucia	President, deLucia Associates, Cambridge, Massachusetts
Marc Dourojeanni	Senior Environmental Officer, Latin America & Caribbean Environmental Division, World Bank, Washington, D.C.
Susan Drake	Presidential Fellow, Office of Senator Terry Sanford, U.S. Senate, Washington, D.C.
Steven Ebbin	Vice President for Science & Technology, Institute of International Education, Washington, D.C.
Clive Edwards	Chairman, Department of Entomology, Ohio State University, Columbus, Ohio
Margaret Fahs	Assistant Director, Federal Relations & International Affairs, National Association of State Universities & Land Grant Colleges, Washington, D.C.
Howard Geller	Associate Director, American Council for an Energy Efficient Economy (ACEEE), Washington, D.C.
Margaret Goodman	Staff Consultant, Committee on Foreign Affairs, U.S. House of Representatives, Washington, D.C.
David Gordon	Associate Professor, James Madison College, Michigan State University, East Lansing, Michigan
Peter Hakim	Staff Director, Inter-American Dialogue, Washington, D.C.
Khristine L. Hall	Program Manager, Government Programs, IBM Washington, D.C.; representing the U.S. Council for International Business, New York City

John Maxwell Hamilton	Specialist, Division of Public Affairs, World Bank, Washington, D.C.
Abdelhalim Hammat	Counsel, Cultural Affairs, Embassy of Algeria, Washington, D.C.
Richard Harley	Research Associate, Institute for International Development, Harvard University, Cambridge, Massachusetts
Stephen Hellinger	Co-Director, Development Group for Alternative Policies, Washington, D.C.
Luther H. Hodges, Jr.	Chairman of the Board and Chief Executive Officer, The National Bank of Washington, Washington, D.C.
Ken Hughes	Washington Representative on Population, Sierra Club, Washington, D.C.
Walter Jackson	Director, Environmental Legislation & Regulation, USX Corporation, Monroeville, Pennsylvania
Jon Hensen	Senior Program Officer, The Pew Charitable Trusts, Philadelphia, Pennsylvania
H. Jeffrey Leonard	Director, International Program, World Wildlife Fund/The Conservation Foundation, Inc., Washington, D.C.
Souad Mahammad	Humphrey Fellow, American University, Washington, D.C.; Director, Food Programs Directorate, State Planning Commission, Syria
Janet Maughan	Program Officer, The Ford Foundation, New York City
John W. Mellor	Director, International Food Policy Research Institute, Washington, D.C.
Arun Misra	Humphrey Fellow, American University, Washington, D.C.; Administrative Service, India
David Mog	Senior Program Officer, Board on Science & Technology for International Development (BOSTID), National Research Council, Washington, D.C.
Katy Moran	Legislative Assistant, Office of Representative John Porter, U.S. House of Representatives, Washington, D.C.

Ned Raun	Regional Representative, Washington, D.C., Winrock International, Arlington, Virginia
Addison E. Richmond, Jr.	Consultant, Graduate Program in Science, Technology & Public Policy, George Washington University, Washington, D.C.
Rick Samans	Legislative Assistant, Office of Representative Donald J. Pease, U.S. House of Representatives, Washington, D.C.
Charles Savitt	President, The Island Press, Washington, D.C.
John W. Sewell	President, Overseas Development Council, Washington, D.C.
Joseph Speidel	President, Population Crisis Committee, Washington, D.C.
Frances Spivy-Weber	Director, International Issues, National Audubon Society, Washington, D.C.
Thomas B. Stoel, Jr.	Director, International Program, Natural Resources Defense Council, Washington, D.C.
Jack Sullivan	Vice President for International Activities, Development Associates, Arlington, Virginia
Jack K. Vaughn	Vice President for Conservation Programs, Conservation International, Washington, D.C.
Martha Walsh	Board of Directors, Rare Animal Relief Effort, Washington, D.C.
Geoff Webb	International Director, Friends of the Earth, Washington, D.C.
Stephen R. Weissman	Staff Director, Subcommittee on Africa, Committee on Foreign Affairs, U.S. Hosue of Representatives, Washington, D.C.
Phyllis Windle	Project Director, Food and Renewable Resources Program, Office of Technology Assessment, Washington, D.C.
Rebecca Wong	Assistant Professor, School of Hygiene & Public Health, Johns Hopkins University, Baltimore, Maryland
R. Michael Wright	Vice President, World Wildlife Fund, Washington, D.C.
George Zeidenstein	President, Population Council, New York City

Index